The Hardware Guide for Novell NetWare®

Jennifer Foster

John Wiley & Sons, Inc.

New York ▪ Chichester ▪ Brisbane ▪ Toronto ▪ Singapore

Publisher: Therese A. Zak
Executive Editor: Katherine Schowalter
Assistant Editor: Laura Lewin
Managing Editor: Ruth Greif
Editing, Design, and Production: Impressions, Inc.

Recognizing the importance of preserving what has been written, it is a policy of John Wiley & Sons, Inc. to have books of enduring value published in the United States printed on acid-free paper, and we exert our best efforts to that end.

Foster, Jennifer
The hardware guide for
Novell NetWare/Jennifer Foster
p. cm.
Includes index.
ISBN 0-471-53511-7

Printed the United States of America
10 9 8 7 6 5 4 3 2 1

Preface

The idea behind networking your computers is not new. In fact, the idea has been around for so long that you could be forgiven for thinking that networking technology is cut and dried and that it will be a real snap (literally) to connect your computers to each other.

A little more thought will remind you that networking is brought to you by the same industry that brought you your latest software package. Remember the program that gave you so many hours of . . . um, stimulation . . . as you struggled to master what was advertised as the program's simplest concepts? Networking comes from the same place.

Therefore, connecting computers to each other is not a snap, and it never will be until you learn to think like the computer programmer who came up with the original idea and all the people who have fiddled with it since. However, networking technology has steadily improved the last few years, and, even without the ability to think like the original computer programmer or a professional network administrator, there are things you can do to make installation of your network possible:

- Hire someone who thinks like a network administrator. This is the simplest solution and the most trouble-free. It's also the most expensive.

- Do it all yourself. Unless you're a network techie, this is not practical. If you have to hire somebody to correct your mistakes, it won't be any cheaper than starting out with a professional, and it may be more expensive.

- Arm yourself with knowledge. Decide what you can do and what you had better leave to the professionals. It may be that you can plan the network, buy the components, and then let someone who does that sort of thing for a living hook them all together.

This book is aimed at those of you who are choosing the third option.

Networking is a large subject, divided basically into two parts, like everything else in the computer industry: hardware and software. This book assumes that the software issue is settled: you've decided on a version of Novell's NetWare for your network operating system, and you are either upgrading your existing hardware or you want to choose the best hardware available for your original installation.

The focus of *Choosing Hardware for Novell's NetWare* is on the hardware you will need for each version of NetWare, aimed most specifically at those of you using Novell's Entry Level Software (ELS) operating system. Along the way, it provides answers to such weighty questions as:

- What are the basic system requirements for a file server that runs NetWare 386? SFT NetWare 286? ELS NetWare? What kinds of computers work with each version?
- What is Novell's IMSP program? Why should you care?
- What is the best cabling system to use? Why? The best topology? Should you try to install the cabling yourself?
- What boards should you install for your file server? For your workstation?
- What about a UPS (Uninterruptible Power Supply)? A tape backup? What about upgrading the hard disk drive?
- What about Portable NetWare? How does it affect you?

Armed with this knowledge, you should be able to obtain the best hardware for your version of NetWare, and therefore, the best results from your network. You may even be able to fool your local network administrator into thinking that you think like a computer programmer, too.

Acknowledgments

It's a cliche to say "Without these people, this book couldn't have been written." However, a cliche is a cliche because it's so often true. The help of members of the Novell Alumni Association was invaluable, particularly the advice of Ed Murray, Frank Quinn, Fred Garcia, Deni Conner, and Bob Murray, who've all moved on to bigger and better things after leaving Novell. Thanks also to Novell Alumni Association member Tom O'Neill, who not only contributed advice and answered technical questions, but provided a technical edit as well.

Current employees of Novell who took the time to clarify technical issues for me included Elson Park, product manager of Entry Level System; Dave Owen, vice president of hardware engineering; Steve Boren, IMSP engineering manager; Mike Dahlgren, the product manager for IMSP; and Patti Heisser and Kelli Christensen, my official liaisons with Novell.

Taking time from their duties to explain various facets of networking were John Trafari, Robert Lent, Ann Revell-Pechar, and Bill North, hard disk drives and data storage; Don Johnson, Bill Swift, and Kumar Shar, LAN boards; Cathy Scott, Bill Moldozan, and Paul Mattucci, disk controller boards and data storage; Suresh Panikar and William Chiu, workstations and file servers; Martha Graham, Denise Perdue, and Robert Schneider, power surge suppressors and uninterruptible power supply units; and Nancy Chirafisi, backup units.

A special thanks goes to Paul Worthington, who provided most of the line art and the cartoons for my book, and to Robert Roeder, who provided the rest. Most of the people listed also provided photographs when I sent out a plea for illustrations; I'm very grateful.

Trademarks

Every attempt has been made to include trademarks of the various firms and products listed in this book, through checking with the vendors in question, through reading ads and brochures, and through several trips to the library. Still, I didn't find everyone. Nevertheless, all brand and product names mentioned in this book should be considered trademarks or registered trademarks of their respective firms, whether or not they are listed below.

286, 386, and 486 are trademarks of Intel Corporation; Intel is a registered trademark of Intel Corporation.
3Com and EtherLink are trademarks of 3Com Corporation.

Acer is a registered trademark of Acer, Inc., and Acer America Corporation.
Adaptec is a trademark of Adaptec, Inc.
ADIC is a trademark of Advanced Digital Information Corporation.
ALR is a registered trademark of Advanced Logic Research, Inc.; Flex Cache is a trademark of Advanced Logic Research, Inc.
Apple, AppleTalk, Macintosh, and Mac are registered trademarks of Apple Computer, Inc.
ARCNET is a registered trademark of Datapoint Corporation.
AST is a registered trademark of AST Research, Inc.
AT&T and StarLAN are trademarks of AT&T; UNIX is a registered trademark of AT&T.

Canon is a registered trademark of Canon, Inc.
Central Point Software and Deluxe Option Board are trademarks of Central Point Software, Inc.
Chips and Technologies is a registered trademark of Chips and Technologies, Inc.
Club American Technologies is a trademark of CLUB American Technologies, Inc.
Compaq is a registered trademark of Compaq Computer Corporation; Systempro is a trademark of Compaq Computer Corporation.
Corel OptiStar and CorelDRAW! are trademarks of Corel Systems Corporation.

DEC and DECnet are registered trademarks of Digital Equipment Corporation.
Dell is a trademark of Dell Computer Corporation.

FaxPress and LANpress are trademarks of Castelle, Inc.
FileMaster is a trademark of Storage Dimensions.

GoldStar is a trademark of GoldStar Technology, Inc.

Hayes Smartmodem 2400 is a trademark of Hayes Microcomputer Products, Inc.

Contents

Introduction

NetWare is by far the best-selling network operating system on the market today. Depending on who you are listening to, between 50 and 80 percent of the network operating systems currently sold are sold by Novell, from the version that supports only four users to the version that supports hundreds. Altogether, more than one million NetWare systems, in all versions, are installed.

As you might expect, the version that supports only four users isn't as powerful (and doesn't require as powerful hardware) as the version that supports hundreds of users. In fact, the version that supports only four users will only let you use the most powerful hardware on the market if you are extremely careful; no SCSI hard disk drives, for example, and no disk arrays. (But if you have a 486 computer that you're using as a file server, why try to attach it to the most elementary version of NetWare around?)

A network operating system, starting with the basics, runs the network the same way that MS-DOS runs your computer. It controls access to the printer and the hard disk, it provides a way for electronic mail to get to your workstation, and it allows applications (such as spreadsheets and word processors) to be used by a number of people simultaneously. And it does these things transparently, for the most part. You never know that 16 other people are using your word processing package while you are, or that everyone on the network is, at this moment, writing and sending mail through the system. (Well, maybe if *everyone* on the network is trying to send mail you would notice. One of the management features of a network is based on the fact that people are diverse and are not going to be doing the same things at the same time.)

Figure 1.1. 486 Computers and Novell's Entry-Level System

Novell is largely responsible for the concept of a networking operating system. In 1983, Novell came up with file server software to manage disk input/output in a way that forced the workstations to call the file server for disk input/output. (A workstation "calls" the file server to request that a file be opened or saved.) Some critics felt that this was not a mainstream technology and labeled NetWare as just another proprietary networking system. (It can be said that the difference between "proprietary" and "standard" is in the number of users.) However, this concept, whether proprietary or not, was soon adopted by industry giants IBM and Microsoft, followed by most of the other vendors interested in networking.

The fact that this concept gained wide acceptance was (and remains) a real boon for application programmers. Previous to the adoption of the file server method of network management, vendors used a variety of disk server management systems, which meant that programmers had to create a different version of their application for each networking operating system. Today, Novell has expanded that compatibility to encompass things that the company didn't imagine eight years ago—offering compatibility with a larger number of applications, computing environments, and hardware than ever before.

But one of the main strengths of any networking operating system and one that Novell has been boasting about lately is its security (Novell has enhanced its security features for NetWare 386). A desktop computer that is neither networked nor locked away is a computer that is very vulnerable to outsiders accessing, changing, deleting, and/or removing its files. Certain departments in many businesses—personnel and finance, say—need to be able to keep their files secure from those who are not authorized to see them. Putting them on a file server is usually the answer. Even if someone can get to the appropriate directory on the network, the files cannot be accessed or even copied without the correct password.

Networks whose users have workstations without any disks at all have doubled their security precautions; a file can't be copied from a file server to a workstation if the workstation has no place to copy it to. (Users enjoy using diskless workstations in direct inverse proportion to their knowledge of computers—the more they know, the less they like diskless computers—but that's another story, discussed in Chapter III.)

If you're really concerned about security, you can use software that encrypts and decrypts files, which works by using a complex mathematical algorithm to change each of the characters in a file. Novell is licensing a public key encryption scheme (where both the originator and recipient must have the exact same key to decrypt a file) for NetWare 386 that builds in password encryption.

Novell, as mentioned earlier, has been phenomenally successful, and NetWare is now in its eighth generation, something that not many other software applications, networked or not, can say.

However, a system as complex as NetWare is going to have some requirements of its own, mostly concerning hardware. These hardware requirements are discussed in the next few sections.

DETERMINING HARDWARE COMPATIBILITY

Hardware requirements for a computer that can run NetWare can be complex. Not only do the systems have to run the appropriate version of NetWare and whatever other software you want to put on the network, but they also have to run the boards that allow the computers to be hooked up to each other. In other words, the best computers must be able to mix hardware and software from various vendors into a cohesive package, no easy feat since most software *and* hardware products have bugs and various incompatibilities built in, whether inadvertently or deliberately.

Novell has tried to make it easier to buy proper components by maintaining a testing program and certifying computers, local area network (LAN) boards, hard disk drives, and other peripherals for use with different versions of NetWare. This information is released to Novell's authorized dealers, who are supposed to pass it on to their local outlets and resellers. (Novell's testing program is discussed later in this chapter.)

Others have also implemented a testing lab to test hardware and software for compatibility; these outlets may or may not be interested in Novell's test lab. One store in a Novell-authorized chain said that it had heard of Novell's testing program, but that only the headquarters office received the test bulletins. The store was unconcerned about this oversight because it, like many other computer-specialty stores, maintain a compatibility lab for those products that it is authorized to sell. The results from *that* lab are broadcast chainwide. Of course, these dealers don't care about the compatibility of products they aren't authorized to sell. In other words, woe unto you if you decide to buy a computer from one authorized dealer and a LAN board from another, even if both stores (or their headquarters) receive Novell's compatibility test bulletins and those bulletins say "THIS BOARD DOESN'T WORK WITH THAT COMPUTER."

All this means is that the buyer should beware, which you already know. The best thing you can do is figure it out yourself, learning the categories and base requirements for each version of NetWare and then determining where you and your current and/or proposed equipment fit in.

CHOOSING NETWARE

Two general categories of NetWare currently exist: NetWare 386 and NetWare 286. (Novell hasn't mentioned NetWare 486 yet. Just wait.)

The numbers 286 and 386 in NetWare, as in 286 and 386 computers, refer to the kind of CPU chip that runs the computer. These chips are usually manufactured by Intel Corporation, but several other manufacturers are coming out with their own versions of Intel's 80386 and 80486 chips. Roughly, Novell says you should use 286 or 386 computers as file servers for NetWare 286 and 386 or 486 computers as file servers for NetWare 386. (They say. I say you'll be happier if you use a 386 for a NetWare 286 file server and a 486 for a NetWare 386 file server. Save your 286 computers for workstations.)

Of course, each of these NetWare categories is broken down further into publicly announced versions. And sometimes unannounced versions, known as "bug fixes," pop up because of problems that showed up in the announced version.

OSI MODEL

Before getting to the details of networking and NetWare, let me take time out here for a review of some of networking's background, specifically the

OSI model, which is so important to programmer types. (If you want to think like a programmer, you have to know what programmers think about.)

OSI stands for Open Systems Interconnection, and it represents how the International Standards Organization thinks communications functions should work. Ideally, LAN manufacturers strive to fit their products into this communications model, but it's not a showstopper to the vendor if the product doesn't seem to fit anywhere. (This is one reason that networking is confusing.)

Briefly, the OSI is divided into seven layers that in turn fit nicely into three categories:

- Physical
- Communications
- Services

The formal OSI model is illustrated and discussed on the following pages.

The layers are listed in order of complexity, with each succeeding layer built on the level below it; therefore, Layers 1 and 2 are at the bottom. Also, each layer can only communicate with the layer below it.

PHYSICAL

The first two layers of the OSI model make up the hardware and low-level software of a network: the cable, the connectors and transceivers, the voltage and current levels, the hardware (usually a board in a computer but sometimes just a chipset) that talks to the cable, and the software (frequently stored on the board) that manages communications between the computer and the cable. Layer 1 has the hardware specifications; Layer 2 contains the software.

As someone said, cable is just cable; it's the kind of network that determines how the cable behaves. The kind of network that is being used and how the data on the cable are sent and received depends on the kind of network interface board you have in your system: Ethernet, ARCNET, or Token-Ring. (There are others, but these are the only ones that will be discussed in detail in this book.)

The board contains the physical connection to the cable for the computer; it also frequently contains the software that manages, usually to a low-level extent, communications to the cable and computer. This low-level software is designed to maintain a reliable connection between adjacent nodes. (A node is any device-computer or printer-on the network.)

Figure 1.2. OSI Model

Layer 7:	Application (Protocols used by an application)
Layer 6:	Presentation (Application program code, data conversions)
Layer 5:	Session (Maintenance of data links between nodes)
Layer 4:	Transport (Error handling/retransmission of data)
Layer 3:	Network (The way data is routed)
Layer 2:	Datalink (Hardware/software that accesses and manages the cable)
Layer 1:	Physical (Cabling, signal strength)

For local area networks, cabling is usually copper-based wire (twisted-pair or coaxial wiring), although fiber optic wiring is rapidly gaining popularity as the price comes down.

These first two levels are the only hardware layers in the OSI model; the other five are entirely software-driven, and even part of Layer 2 concerns software.

COMMUNICATIONS

Layers 3 and 4 specify how data are routed and how errors should be corrected, and these two layers are referred to as communications protocols and controlled by software drivers. NetWare's communications protocol/software driver is called IPX/SPX, and you see those letters flash on your screen every time you boot your system. IPX/SPX stands for Internetwork Packet Exchange/Sequenced Packet Exchange, which is a way of identifying the network, the station address, and the application.

Layer 3 controls the data channel between two hosts; if your network is small, with only one file server, this layer is relatively unimportant. It's when you are dealing in wide-area networks, with different protocols, that this layer takes on a new importance. A communications protocol that usually runs on wide-area networks is TCP/IP. TCP/IP and IPX/SPX can talk to each other, but it isn't easy. NetWare handles this kind of internetwork communications through Portable NetWare, discussed in more detail in Chapter VII, and through bridges and gateways.

SERVICES

The last three layers in the OSI model provide services to applications; specifically, they provide for the establishment and termination of a communication session (Layer 5), a way to translate the data format so that both the sender and receiver can understand (Layer 6), and protocols for end-user applications, including NetWare itself (Layer 7). Protocols affected by Layer 7 include E-mail and remote access to a network, among others.

Layers 6 and 7 are usually implemented by MS-DOS (or OS/2) and NetWare, while the network BIOS (NetBIOS) handles the establishment and termination of a communication session. NetWare, unlike most other networks (specifically LAN Manager), is not dependent on the NetBIOS; the NetBIOS passes the establishment/termination requests to IPX/SPX.

Keep in mind that this is Novell's idea of the way the OSI model should behave. Apple has a different idea and Microsoft has still a different one. Apple's AppleTalk seems to come closest to sticking to the boundaries set up by the OSI model, probably because it only runs on one hardware platform. Both NetWare and Microsoft's LAN Manager have had to make accommodations, since they run on different hardware platforms.

The next few sections discuss the hardware requirements for each version of NetWare. They also discuss testing programs, both Novell's and those of other vendors.

NETWARE HARDWARE REQUIREMENTS

Novell ships different versions of NetWare, each more powerful than the last. Each of these systems has different hardware requirements. The lowest (and, not coincidentally, the oldest) version of NetWare has much less powerful hardware requirements and many more hardware limitations than the newer versions, which is only logical. It is very difficult for a hardware product to be upwardly compatible with software. It's a lot easier for a product, such as NetWare, to be downwardly compatible, and NetWare usually is.

NETWARE 386

Currently, Novell has three versions of NetWare 386: v3.0, v3.1 and 3.11. However, v3.1 and 3.11, while adding some new network management features, are basically still NetWare 386, so computers and peripherals that support v3.0 will work with v3.1. (Portable NetWare, although it is version of NetWare 386, is shipped by vendors who have licensed it and not by Novell. Portable NetWare is discussed in Chapter VII.)

NetWare 386 supports hundreds of users, specifically 250 per file server. With bridges and gateways, the total number of users on a network can be a lot higher. This is also the version of NetWare that has eliminated some software constraints—such as limits to data storage and limits on boards in the system. Where NetWare 286 only allows 2 gigabytes (GB) of data storage, NetWare 386 allows up to 32 terabytes (32,000GB). Where NetWare 286 allows only four disk controller boards with different I/O addresses, NetWare 386 removes all limits on the number of boards in the system. (Limits still exist, but the constraints are caused by the hardware, not NetWare.)

NETWARE 386 REQUIREMENTS

Novell says that the file server, the machine that will run NetWare 386, must be either a Compaq 386/20 with two megabytes of memory on the motherboard, or an IBM model 70 or 80 that runs OS/2 (or a fully compatible computer).

Of course, you can't find a more expensive system than a Compaq or an IBM. And, if you ask Compaq or IBM or Novell, you'll be told that no other machine is "fully" compatible. (Which is true, but it's the "fully" they emphasize—functionality they don't mention.) However, Novell's testing program lists lots of other machines that can run NetWare 386.

SFT NetWare 286 and NetWare 386 require additional hardware to support all their options. For example, if you use disk mirroring, you must have two hard disk drives within the file server; if you use disk duplexing, you need either a disk subsystem or another file server. (You have other options if you want to duplex disks, but the two mentioned are the most common.) Disk mirroring and duplexing are discussed in more detail in Chapter IV. Figure 1.3 shows a file server that can easily handle the hardware required for SFT NetWare 286 and NetWare 386.

Workstations can be any MS-DOS industry-standard IBM PC, PC XT, PC AT, or compatible or Personal System/2 (PS/2) or compatible with 512KB of memory on the motherboard. Basically, this list of computers is all-encompassing.

If you are using NetWare to network Macintosh computers, you can use a Macintosh Plus, a Macintosh II, or a Macintosh SE as a workstation. (Consult with a Mac expert before buying an MS-DOS–based network operating sys-

Figure 1.3. Interior of the Syntrex 386/486 Deskside Server
Courtesy of Syntrex, Inc., Eatontown, NJ 07724

tem; the expert may think of a better networking solution. Mac users don't generally think of DOS as a solution to anything.)

While NetWare 386 has general hardware requirements, they are not always the only hardware limitations. NetWare Access, v1.0, which strictly speaking is not NetWare 386 (but requires a 386 computer), has limitations too, above and beyond that of the network operating system.

NETWARE ACCESS V1.0

NetWare Access Server (v1.0) is a version of NetWare that allows you to dial into the network with a PC and a modem. Basic hardware requirements for NetWare Access include a 386 computer with multiport WNIM (Wide-area Network Interface Module) boards used in workstations to route asynchronous communications. In addition, the server has to have 3MB RAM for every four users, up to a maximum of 15 remote users and 12MB RAM. Also, each user has to have a modem and 640KB of RAM. So far, so good, with the RAM requirement just a little higher than that of NetWare 386 workstations; the additional hardware limitation is that each user can only have one hard disk enabled. This is a problem for the power users out there.

However, the NetWare Access has another hardware problem, one that is likely to affect most people, not just the power users, and that is if you have a VGA monitor on your system. If you want to use Access Server, you have to modify your CONFIG.SYS file to exclude C600-C7FF and E000-E7FF conflicting memory addresses.

If this is a problem for you, check with Novell to see if they've fixed this bug yet. A large number of people use VGA monitors; while fewer of them dial their home network from a remote location (or vice versa), I think that most of the people using NetWare Access have VGA monitors.

NETWARE 286

NetWare 286 comes in several flavors: Entry Level System, Advanced, and System Fault Tolerant (SFT). Advanced and SFT are dedicated (your file server can't do anything else but run NetWare) and Entry Level System (ELS) comes in both versions, dedicated and non-dedicated (you can use your file server as a workstation, too). And all of these flavors come in versions: v2.0a, v2.11, v2.12, v2.15, and v2.15c (which is very different from the vanilla v2.15).

NetWare versions 2.0a, 2.11, and v2.15 are obsolete, leaving only NetWare v2.12 and NetWare v2.15c to carry on the 286 line. Novell has another version of NetWare 286 in the works, but it hasn't been announced yet and won't be discussed here.

NetWare 286 limits data storage to 2GB and the number of disk controller boards to four. Since the latest and greatest hardware has far outstripped the limits set by NetWare, be careful that the hardware chosen to run NetWare doesn't exceed the software restrictions. For example, an EISA machine with a disk array is a good example of a machine that can exceed NetWare 286 storage limitations. (The Compaq Systempro, using all its data storage options, can support more than 4GB.)

Theoretically, up to 100 users can be supported by a NetWare 286 network, but on an already large network (70 users or so), with mirrored disk drives, additional users are sometimes prevented from logging on. Novell is said to be working on an upgrade (that new version of NetWare 286 mentioned earlier) that will correct this problem. If it is a problem for you, send in your warranty registration card, hang onto your receipts, and check with your authorized Novell reseller every so often.

GENERAL NETWARE REQUIREMENTS

Your NetWare 286 file server (for whichever version) should be an IBM PC AT or compatible or an IBM Personal System/2 Model 30 (286), 50Z, 65, 70, or 80 with at least 1MB of memory on the motherboard (if you are running your file server in dedicated mode, as a file server only) or at least 2MB of memory (if you are running your file server in non-dedicated mode, as a workstation sometimes). That's what Novell says; I think the Model 30 makes a fine workstation, but I don't think it should ever be used as a file server.

A NetWare 286 workstation should be an IBM PC/XT/AT or compatible or an IBM PS/2 (any model) with 384KB on the motherboard. (You'll also need enough memory to run whatever applications are resident on your system.)

Novell's manuals add the disclaimer that if you intend to use an IBM-compatible machine (as opposed to a *real* IBM machine) as a file server *or* as a workstation, make sure it's UL-recognized and tested and approved by Novell. In other words, make sure it's "fully" compatible.

Beyond the general NetWare 286 requirements are some hardware requirements that are specific to some versions of NetWare 286, such as a dedicated workstation, 256KB RAM and a modem to use NetWare Anyware, which allows you to dial into a network. However, most hardware restrictions are aimed at ELS Level I and Level II.

ELS LEVEL I AND LEVEL II

Entry Level System, Levels I and II, is meant for those who are just starting out in the networking field or for small area workgroup networks. These two versions of NetWare support a limited number of users and a subset of the features that full-fledged versions of NetWare support. Since ELS is a closed system (meaning that Novell didn't provide any developers' kits for this product), it's very difficult for those outside Novell to make enhancements to the software that would make ELS more attractive long term. The idea, on Novell's part, is for the network administrator to quickly outgrow ELS and upgrade to a network operating system with many more options.

In the next release of NetWare 286, Novell plans to strongly encourage the small network administrator to upgrade to the full-fledged version of NetWare 286 by no longer offering ELS at all. Instead, network administrators can choose NetWare 286 for a certain number of users.

However, in the meantime, if you are a beginning network administrator, you have a small number of people to network, and you don't need the most sophisticated machines or networking techniques (mirroring and duplexing, for example), then ELS may be just the right package for you if you can find it in the stores.

With the current revision of ELS, the operating system supports the same network types as Advanced and SFT NetWare 286. Previously, NetWare ELS was limited to three network types (Ethernet, ARCNET, and IBM's PC LAN). Now ELS Level II, v2.15, can use the same types that any other version of NetWare 286 can support. ELS Level I, v2.12, can use everything except for the Macintosh value-added driver, meaning that you can't add Macintosh machines to the network. (The comparable full-fledged version of NetWare v2.12 does not support that value-added driver either.)

ELS Level I

ELS Level I, v2.12 for four users is old NetWare technology; it shouldn't come as much of a surprise that it does not support a lot of the newer networking technology. A more complete list of what ELS does and does not support is in Appendix B, but following are two examples of what ELS I won't support:

- Hard disk drives with a Small Computer Systems Interface (SCSI)

- Third-party device drivers (software written by non-Novell types that allow hardware to work)

What this means in practical terms is that you cannot add a disk subsystem (a box containing extra hard disk drives) to your ELS I networks, because disk subsystems use SCSI drives and require a special disk controller board (third-party device driver) in the file server. Disk duplexing isn't supported for the same reason, and 486 EISA computers also run afoul of the ELS rules for hard disk drives and third-party device drivers.

ELS Level I is limited to two ISA-compatible (PC/AT) drives for the network file server, and Novell wants you to figure out what "ISA-compatible" means. The Novell spokesman agreed that some types of hard disk drives are ISA-compatible, such as those labeled MFM, RLL, and ESDI, but things grew fuzzy when we started discussing the IDE-type hard disk drive. Most IDE drives do work with ELS, but several have driver problems that preclude their use. Check for compatibility before installing an IDE drive into an ELS file server.

No matter which hard disk drive type you install on your ELS network server, you are going to have file storage problems from the beginning, unless your network users each have a hard disk drive on their workstations and unless they are trained to keep as much data as they can *off* the network. It also helps if you buy the largest capacity hard disk drive that is compatible with both your file server and ELS. (Two ESDI drives, supported by ELS I, will give you more than 1GB data storage.)

ELS Level II

ELS Level II, for eight simultaneous NetWare users, thanks to some improvements made in March and August 1990, does support SCSI drives (as long as they are IBM PS/2 compatible SCSI), although it still does not support third-party device drivers, and it has the same IDE driver problem as ELS I. Since the IBM PS/2 SCSI host adapter board supports eight hard disk drives (currently up to 660MB each), the data storage problems faced by ELS II networks are not as severe as those faced by ELS I. In fact, your data storage problems should be nearly non existent because NetWare 286 only supports 2GB, and you can get about 1GB into an ELS file server with large-capacity ESDI hard disk drives. If you use the IBM PS/2 option, you can theoretically install up to 3.5GB. (Theoretically means that no version of NetWare 286 supports that much data storage.)

In addition, several companies, among them Plus Development, have developed workarounds so that ELS II can support disk subsystems, if you feel you have to have them. Refer to Chapter IV for a discussion of hard disk drives, disk subsystems, and disk drive alternatives.

Dedicated and Non-Dedicated ELS

Both ELS Level I and Level II give you the option of running in either dedicated or non-dedicated mode, which means that the file server can either be used as a file server exclusively or that it can also be used as a workstation, giving you an extra computer. Non-dedicated mode also means that the network, even with the additional motherboard memory required by a non-dedicated system, is going to be slower than a network whose file server is only doing one thing.

Be advised that a number of systems ran into difficulty with slow keyboard input running in non-dedicated mode because of the keyboard and/or keyboard chip. The manufacturers I checked with dismissed this limitation as not affecting their sales. This means they aren't going to fix it; if running in non-dedicated mode is important to you, find a vendor to give you guarantees that a particular machine works with ELS in non-dedicated mode before you buy it.

Another operating problem of non-dedicated ELS, in addition to a slower network, is that some applications run from the file server when it is serving as a workstation can crash not only the file server/workstation but the network as well. If, for example, you're using WordPerfect in workstation mode and WordPerfect freezes the screen and the keyboard, you have no choice but to reboot. However, doing so also reboots the network, so all files open at the time also have to be recalled; new information in those files that was not saved before the reboot is lost.

Other applications currently require a PRFIX.COM package (available from NetWire or LANSWER) in order to run in non-dedicated mode. Before running some big application programs in non-dedicated mode (database programs, for example), check with NetWire or your NetWare reseller. (You can also check with LANSWER, but it's expensive.)

Future of ELS

In spite of the drawbacks, ELS is a rip-roaring success, accounting for roughly 50% of NetWare sales and more than 25% of Novell's revenue. As far as Novell is concerned, however, it's too much of a good thing. ELS is by far the cheapest of the NetWare versions, costing around $695–$1,495; NetWare

386 costs about $8000 and NetWare 386, v 3.11 for 250 users, will cost $12,500.

When ELS was introduced, sales of Advanced NetWare 286 (the most powerful version at the time) tumbled, because as those network administrators with a small number of users decided they could do without some of the fancier features the full-fledged version of NetWare offered.

It's an open secret that Novell would prefer that ELS not be there.

With the next release of NetWare 286, ELS will be eliminated or farmed out to a distributor; Novell will start charging for NetWare on a "per node" basis the way that vendors of other networking software do. This will eliminate connectivity hassles when administrators try to attach ELS to other versions of NetWare. It will also relieve technical support of the task of keeping track of a non-standard version of NetWare and maintaining a growing list (as technology moves on) of products incompatible with ELS. Finally, by raising the lowest common denominator, Novell will make more money.

WHERE DO YOU FIT?

If you are upgrading your network you probably have different concerns than if you are hooking up your computers for the first time. For one thing, you're a veteran of the compatibility wars. You already have a cabling system, complete with the appropriate LAN boards, and you have meshed your computers and peripherals into a network.

If you are hooking up your computers for the first time, it's a different story. You have a bunch of computers at different stages of technological sophistication. Some may be suitable for file servers, some for workstations, and some, like your 8086s, may only be suitable for your kids to play with.

WORKSTATIONS

How much memory you need depends on the applications you run from the workstation. If your application requires 1MB, then you must install 1MB on the system, no matter how much or how little memory NetWare itself requires; however, you have to include NetWare in your calculations. If your application requires 384KB memory to run and NetWare 386 requires 384KB to run, you're going to need 1MB of memory. (System memory doesn't come in increments between 640KB and 1MB.) Besides memory, the workstations themselves should be chosen with an eye toward the applications they will run; if you do a lot of graphics-intensive work, you'll need a more powerful machine than one that is running an older word processing package.

Above and beyond local applications, if you want to use the "latest and greatest" network operating system, NetWare 386, each and every workstation on the network will have to have 512KB. Your IBM PC/XT types may not be capable of having that much memory installed on the motherboard. However, the memory requirement for NetWare 286 workstations is only 384KB, so your old PC/XT (or clone) may still be able to do the job if you run NetWare 286.

For NetWare 386, Novell says the IBM PC/XT-type machine will serve as a workstation. What Novell doesn't say is that you'll be a lot happier if you use a AT-type system. It's not just the memory requirements (and there's only so much memory you can buy before you have repurchased the old, clunky computer), it's the technological improvements in computers made since the PC/XT systems came out. An old, clunky computer with a lot of memory is still an old, clunky computer that's going to be slow.

FILE SERVERS

File servers are another story, one where functional compatibility is really important. NetWare 286 requires 1MB RAM on the system (except for non-dedicated versions, which require 2MB) and NetWare 386 requires 2MB of memory, and more does not hurt. A 386SX may make a fine file server for NetWare 286, but it probably is not satisfactory for NetWare 386, even if you upgraded the memory. For one thing, larger-capacity hard disk drives require more memory on the system even before you start adding memory for NetWare and the various applications you want to run.

As a general rule, the bigger the network, the more powerful the file server should be. A file server that has the minimum amount of memory does fine on small networks, but gets slower and slower as you get closer to the maximum number of users.

NetWare 386 has lots of wondrous features and more are promised. (Any wondrous feature that is promised but not here yet is VaporWare.) Even many of the most powerful machines on the market today, the 486 computers, won't be able to take advantage of some of these planned features, such as multi-processing, without upgrading. A 386-based computer, especially a 386SX, will be outclassed by many of these features. You will never be able to upgrade it enough to take advantage of all that NetWare 386 can (or will be able to) offer.

If you aren't interested in features like multi-processing and you aren't planning on a giant network, a computer with the full 386 chip and at least the recommended amount of memory will do just fine as a file server for NetWare 386. Just be aware that you will not be able to take advantage of many of the future wondrous NetWare 386 features.

If you are interested in features like multi-processing, get a 486 system that is designed for that feature and hope that you can upgrade it when the time comes. There are a couple of them out there and more planned every day; the problem is that, since multi-processing isn't implemented yet on NetWare, the manufacturers of those systems are guessing what Novell is going to do. Guessing leads to new versions of the hardware when it arrives. *I* would wait.

NOVELL'S TESTING PROGRAM

Novell used to sell not only the network operating system but also the hardware that went with it. As it became apparent that the company was competing with some of its best customers (Compaq and IBM) and also that resources were being diluted to the detriment of NetWare, Novell started phasing out the hardware end of the business. The IMSP (Independent Manufacturer Support Program) came into being to redirect Novell's hardware engineering expertise to support the development of networking hardware.

THREE ASPECTS OF IMSP

Through IMSP, Novell tests networking hardware submitted by industry manufacturers for compatibility with NetWare. In addition to product testing, Novell's IMSP also provides engineering support programs that can make life simpler for manufacturers (and, when you start talking about NetWare Ready disk drives, for the customer as well). The third function of the IMSP is to occasionally co-develop networking hardware that otherwise would never come into existence. The next few sections discuss the three aspects of the IMSP program.

PRODUCT TESTING

Novell, in its testing program, tests computers and workstations; LAN boards and drivers; disk drives, disk controllers, and disk subsystems; backup systems and Uninterruptible Power Supplies (UPS); and printers and other peripherals, such as keyboards. When it certifies a product through the testing program, Novell sells the vendors stickers that proclaims the product to be "Novell Labs Tested and Approved," as illustrated in Figure 1.4. These stickers can then be placed on the product and in ads, and used by the public as a guideline for networking purchases.

This testing is done for several reasons:

- It allows Novell to establish closer ties with hardware vendors in the marketplace.
- It allows Novell to gauge market direction.
- It allows Novell to ensure compatibility, to some degree, between NetWare and the various industry standard platforms.

Product testing has made an impact upon volume buyers of LAN products, giving them an easy guideline to follow when making LAN decisions. (It shouldn't be the only guideline by any means, and those who treat it as if it were are being shortsighted.)

Figure 1.4. Novell Labs Tested and Approved Sticker Courtesy of Novell, Inc.

Figure 1.4. Novell Labs Tested and Approved Sticker Courtesy of Novell, Inc.

Figure 1.5. Novell Labs NetWare Ready Sticker Courtesy of Novell, Inc.

Figure 1.6. Novell Labs Co-Developed Hardware Sticker Courtesy of Novell, Inc.

If you're buying strictly mainstream, well-known LAN-brand products, the IMSP sticker is probably all you need, as long as you check to make sure that any limitations noted by Novell are not pertinent to your installation. (If you're not buying name-brand products, you need to do some compatibility testing yourself and not leave it up to Novell to be sure that everything in your installation fits together.)

The way you check limitations is to ask to see Novell's certification summaries, known as product test bulletins, for that product. Vendors with IMSP stickers usually have Novell's certification summary for their products. (If not, you can get the test bulletin from Novell's Product Information, NetWire, the Novell Technical Information Database, or, possibly, from the dealer). These bulletins list model number, configuration, options, and brand names and models of any hardware tested with a particular product. They also list any problems, such as a particular board not working with a particular computer.

Any hardware vendor can pay the fees and send products to Novell for this certification testing, which provides an entry-level certification program to everyone who wants to market NetWare-compatible hardware. This open-ended approach can lead to some abuses, wherein some vendors (usually those outside the networking mainstream) may use the certification as a cheap way to expand their market without investing much time and effort. Therefore, if you're treating the stickers as gospel, make sure that the product you're considering has some networking knowledge behind it. Otherwise, your networking knowledge should be extensive enough to overcome a possible lack of networking knowledge on the part of the vendor.

If you're feeling really careful, check the product to be sure that all the options (including model number) tested are the same in the box as they are on the certification. Novell requires that any changes (BIOS, different brand or capacity hard disk drive) be recertified. Rather than do that, some vendors may drop the sticker from the box of the hardware in question and delete the sticker from the ad, replacing it with vague phrasing such as "Compatible with Novell's NetWare," which, to someone not focused on words, looks the same as "Novell Labs Tested and Approved."

The final thing to check is whether the manufacturer has a newer product on the market. Vendors have voiced the complaint that Novell's certification takes so long that the just-certified model is two or three revisions behind the currently shipping model. One firm complained that its product went through four revisions in a year, and that Novell was still back on number one or two. This may lead to the kinds of problems that you have when you're trying to follow the recommendations in *Consumer Reports*; you can't find the exact model that was listed in the magazine, and the salesman tells you that those recommendations are at least a year old and that this product over here is a much better buy anyway. Like *Consumer Reports*, though, Novell's certification is a place to start when you're looking for new networking products.

ENGINEERING SUPPORT PROGRAMS

Novell provides a couple of programs to make a vendor's life easier, and one that definitely makes the end user's life easier. The two that make the vendors' lives easier are a driver development program to assist developers in the creation of NetWare drivers (a driver tells NetWare what the product is and how it's going to behave with NetWare) and an engineering support program for large, multi-product companies with an established commitment to the NetWare market.

The program that makes the end user's life easier is the NetWare Ready program, open to drive, disk controller (host adapter) board, and subsystem manufacturers. The result for the end user is that the disk or subsystem has had all of the preliminary NetWare installation steps done before being shipped to market. Many hours of work go into making a hard disk drive ready for NetWare, so drives and subsystems that ship with these steps already done are a real boon for anyone who has better things to do than fuss with a hard disk drive for 24 or 48 or more hours. Unless you have a person who spends his or her time fussing with hard disk drives, it's worth the extra money to buy a product that is ready to work.

Drives and subsystems that are certified "NetWare Ready" ship with a sticker that says "Novell Labs NetWare Ready," as shown in Figure 1.5.

The thing to watch out for here is that some vendors claim that their drives are NetWare ready, when what they mean is that the drives have been pre-COMPSURFed. (COMPSURF is a NetWare 286 utility used to verify the integrity of the drive; it can take up to two days and isn't designed for ESDI drives, which weren't around when NetWare 286 was first created.) These drives lack the sticker of drives that have been through Novell's NetWare Ready program. However, a vendor who pre-COMPSURFs a drive has performed a valuable service for you if you are using NetWare 286. If the drive under discussion is not on the cutting edge of technology, COMPSURFing may be all you need.

However, Novell claims that drives and subsystems that have been through Novell's NetWare Ready program have achieved the proper integration of the drive, disk controller board, and driver for the tested version of

NetWare. An added bonus to a NetWare Ready drive, especially those on the cutting edge of technology, is that NetWare's disk drive support tables do not have to be upgraded, because "NetWare Ready" becomes an installation option in NetWare. (The drive ships with a software driver to make "NetWare Ready" a viable option.)

The real catch to the NetWare Ready installation option is that you must use a disk controller board supported by the NetWare Ready driver. As of December 1990, the following boards are supported: the co-developed ADIC/Novell DCB, the ADIC/Novell DCB/2, the ADIC/Novell EDCB, Adaptec's 1540 and 1640 series, and the Always IN-2000.

CO-DEVELOPED PRODUCTS

The IMSP provides original engineering knowledge for very few products, products that would not exist without a joint effort from Novell and the hardware vendor. An Ethernet board by Compaq/Novell, disk subsystems by Storage Dimensions/Novell, and a disk controller board for PS/2 systems by ADIC/Novell are among recent examples.

This program has a sticker too, one that says "Novell Labs Co-Developed Hardware," as shown in Figure 1.6. You can bet that products with that sticker are going to work and work well with the versions of NetWare that the vendors say these products work with. Since they're co-developed products, it's probable that the version in the stores with the sticker on it is the latest version, overcoming one of the problems (for end users) of the IMSP certification.

OTHER TESTING PROGRAMS

While Novell, the biggest player in its field, has the biggest testing program, it certainly doesn't have the only testing program. Most other programs are much more informal than Novell's, and the testing is strictly for internal use, unlike Novell, which is beginning to market the results of its testing program. (When available, you can buy the test bulletin book through NetWire or in hard copy form by calling 1-801-429-7670.) But the reputable firms test their products for compatibility with as many products as possible; for example, Samsung Information Systems America, a division of Korea's Samsung heavy industries, tests its computer products against the main network interface boards in each of the main network types; it also tests for compatibility with RAM and disk controller boards, modems, and bridges. And they do it for the same reasons that Novell does its testing: to ensure compatibility and to keep up with the market.

In addition, several magazines have testing programs of their own. (You can check a magazine's test review a lot easier than you can check the reviews of products that were done for private purposes.) *InfoWorld* and *PC Magazine*, two of the computer industry's biggest trade publications, each test hardware and software products and print the results. These firms are not as network-oriented as Novell and testing hardware for compatibility with NetWare isn't in depth, but each can tell you about the best and worst products in the field.

Also, when you go to various computer stores, ask if the store has a testing program. As discussed earlier, many stores run compatibility testing on the products they sell. And while all the products in the store are, of course, far superior to the products in any other store, the salesman won't tell you that a product is compatible with NetWare if he or she knows it isn't.

II

Network Type and Cabling

OVERVIEW

Network type and its attendant cabling is the first step when you're determining your network requirements. Choosing the network type (token passing, collision avoidance, etc.) is the decision that determines the direction of many other networking purchases.

How you make this decision, of course, depends on several circumstances, all of them individual: Do you already have a network installed? Is price the most important thing? How about performance (speed)? Troubleshooting? Name brands?

There's nothing intrinsic to a network type that makes it mandatory for a particular situation. NetWare supports all of the baseband standards—Ethernet (including StarLAN), ARCNET, Token-Ring—and some of the not-so-standards, such as IBM's PC LAN, which is "kinda-like" Ethernet. NetWare supports other network types, including broadband, proprietary, and wide-area network, but these won't be discussed here. Each of these types has its own strengths and weaknesses, and you probably are going to have to make tradeoffs, going with the factors that are most important to you and letting the rest go.

If you're working with an already-established network, continue using the same network type and the same wiring; your life will be simpler. If you have ARCNET, you can keep the type and change the wiring without starting over, one of ARCNET's strengths. It doesn't make sense to throw out perfectly good cable and start over from scratch without a strong reason.

If price, the up-front cost, is the most important factor in your networking decisions, then the ARCNET network type is probably the cabling scheme for you. ARCNET is the oldest of the established network types, and it is the least expensive. It's also easy to install and troubleshoot. Ethernet has the most installations, thanks to its connections to DECnet, and, because of the advent of unshielded twisted-pair wiring, it is enjoying a resurgence of popularity. Token-Ring, on the other hand, is the newest and the most expensive, partly because of the built-in intelligence on the board (chips with intelligence are expensive) and partly because not many vendors are making the faster board yet.

If troubleshooting is the most important feature for you, consider Token-Ring, whose network management capabilities make troubleshooting very easy. Token-Ring has the most expensive up-front costs, but Token-Ring vendors claim that the up-front costs are more than offset by the life-of-network costs.

If your product has to be a name brand, remember that IBM is the biggest player in the computer industry today and is the father of Token-Ring. IBM makes Token-Ring boards as well as the all-but-abandoned PC LAN, and they have just introduced a Micro Channel Ethernet board. Of course, IBM charges more for its products than anybody else on the market, and their products tend not to work too well with products not made by IBM. (IBM strolls along to its own drummer, frequently oblivious to the dictates of the marketplace.)

If performance is the most important criteria, and all other things being equal it should be, then you have a problem. Every vendor out there will tell you that his network type is the best and will cite reasons. You have to evaluate all the performance issues—speed, network stability, flexibility, troubleshooting, network management—and make the tradeoffs to get the network type that is best for you.

In a nutshell, the reasons for choosing (or not choosing) each network type are listed below:

- ARCNET networks are easy to install, give you a choice of wiring topologies (bus, star, daisy chain), and the boards themselves are cheap. On the other hand, ARCNET boards don't feature much in the way of network management.

- Ethernet is best for environments with a small number of large data accesses (computerese for "going to the network infrequently but for big jobs"). It also has DEC connectivity, since DECnet networks use Ethernet cabling, and it's the cabling of choice for Portable NetWare. The new unshielded twisted-pair wiring standard (10Base-T) also features networking management capabilities that, along with the star topology, make troubleshooting a much more viable proposition than Ethernet's traditional bus topology with coaxial cable.

- Token-Ring networks feature dependable performance and IBM connectivity, as well as sophisticated network management capabilities. The main drawback is the cost, which should drop as more vendors enter the marketplace.

Performance and other issues of each networking type are discussed in more detail in the sections that follow. A general discussion on cabling begins later in this chapter.

IEEE STANDARDS

The Institute of Electrical and Electronic Engineers (IEEE), in conjunction with the American National Standards Institute (ANSI), publishes standards that control the Ethernet and Token-Ring topologies. ARCNET's standards have never been controlled by the IEEE.

Ethernet and Token-Ring standards fall under the auspices of the IEEE's 802.xx committee. The subcommittee governing Ethernet standards is known as 802.3, and the subcommittee governing Token-Ring is 802.5. These standards have been accepted by the industry, and most vendors I spoke with talked about how their products not only met but exceeded the standards set by the IEEE. (It's not that the IEEE is setting low standards. Most manufacturers just make it a point of pride to do better than minimum standards.)

ARCNET TRADE ASSOCIATION (ATA) STANDARDS

The ARCNET Trade Association (ATA), a group of ARCNET component manufacturers, controls the standards for the ARCNET networking type, although this hasn't always been the case. ARCNET was originally created by Datapoint Corporation, and Datapoint has historically controlled the specifications for that networking type. Today, however, the ATA says that Datapoint has given up control of ARCNET and claims that every ARCNET vendor in the association has as much right as Datapoint to propose revisions. The ATA publishes the ARCNET specifications and doesn't understand why the rest of the networking world thinks that these standards are any less valid than those issued by the IEEE. However, when asked what would happen if Datapoint went right ahead and created a new revision without the ATA, the spokesman said that the ATA would write up a new ARCNET specification draft incorporating that standard.

PC LAN

PC LAN is a proprietary network operating system that belongs to IBM. Until March 1990, when Novell released an upgrade to NetWare Entry Level System, Level I, PC LAN was one of only three network types supported by ELS. The PC LAN operating system is mentioned here only because of its historical connection to ELS.

When you look at the testing done by Novell, it seems that the IBM PC LAN Adapter II (PCNII) board is extremely popular. However, that's misleading. Novell writes the NetWare drivers for IBM's PC LAN Adapter and PC LAN Adapter II boards and therefore tests all systems against them (as Novell does with all drivers that ship in its "red box"). As a matter of fact, many systems did not do well in running the PC LAN Adapter II board, and all of the vendors I checked with were indifferent to that fact, saying that the PC LAN market was not important to them.

IBM is still supporting the PC LAN network type (the IBM'er I spoke with said that IBM provides five years of support for each of its products after they stop shipping), but obviously has positioned Token-Ring as its network type of the future. Fortunately, ELS now can use the same network types as any other version of NetWare 286, so your ability to find a computer that can run the PC LAN board becomes less critical. (Computers that can't run the PC LAN board are listed in Appendix F.)

NETWORK TOPOLOGIES

A network topology is the way that the network is logically connected, never mind what it looks like when you've finished physically connecting it. You have three choices—bus, star, or ring—each named for the way they logically look.

BUS TOPOLOGY

A bus usually runs on coaxial cable and is used most often with Ethernet, although ARCNET sometimes uses it if the network involved is small enough (no more than 1,000 feet, 8 users). A bus is named because of its similarity to the buses on our streets; you can get on or get off when you want, but when the bus stops or breaks, you stop, too, along with every other person on the bus at the time. That, of course, is the main drawback to using a bus topology; on a star or a ring, the whole network does not go dead if a problem develops on one portion of the network. With a bus, however, the network does go dead, which means that you are going to have a hard time figuring out what and where the problem is.

The advantage to a bus network is that it uses the least amount of cable, and, if you can keep the network small and use thin cable, the least amount of additional hardware. This keeps the up-front network costs down. (Remember, however, that up-front network costs pale beside life-of-network costs; if you're unlucky, you can spend all your up-front cost savings troubleshooting your bus network and buying equipment to make that troubleshooting job easier.)

While coaxial cable is usually used on a bus network, fiber optic can also be used as a backbone or for connectivity between buildings.

STAR TOPOLOGY

A star topology usually runs on unshielded twisted-pair cable and is most often used with ARCNET networks, (although Ethernet specifications have just been expanded to include unshielded twisted-pair and thc star topology.) This specification is expected to boost the popularity of Ethernet, because suddenly it's now as easy to troubleshoot an Ethernet network as an ARCNET network.

ARCNET's star topology is most often described as a "string of stars," which is also used by Ethernet's unshielded twisted-pair wiring. This string is created by attaching the devices on the network to a passive or active hub, which in turn is connected (daisy-chained) to another active hub. (Ethernet's twisted-pair wiring uses concentrators instead of active or passive hubs.)

RING TOPOLOGY

Only Token-Ring uses the ring topology. In a ring topology, each station on the network acts as a repeater for the station physically connected to it. Each station is also physically connected to a central device called a Multistation Access Unit (MAU). Because of the way it connects to the MAU, the Token-Ring topology is called a star-wired ring.

Token-Ring usually uses shielded twisted pair, although an IEEE specification has been proposed that will allow it to run on unshielded twisted pair.

CABLING OVERVIEW

Once you've decided upon a network type and topology, you're two-thirds done. All you have to think about is choosing among the different wiring types that are supported: coaxial, twisted pair, or fiber optic.

To a limited degree, this choice is made for you; that is, if you have a Token-Ring network, you can't choose coaxial cable, but you can choose from two different kinds of twisted-pair wiring and one kind of fiber-optic wiring. If you have ARCNET or Ethernet (including AT&T's StarLAN), you can use twisted pair (including telephone wiring already in the building if you know what you're doing or have hired a consultant), coaxial, or fiber optic.

And of course, if you've already got an established network, you are bound by compatibility constraints. For example, you can only mix and match the two kinds of Ethernet coaxial cable according to strict limitations. (Simply put, the cheaper cable doesn't cover as much distance as the more expensive.) And no matter what cabling you choose, check with local regulations to make sure you will be in compliance with local building codes.

Each of the wiring systems discussed in the following sections has strengths and weaknesses. How important each strength or weakness is depends on the kind of network and the number of nodes you're installing.

TWISTED PAIR

Twisted-pair wiring comes in two variations, shielded and unshielded. Shielded is most often used in Token-Ring, while ARCNET and Ethernet (including StarLAN) use unshielded. The advantage of shielded over unshielded is in electronic noise/crosstalk immunity. On the other hand, shielded twisted-pair wiring is expensive to buy, and it requires much more knowledge to run. (Everybody who cares knows how to run unshielded twisted-pair wiring: as telephone cable, it's been around forever.)

The unshielded twisted-pair (UTP) cabling option, while long the StarLAN standard and popular as an ARCNET cabling media, has just been approved by the IEEE Ethernet subcommittee and is in the beginning stages of approval for Token-Ring. Even before official sanction, it gained in popularity as an Ethernet option for several important reasons: UTP wire is telephone cable, and you can make use of the telephone wiring closet for your network. (Telephone wiring closets are usually centrally located in an office, making them very convenient for network cabling.)

Twisted pair is also cheaper than thick coaxial cable, and it's considerably easier to work with.

The main drawback to unshielded twisted-pair wiring is mune to radio frequency interference. If you have an electron network environment, you will need a shielded cable. The only shield supported by the IEEE for Ethernet is coaxial cable or fiber optic, each which has a drawback (price and/or flexibility).

Specific rules for twisted-pair cabling are listed in Chapter III, with the discussions on ARCNET, Ethernet, and Token-Ring.

COAXIAL CABLE

Coaxial cable, more familiarly known as co ax cable, is used in Ethernet and ARCNET networks, although you can't use an Ethernet-specified coax cable in your ARCNET network. ARCNET cable is specified as RG-62; Ethernet cable, which comes in two varieties, is specified as RG-8 (commonly known as thick, thicknet, or Ethernet, depending on where you're from) and RG-58 (thin, thinnet, or cheapernet). Coax carries higher frequencies and offers a broader bandwidth than twisted-pair cable. It's also expensive (although the price is coming down) and horrendously hard to work with, especially the thick cable, according to several vendors. Thick coax cable is not being recommended by any of the vendors I spoke with; instead, they all recommended thin coax cable for small networks (25 or so users) and unshielded twisted-pair wiring for larger networks.

FIBER OPTIC

Fiber-optic cable has three advantages:

- It's designed for distance.
- It's almost impossible to tap.
- Being shielded, it's meant for use in electronically noisy environments.

It also has one great disadvantage:

- It's expensive (but getting cheaper).

Almost everyone agrees that fiber-optic cable is the best cable out there. It's so heavy duty that it is probably more than the average network needs, and it's certainly more expensive than the average network administrator needs, although the price is dropping.

If you are connecting networks between two buildings, say on a college campus, fiber-optic wiring is the perfect choice. If you're in charge of the Air

Force 1 LAN and need a cabling type that is difficult to tap, choose fiber optic. If your networking environment has a lot of electromagnetic and radio frequency interference, fiber optic can block it out. Fiber optic is also the cabling of choice for broadband and high-speed networks.

If you have a lot of network users with database and word processing needs, fiber-optic wiring is overkill unless your network has a large number of users or the fiber-optic cable can be used as a backbone.

The next few sections discuss the three most popular network types used by Novell's NetWare—ARCNET, Ethernet, and Token-Ring—giving the pros and cons of each network type as well as rules for cabling each one.

ARCNET

ARCNET (Attached Resource Computer NETwork) is one of the oldest network types around, created in 1977 as a proprietary network type by Datapoint. Later technologies copied it when they came on the scene. Token-Ring took a page from the ARCNET book to use a token passing scheme, while Ethernet took a page to use a bus-type broadcast scheme.

But ARCNET's implementation of the token passing scheme and the bus topology resulted in a surprisingly efficient network whose only drawback, once it's installed, is speed. Not surprisingly, high technology is currently addressing this slow-speed drawback and ARCNET is planning on a network protocol that can run at 20 megabits per second (Mbps) instead of 2.5 Mbps. "Mbps" is the speed with which traffic is moved over the network; the higher the number, the faster the network.

ARCNET, although easily installed, does have a drawback for the mechanically klutzy—you, the network administrator, have to manually set the address on each and every ARCNET board in the network. Every device on the network must have a unique identification address. Every Ethernet and Token-Ring board comes with a unique set of addresses already configured, eliminating the likelihood that you will get every address right but one. Duplicating an address means you have to check up to 255 boards to find out just which two have disabled the network. This is the best reason I can think of to maintain good records of your station addresses and to label the boards as you go.

One of ARCNET's great virtues, in addition to its ease of installation (most cable installers aren't mechanical klutzes), is its ability to mix and match the various wiring media—coaxial, twisted pair, fiber optic. This virtue is not important if you have a small network, of course, but it becomes more critical if you have to make additional cabling decisions because you are going beyond the eight- or ten-user limit that one segment of wire media supports. Whether the limit is eight or ten users per segment depends on whether the wiring is coaxial cable or twisted pair. Fiber-optic wiring supports as many users as the network operating system allows. (Wiring limitations for ARCNET are discussed later in this chapter.)

Network experts who don't like ARCNET talk about "standards" and compatibility, claiming that ARCNET lacks a set-in-concrete standard and also that the new 20-Mbps board will be so fast that it won't be compatible with the networks running at a slower speed.

ARCNET was invented by Datapoint Corporation, and while historically only Datapoint maintained the standards for the network type, the standards are now being controlled by the membership of the ARCNET Trade Association (ATA). However, proponents of other network types keep talking about the IEEE subcommittees as the place where true network-type standards are set. The general manager of the ATA points out that the IEEE is a trade association just like the ATA, with the difference being that the ATA is devoted exclusively to one network type's issues, unlike the IEEE, whose energies are diffused.

The other problem, say ARCNET's critics, is whether the 2.5-megabit board will work with the future 20-megabit board. This is currently only a hypothetical problem, since the 20-Mbps board seems to have hit a snag somewhere between the drawing board and the execution and won't be shipped until the fall of 1991, if then. But it's a valid consideration and something to ask the vendors if you are thinking of combining the two kinds of boards onto one network; however, rest assured that ARCNET manufacturers are not going to alienate their established base to embrace an untried high-end technology. (Thomas-Conrad has a 100-Mbps board for fiber-optic wiring that uses the same drivers as its 2.5-Mbps board. The 100-Mbps board is not meant for use in traditional ARCNET networks, just in case you were thinking of getting a really high performance network interface board meant for the next generation of data-intensive and transaction-oriented applications. See Chapter VIII for a discussion on FDDI technology.)

Token-Ring vendors, who were quick to bring up the compatibility issue about ARCNET, are marketing a 16-Mbps board that is much faster than the 4-Mbps boards running to the old Token-Ring standard. They insist that compatibility isn't a problem, since the two boards can run on the same network. And so it is a similar issue with the faster board manufactured by ARCNET vendors; it will be compatible with the lower standard.

The real question is likely to be: do you want to add a high-end, more expensive solution to a network that is running satisfactorily at the lower speed? The real answer is: probably not, unless you change the applications that are being run on the network.

ARCNET NETWORK TYPE

Although ARCNET is technically a bus topology and can look like a linear bus, it is usually "a string of stars" through the use of hubs, active and passive, that relay the network signal. (Refer to the chapter overview for a discussion of the various topologies.)

If you have a choice, cable your network in a star, assuming that you don't mind a little additional up-front cost. A star-wiring scheme uses more cable than other wiring schemes, so the cable costs are more expensive. The nice thing about a star is that, if you want to add users, it's easy to do. Also, when a cable breaks, only the station directly connected is affected; the network continues to function. And because everything works but the station affected, it's easy to determine the problem.

On the other hand, if you cable your ARCNET network in a linear bus, the network is dead if a cable breaks, which is only the first difficulty. No easy way exists to isolate the problem, since nothing is working. The advantage of a linear bus is that hubs are not needed if you have a small network (eight or fewer actual users and a maximum network length of 1,000 feet), which saves you some hardware costs.

These two cabling schemes are illustrated in Figures 2.1 and 2.2.

ARCNET HARDWARE REQUIREMENTS

Unfortunately, even though ARCNET is easy to use, it requires a lot of hardware. And each topology requires different hardware.

Hardware Required for ARCNET Bus Topology

To run ARCNET with coaxial cable, you need:

- RG-62 coaxial cable
- ARCNET interface board that supports coaxial cable
- BNC T-connectors (to attach the board to the cable)
- 93-ohm BNC terminators (to attach to each end of the cable)

Figure 2.1. ARCNET Configured in a Bus

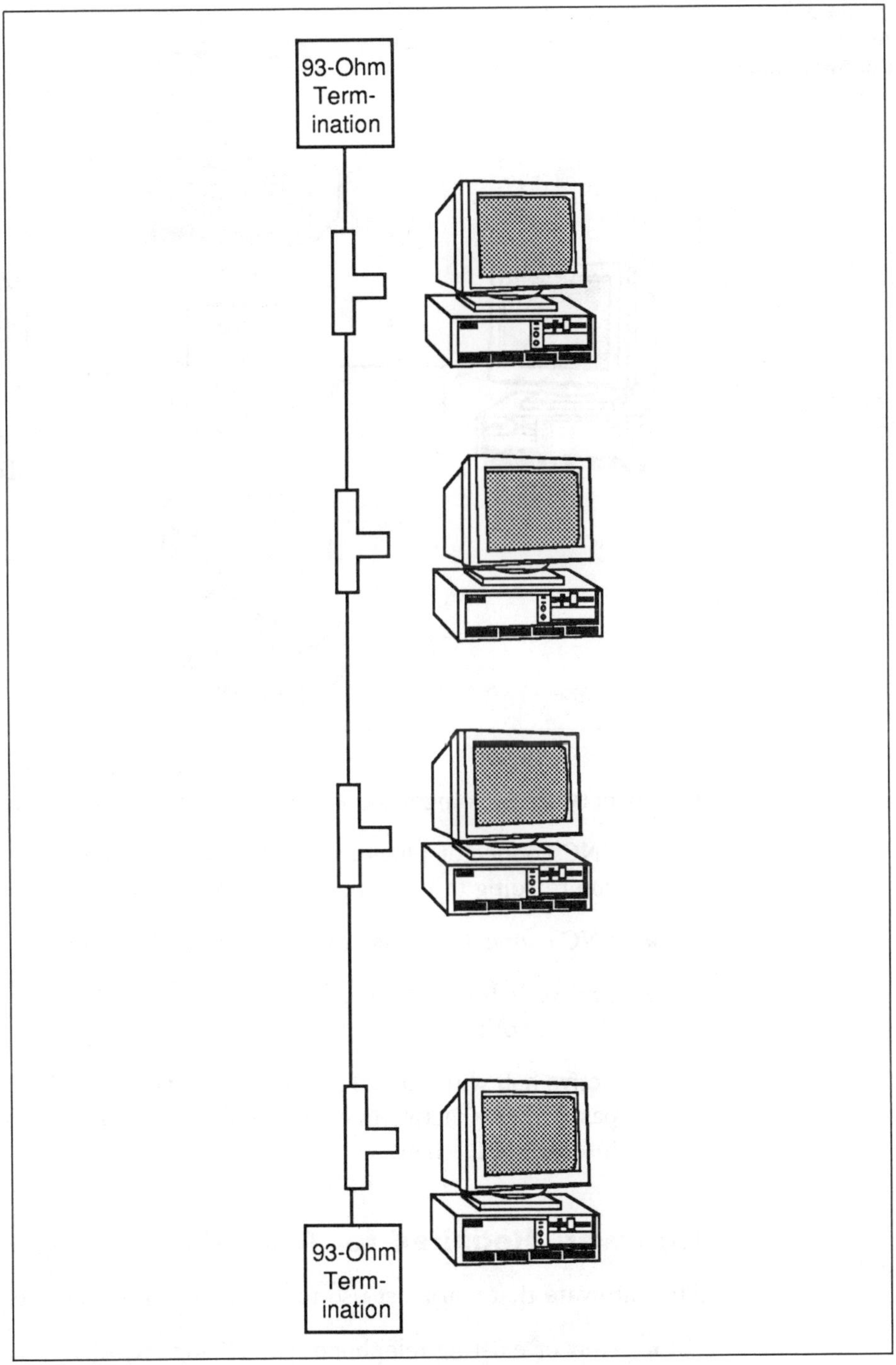

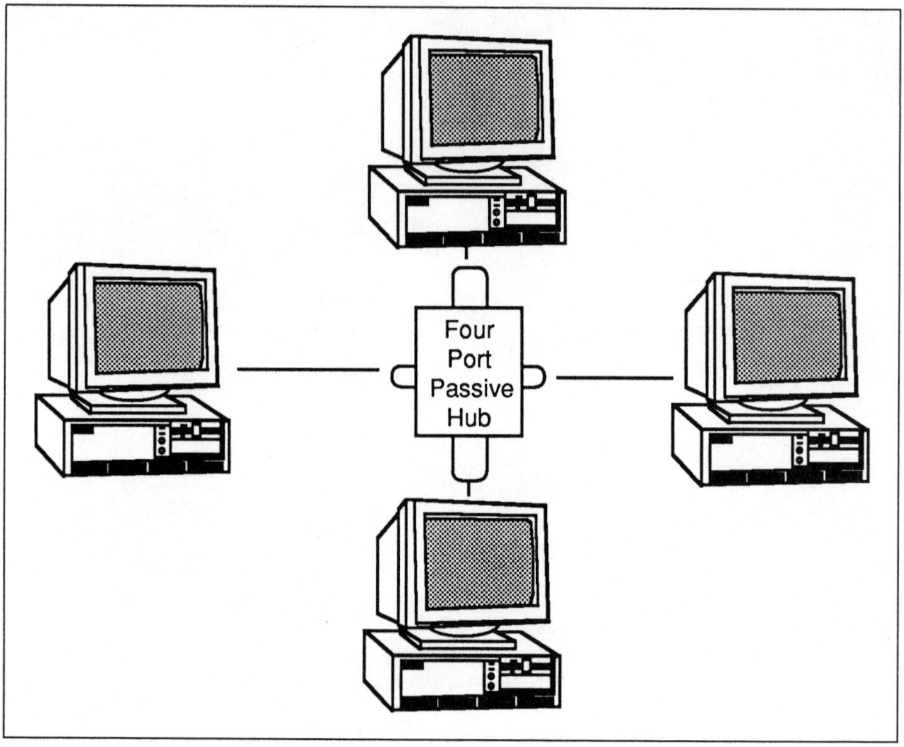

Figure 2.2. ARCNET Configured in a Star

If your network is going to be larger than eight stations, you may also need:

- BNC connector plugs to attach to each end of each cable length (if you're going to have more than one segment)
- BNC connector jacks (to attach to BNC connector plugs)
- Passive hub with four cable ports (one computer to a port) to relay the network signal
- Active hub with up to 16 cable ports, which can be connected to 128 passive hubs, active hubs, and computers (unless your board has an internal active hub)

Hardware Required for ARCNET Star Topology

The hardware that you must use for twisted-pair wiring includes:

- New or existing telephone-type wiring (RJ-45)

- ARCNET interface board that supports twisted-pair wire
- 93-ohm terminators

If you are connecting more than eight or so stations, you may also need:

- Twisted-pair active hub
- Twisted-pair link (if you connect twisted-pair to coaxial cable)
- Baluns (if you want to use coaxial ARCNET products with twisted-pair cable)

The family that makes up the cabling hardware for an ARCNET network is illustrated in Figure 2.3.

CABLE ACCESS

Cable access on an ARCNET network is controlled by whichever node has the token. The token is passed from node to node in a predetermined order, which usually has nothing to do with physical location. When a node has the

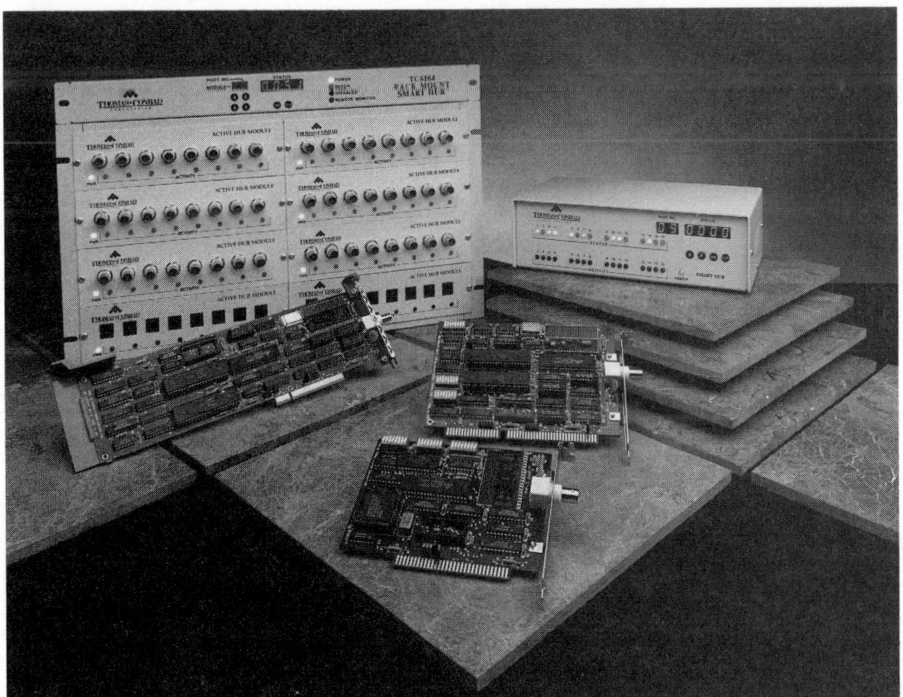

Figure 2.3. Family of Products Needed for an ARCNET Network Cable
Reprinted by Permission of Thomas-Conrad

token, it can send data (called a packet) over the network. If the node doesn't have the token, it cannot send the packet and is required to wait its turn.

The order of token passing is determined by the address that each node on a network is given (from 1 to 255). As each node receives the token, the next highest node address is written into the node's Next Identifier. When the node is through with the token (either having sent its packet or not having a packet to send), the token is passed to the address in the Next Identifier. This cable access method is illustrated in Figure 2.4.

ARCNET's token passing scheme gives it a performance advantage over both Ethernet and Token-Ring (different kinds of advantages, of course, since those two network types are so different from each other).

Ethernet, which has a collision-detection cable access scheme, has difficulties when a lot of traffic is on the network, and its performance goes steeply downhill. A collision-detection cable access scheme doesn't prevent anybody who wants to from getting on the network at any time on a first-come, first-served basis. But every time a packet of information collides with another packet of information, both packets die in a collision that is heard by every node on the network. This forces the nodes involved to retransmit their packets from the beginning. Using a token-passing system avoids the whole issue of collisions by controlling network access.

However, Token-Ring's token passing scheme causes a lot of overhead on the network because Token-Ring nodes can only talk to the next directly

Figure 2.4. ARCNET Token Passing Scheme

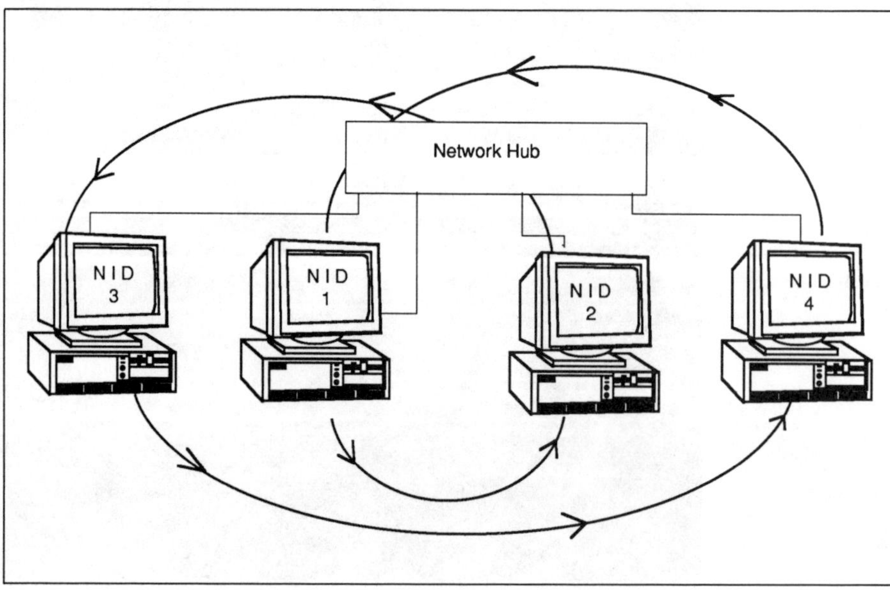

connected node, forcing each one to act, in essence, as a repeater. ARCNET, on the other hand, allows its nodes to broadcast to every node in the network; only the node whose address is broadcast in the packet gets the whole message.

The ability to broadcast generally, the way ARCNET does, is its virtue, offering slightly higher performances than other star-wired networks.

ARCNET CABLING

ARCNET can use any of the three wiring media (coax, twisted pair, or fiber optic) to connect its network, but the cable of choice is usually unshielded twisted pair because of its ability to be used in a star topology. Coax cable for ARCNET (or for Ethernet, for that matter) is expensive (but getting less so) and difficult to work with. Fiber-optic wiring is just as expensive; but like coax cable, it's getting cheaper.

Cabling Rules

Installing an ARCNET network is easier than installing any other network type. However, rules are everywhere, and ARCNET is no exception. When you are ready to cable, keep the following guidelines in mind.

The most important rule is the limit on the number of nodes: only 255 nodes are allowed on the entire network (but you can place those 255 over 20,000 feet of cable).

The rules in the following sections only pertain to the wiring. Other hardware, such as the passive and active hubs, also has limitations. If you decide on ARCNET, or any other networking type, talk to a professional first.

Copper-Based Wiring

A number of general rules pertain to all ARCNET networks that use copper wiring. (That is, all networks running any cable but fiber optic. Coax and twisted-pair cable are made from copper.)

- The maximum number of copper segments in a series is three.
- Each end of each copper segment must be terminated with a 93-ohm terminator.
- Each copper segment can be grounded at only one point.

Unshielded Twisted Pair (UTP)

These rules are in addition to the rules regarding copper-based wire.

- The maximum length of an UTP cable or daisy chain is 130 meters. (Daisy chain is the method by which the stations are connected.)
- Ten stations are allowed on a UTP daisy chain.
- Each twisted-pair hub counts as a node on the network; i.e., if you have three twisted-pair hubs, you can only have 252 other nodes (totalling 255).
- Twisted-pair cable or daisy chain must be terminated at both ends with 93-ohm terminators or with a terminator and an active hub.

Coaxial

These rules are in addition to those regarding copper-based wire.

- The maximum length of a coaxial cable bus is 300 meters.
- Eight stations are allowed on a coaxial cable bus segment.
- Coaxial cable must be terminated at each end with 93-ohm terminators or with a terminator and an active hub.

Fiber Optic

- The maximum distance between boards, hubs, and other ARCNET hardware devices is 2,000 feet.

ETHERNET

Ethernet is the networking type in the middle—neither fastest nor slowest, neither cheapest nor most expensive, neither youngest nor oldest. Originally created by Xerox, Intel, and DEC, DEC today still uses Ethernet to connect its minicomputers; if you have DEC systems to network, Ethernet is probably the networking choice. By the same token, if you're thinking about using Portable NetWare to connect to a UNIX network, now or in the future, Ethernet connections can expand the data processing options open to your users.

Ethernet is also the network type to use if your network is fairly small and the applications on the network don't require constant access. That is, Ethernet is designed to allow the people on your network to turn the machines on in the morning, check their mail, call up their applications, save the work created, print their efforts, and exit the network at the end of the day. Between each of these accesses (turn on, call up, save, print, exit), nothing much is happening on the network.

(I have been told that network performance is not an objective matter—it's a religious issue, with people taking strong stands on faith. On the other hand, I have come across several people who say no performance difference exists between Ethernet and Token-Ring networks.)

At 10 Mbps, Ethernet can feel the high-tech wolf snapping at its heels, because Token-Ring is mastering a 16-Mbps technology and ARCNET is working on a 20 Mbps. One manufacturer told me that when Token-Ring and ARCNET are faster than Ethernet, then Ethernet will come up with new standards. The same vendor said that Token-Ring's 16-Mbps board didn't test faster than Ethernet in throughput tests, so he didn't think the Ethernet IEEE committee would bestir itself to catch up with Token-Ring, at least for now. (This vendor also said that since the 20-Mbps ARCNET board wasn't shipping yet, ARCNET competition was also nothing to worry about. He may be right, since the 20-Mbps ARCNET board has hit a roadblock.

IEEE STANDARDS FOR ETHERNET

The IEEE standard that affects Ethernet as a local area network type has four categories that concern this book. The standards listed below are for baseband signaling; all but the StarLAN standard is for a 10-Mbps transmission rate.

- 1Base5: Known as the StarLAN standard, this category allows for 1-Mbps transmission over unshielded twisted-pair wiring.
- 10Base-T: The newest standard, approved in late 1990, describes unshielded twisted-pair wiring specifications.
- 10Base2: This category sets the standard for thin coaxial cable.
- 10Base5: This category sets the standard for thick coaxial cable.

The last two categories are always lumped together, just as they are sometimes used together. The first two standards are rarely used together or with coaxial cable, although you can do so, if you want to complicate your life.

Figure 2.5. High-Tech Wolf

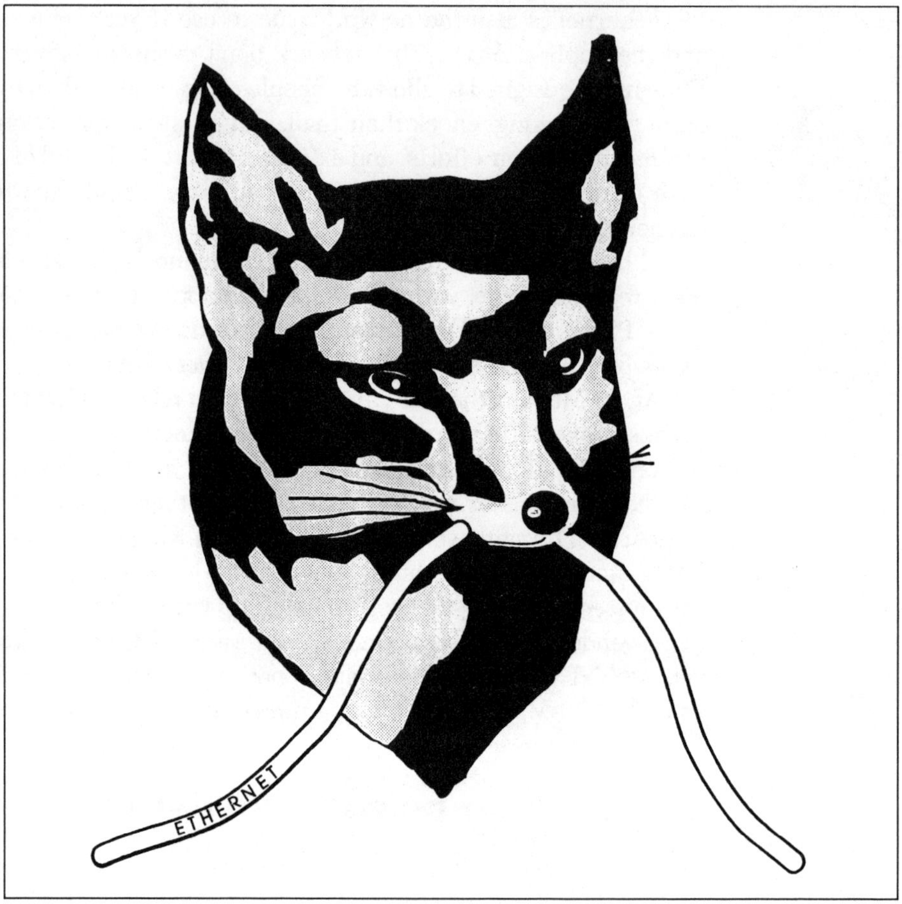

StarLAN

StarLAN was created by AT&T to use twisted-pair wiring long before the 10Base-T standard was proposed by the IEEE. StarLAN was meant to take advantage of the millions of miles of telephone wire that is located in most of the country's buildings.

However, the 1-Mbps transmission rate means that it is slow, compared to the other three Ethernet standards of 10 Mbps or to the new ARCNET and Token-Ring boards. When the 10Base-T standard was proposed, with a transmission speed of 10 Mbps, it was eagerly embraced by firms such as Hewlett-Packard, which had previously been limited to the 1-Mbps rate for their StarLAN board. Even AT&T is now utilizing the proposed 10Base-T standard, which combines StarLAN's unshielded twisted-pair option with Ethernet's 10-Mbps speed.

AT&T is still selling the traditional 1Base5 StarLAN board, but perhaps not for much longer. The problem is that the 1Base5 standard is now old technology and is not compatible with the other Ethernet standards, including the new 10Base-T standard, without workarounds and additional hardware.

10Base-T

When you think of Ethernet, thick- and thin-coaxial cable historically comes to mind. But when the 10Base-T standard for unshielded twisted-pair cable was proposed, allowing Ethernet to run at 10 Mbps over ordinary telephone wire, it captured the imaginations of Ethernet LAN vendors everywhere. Every Ethernet vendor I spoke with had several twisted-pair boards, and most of those boards had been shipping for some time.

These firms took their best guess as to what the final standards would be, even before the specifications were finally approved in September 1990, and then implemented those guesses. Since only editorial (not technical) changes had been made to the standard over the previous year, those guesses turned out to be right.

However, SynOptics Communications, Inc., has been shipping its LattisNet product, which is 10 Mbps Ethernet running over unshielded twisted-pair wiring, since August 1987, the same month that the 10Base-T study committee was formed. By now, it has a large customer base. While functionally identical to 10Base-T, LattisNet does not meet the 10Base-T specifications, and SynOptics Communications has begun to also ship a 10Base-T product. SynOptics hastens to mention that LattisNet and 10Base-T products can coexist quite nicely in the same network. SynOptics prides itself on its interoperability and says that not only do its two products work together without problems in the same network, but also that 10Base-T boards from 3Com, Tiara, Racal-Interlan, and Western Digital also work just fine when mixed and matched with SynOptics products. What this means to you, the consumer, is that probably any 10Base-T board will work with any other, although you still should test or get guarantees when mixing and matching different brands of boards.

When it comes to a popularity contest, twisted-pair cable is now the wiring of choice for Ethernet, with thin coaxial cable used for small networks. Thick coaxial cable loses the race because it is difficult to work with, along with being more expensive than unshielded or shielded twisted-pair cable.

Star-based wiring systems are also a key to twisted-pair Ethernet. 10Base-T, with its twisted-pair wiring, has added some network management capabilities that the other Ethernet standards lack. If the line goes quiet, for example, 10Base-T sends pulses down the line to indicate that the link is operative. If the link is no longer operative (i.e., someone has turned off the computer) then 10Base-T takes down the link. This network management feature is similar to that featured by Token-Ring networks. (See the section on Token-Ring for a discussion of that network's network management features.)

Coaxial

Historically the cable choice for Ethernet, coaxial cable is losing ground very rapidly to the 10Base-T standard, not only because coaxial cable is considerably more difficult to use than twisted-pair wiring but also because 10Base-T has much more management capability and is easier to troubleshoot.

Fiber Optic

Fiber-optic cable is used for special situations where the network is large (in terms of distance), security is a top priority, or the network environment is noisy. Otherwise, although everyone agrees that it's the "best" cable out there, its cost is still against it; also, the IEEE doesn't have a standard yet for fiber optic in local area networks, although it does have an advisory group on fiber-optic wiring. This means that boards supporting the cable may not be in compliance with the final standard, so many vendors may be avoiding the fiber-optic issue until the standards are settled.

CABLE ACCESS

Ethernet performs best when a small number of people are using the network or when network traffic is fairly light. The more people on the Ethernet network, the worse the network will perform, due to its first-come, first-served cable access scheme that does not always prevent data from bumping into each other as multiple nodes try to transmit on the network.

Technically called Carrier Sense Multiple Access/Collision Detection (CSMA/CD), Ethernet's cable access scheme is equitable. This means that each station listens to the cable to see if information (called a packet) is being sent by a different station. If a packet is being sent by Station 1, Station 2 waits a random time and then checks again. If a packet is not being sent, Station 2 will then send its own packet. If Station 3 was also listening for a free space on the cable and sends its packet at the same time, the packets from Stations 2 and 3 may collide and die, as illustrated in Figure 2.6. In that

Figure 2.6. Ethernet CSMA/CD Scheme

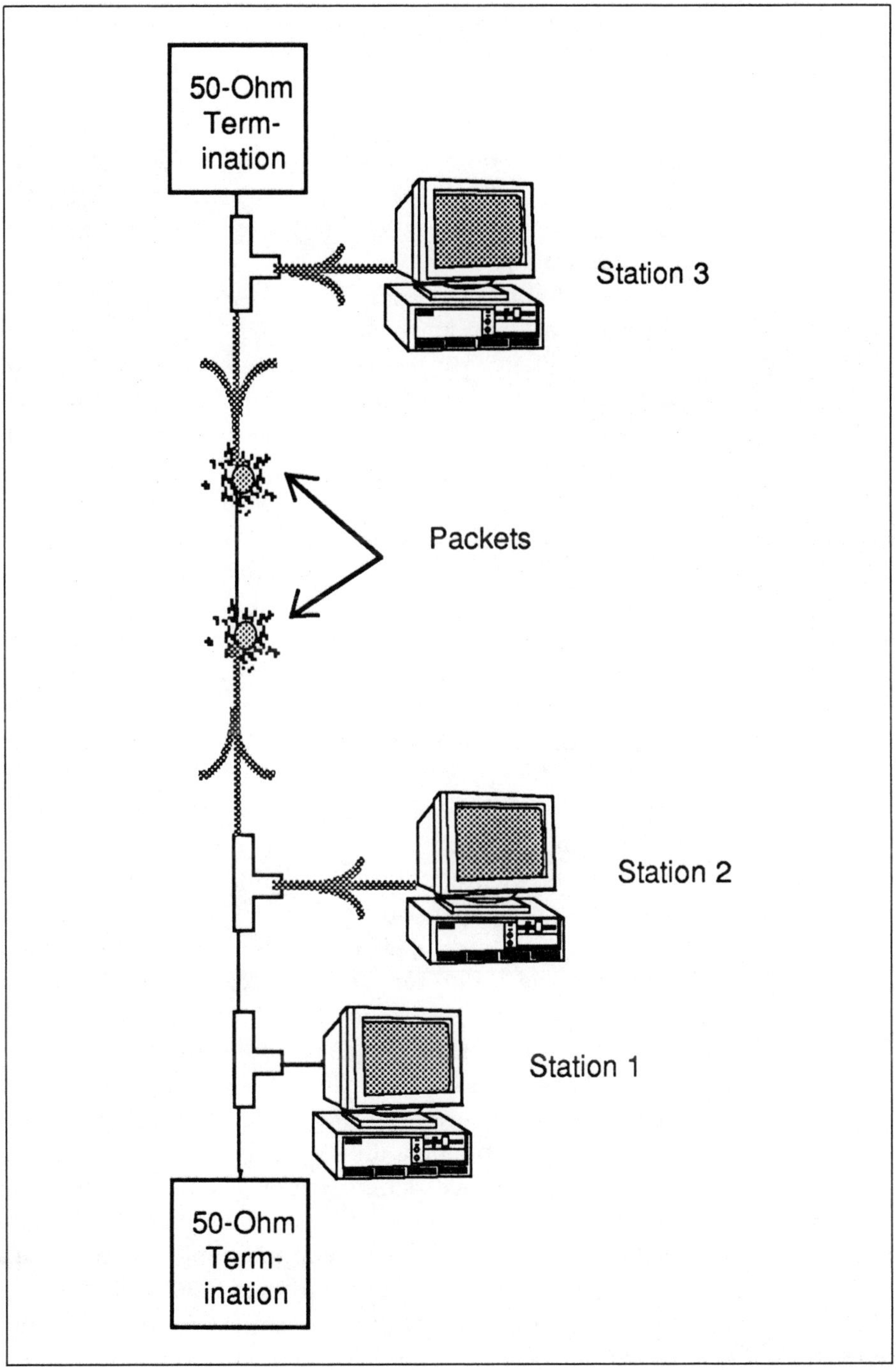

case, Stations 2 and 3 hear the collision, wait a random time, and then retransmit the packets.

This method is practical when not many stations are on the network; as more stations are added and attempt to transmit, it becomes more likely that packets from two or more stations will collide. When everybody has to start over, nobody finishes very quickly, which is another way of saying that the speed on the network takes a nose dive when a large number of stations are trying to send packets.

The advantage to using the CSMA/CD method is that it takes the least amount of cable of any of the methods supported by NetWare, and, for that reason, it's likely to be the lowest-priced of the three network types. (Counting only up-front costs, of course; life-of-network costs on a coaxial bus network are probably going to far surpass those of any network running twisted-pair wiring in a star or ring.)

COAXIAL CABLE

Coaxial cable is used in Ethernet and ARCNET networks, although you can't use an Ethernet-specified coax cable in your ARCNET network. Ethernet cable, which comes in two varieties, is specified as RG-8 (thick, thicknet, or Ethernet, depending on where you're from) and RG-58 (thin, thinnet, or cheapernet). Coax carries higher frequencies and offers a broader bandwidth than twisted-pair cable, supporting broadband transmission as well as baseband. Coax cable, because it been used so much, is well understood and is widely available through pre-existing installations.

However, the traditionally used thick Ethernet cable is rapidly falling from favor. It's fairly expensive and hard to handle, and the rules for using it are complex. It requires a lot of hardware to function—external transceivers, repeaters, and connectors. You can combine thick and thin Ethernet cable, but the rules for doing so are complicated and confusing. (For starters, you must cable thick and thin cable according to a formula with arbitrary numbers that allow you to use very little, relatively speaking, of the cheaper, thinner cable.) With the advent of twisted-pair wiring on the Ethernet scene, the advantages to combining different types of coaxial cable are lost.

3Com, if you ask them, says that if your network is small enough (25 or so users, 185 meters in length) and stable (not likely to grow), thin Ethernet cable is the wiring of choice. For one thing, no repeaters are needed, so the only hardware you need, in addition to the board and the cable, is a BNC T-connector. While every Ethernet connection requires a transceiver, the transceivers for thin Ethernet cable are built into the Ethernet board. However, after you get beyond 185 meters in length, you must switch to thick cable, with the attendant external transceivers and repeaters.

If your network is bigger than 25 or so users or longer than 185 meters, 3Com recommends unshielded twisted-pair wiring rather than thick Ethernet cable.

Hardware for Thick Ethernet Cable

If you're a die-hard traditionalist (or maybe just have a lot of cable that you don't want to throw away), here is a list of the hardware you need to run a standard thick Ethernet cable installation:

- RG-8 cable
- Ethernet interface board that supports thick Ethernet cable
- Drop or transceiver cable (from the board to the transceiver)
- Transceiver (to connect the transceiver cable to the "backbone" network cable)
- N-Series terminators (one grounded) for each end of the network cable
- Repeater (if your backbone cable is going to be longer than 500 meters)

Hardware for Thin Ethernet Cable

If you're going to use thin Ethernet cable, you need the following equipment:

- RG-58 coaxial cable
- Ethernet interface board that supports thin Ethernet cable
- BNC T-connector (to connect the board to the cable)
- BNC terminators (one grounded) for each end of the thin Ethernet cable segment
- BNC barrel connectors (if you decide to ignore 3Com's recommendations and make your network longer than one segment)
- Adapters (if you decide to run thick and thin Ethernet cable lengths together in one segment)

TWISTED-PAIR WIRING

Twisted-pair wiring is the newest wiring supported by Ethernet, and it's being eagerly accepted by Ethernet vendors everywhere. While twisted-pair wiring is indeed telephone wiring, it's not the flat or silver satin telephone wiring that connects the telephone to the transceiver in the wall. Existing twisted-pair wiring is the telephone wiring found in the walls of the buildings all around you. Keep in mind, however, that some unshielded twisted-pair wiring in some buildings is not going to be as satisfactory as some other unshielded twisted-pair wiring. If you want to use existing wiring, be sure that the wiring gives you correct data rates and keeps the errors within allowable ranges. Better yet, hire a consultant who can tell you about the suitability of the unshielded twisted-pair wiring in your building.

Advantages to twisted-pair wiring include the ability to plug and unplug your computer just as you would a telephone that you were moving from one outlet to another. The only downtime in that case is the time that it takes to move the computer and plug it into the twisted-pair transceiver. With coaxial cable, the system administrator has to rewrite the login script for the computer every time that computer is moved to another transceiver.

The cost of a twisted-pair installation is about the same as coaxial as long as you don't take troubleshooting or networking management costs into account. Take troubleshooting costs into account, and the costs of a coaxial installation skyrocket. Since twisted pair is usually cabled into a logical star, you always know which node is down, unlike coaxial cable where the whole network dies if one node has a problem.

Hardware for Twisted-Pair Wiring

The hardware required for a twisted-pair installation is minimal, about the same amount as the hardware for thin Ethernet cable. To run a twisted-pair installation, you will need:

- RJ-45 twisted-pair wiring
- Ethernet interface board that supports twisted-pair wiring
- Transceiver
- Hub

CABLING

For Ethernet, it's not how many nodes on a network that matters the most, but how many nodes on a segment of cable and how many segments. The total number varies depending on your cabling type.

Copper-Based Wire

A number of general rules pertain to all Ethernet networks using coax or twisted-pair wiring, which both are copper based.

- The maximum number of copper segments in a series is three.
- Each end of each copper segment must be terminated with a 50 ohm terminator.
- Each copper segment can be grounded at only one point.

Thin Coax Cable

The rules for copper-based wiring also pertain to rules for thin coax wiring. The following limitations are in addition to the rules for copper-based wiring.

- The maximum length of a thin coax cable segment is 185 meters.
- The maximum number of nodes (including repeaters) on a thin coax segment is 30.
- BNC T-connectors (node connectors) must be no closer than 0.5 meters apart.
- Using repeaters, thin coax cable can be mixed with thick coax cable, fiber optic wiring, and unshielded twisted-pair cable to maximize the network distance.

Thick Coax Cable

Although this cable has fallen into extreme disfavor because of its cost and difficulty of handling, the rules are given here for reference. These rules are in addition to the general rules for copper-based wiring.

- The maximum length of a thick coax cable segment is 500 meters.
- The maximum number of nodes (including repeaters) on a thick coax segment is 100.

- Transceivers (node connectors) must be no closer than 2.5 meters.
- Drop cables (between the external transceiver and the network backbone) can be no more than 50 meters.
- Using repeaters, thick coax cable can be mixed with thin cable and twisted-pair wiring to save costs, although you have to use more thick than thin cable, which is a drawback. (Thick cable can be used with fiber-optic wiring, too, but you won't save any money, unless you already have them both on hand.)

Unshielded Twisted Pair (UTP)

These rules are given in addition to the general rules for copper-based wiring.

- The maximum length of a UTP segment is 100 meters (about the maximum length from a desk to the office telephone wiring closet).
- Transceivers (node connectors) must be no closer than 2.5 meters apart.

Fiber-Optic Wiring

- The maximum length of a fiber optic segment is one kilometer, depending on the number of connectors and splices in the cable.
- Using fiber-optic links and repeaters, fiber-optic wiring can be mixed with thin Ethernet cable, thick Ethernet cable, and twisted-pair wiring to provide connectivity between buildings.

TOKEN-RING

Token-Ring is the newest, the fastest, and the most expensive network type. It also features very reliable performance and IBM connectivity, and, most important from an administrator's viewpoint, it features network management that makes it easy to troubleshoot. If you are an IBM shop with IBM microcomputers, minicomputers, or mainframes, there's no reason for you to choose anything else.

If you're interested in Portable NetWare, be aware that Token-Ring is not currently supported by many of those who licensed Portable NetWare from

Novell; however, since Token-Ring is achieving a growing prominence in the industry, Portable NetWare will soon universally support this network type.

Until recently, Token-Ring's transmission rate was 4 Mbps, not much faster than ARCNET's 2.5-Mbps standard. In the last few years, vendors, led by IBM, have come out with 16/4-Mbps board. The 16/4 board provides a new selling point besides speed: It is switchable, meaning that you can run your network at either 16 or 4 Mbps (but not both simultaneously). This means that if you have the older 4-Mbps boards, you can add the new 16/4 boards and run the network at 4 Mbps until you can replace the older boards with 16-Mbps boards.

Token-Ring's standards committees don't have snazzy names like Ethernet subcommittees. Instead of 10Base-T, Token-Ring vendors talk about the 16-Mbps draft, the 16-Mbps UTP (Unshielded Twisted Pair) draft, and 4-Mbps UTP draft.

While unshielded twisted pair is the glamor kid in the Ethernet world, the 16-Mbps transmission rate is what Token-Ring vendors want to talk about. Even though the standard has not completed the approval process, it's far enough along that vendors feel that they can ship their products, knowing that they will be able to meet the final standards with small revisions to the board, just as the Ethernet vendors did with unshielded twisted-pair cable.

Token-Ring vendors have had a lot of problems with the 16-Mbps speed. Until late 1990, only Proteon and IBM were successfully shipping a 16-Mbps board. No one else was able to overcome a chip problem that crashed the network. But that problem has been resolved, and the 16-Mbps board is being shipped in quantity by most of the Token-Ring vendors in the marketplace. If you're interested in a 16-Mbps board, make sure you get guarantees from the vendor that it will be compatible with the final specification or will be upgraded to the new standards.

NETWORK MANAGEMENT

If you ask Token-Ring vendors why you should purchase Token-Ring instead of Ethernet or ARCNET, you'll be told that Token-Ring, unlike any other networking type, comes with built-in intelligence to make it easy to monitor the network, detect any problems, and correct those problems quickly. (These statements were made without regard for Ethernet's 10Base-T standard, which was not finalized at the time the comments were made. 10Base-T does have some built-in network management capabilities.) The built-in intelligence and the fact that not as many vendors are in the Token-Ring marketplace, makes the boards more expensive than ARCNET or Ethernet boards.

Token-Ring manufacturers say that the built-in intelligence on the board keeps the network running longer. And that when it goes down, the network management capabilities on the board pinpoint the problem quickly, so that the network's down time is minimized. Starting with the lowest level, every node on the ring can serve (if it has the special software) as a ring error monitor and can take itself off the network before any problems affect the network.

Token-Ring can use shielded twisted-pair cable, unshielded twisted pair, or fiber-optic wiring, although shielded twisted pair is the norm. A discussion of the virtues of each of these kinds of wiring is discussed later in this chapter.

CABLE ACCESS

Token-Ring's cable access scheme is similar to ARCNET's in that they both use a token to control which node is broadcasting on the network at any one time. However, Token-Ring networks use a different method to determine which node gets the token. The first node on the network generates the token and passes it to the next physical node in succession, unlike ARCNET, which uses a node identifier to determine which node gets the token next.

The 4-Mbps standard allows one token to be on the network at any one time. The new 16-Mbps draft, subnamed the "early token release," allows data (called a packet) from two different nodes to be on the network at one time. There is little chance of collisions because the packets are not broadcast, as they are in Ethernet; instead, the packets only travel in one direction and, theoretically at least, at the same speed. (The various topologies are discussed in the section overview.)

Token-Ring networks are cabled in a ring, logically enough, although the ring is shaped in a star. Being cabled in a ring means that the network can easily cover longer distances than other network topologies, and that the basic network can cost less than those networks running in a star. The problem, however, is that connecting nodes in a ring is complicated.

In a Token-Ring network, each node is physically attached to the node next to it. Each node is also connected to a transceiver, as well, called a multistation access unit. This is both a strength and a weakness. The way that a node is attached means that if one node malfunctions, only that node is affected, a major improvement over Ethernet bus networks. (In Ethernet bus networks, if one node malfunctions, the network is dead.) The drawback is that each node receives the token and its packet and then has to "repeat" that information to the next node until the packet reaches its destination. This increases the chance that the packet of information could be corrupted by a node whose malfunction has not yet been detected by the network intelligence. The Token-Ring passing scheme is illustrated in Figure 2.7.

CABLING

Token-Ring networks generally use IBM type 1, 2, or 6 shielded twisted-pair cable, although two standards are being drafted for unshielded twisted-pair cable: one at 4 Mbps and one at 16 Mbps.

Shielded twisted-pair cable allows you to install your network quickly and easily, once you understand the system, and, because it's shielded, it protects your network from electrical interference, also one of its strengths.

Unshielded twisted-pair wiring is, as mentioned earlier, still in the proposal stage for Token-Ring. Vendors who are using it now may not be in compliance with the final specifications, which may or may not be a problem for you. If you go with unshielded twisted-pair wiring, get guarantees from the vendor that the wiring will meet specifications and that it will be compatible with other Token-Ring products using unshielded twisted-pair wiring.

Figure 2.7. Token-Ring Token Passing Scheme

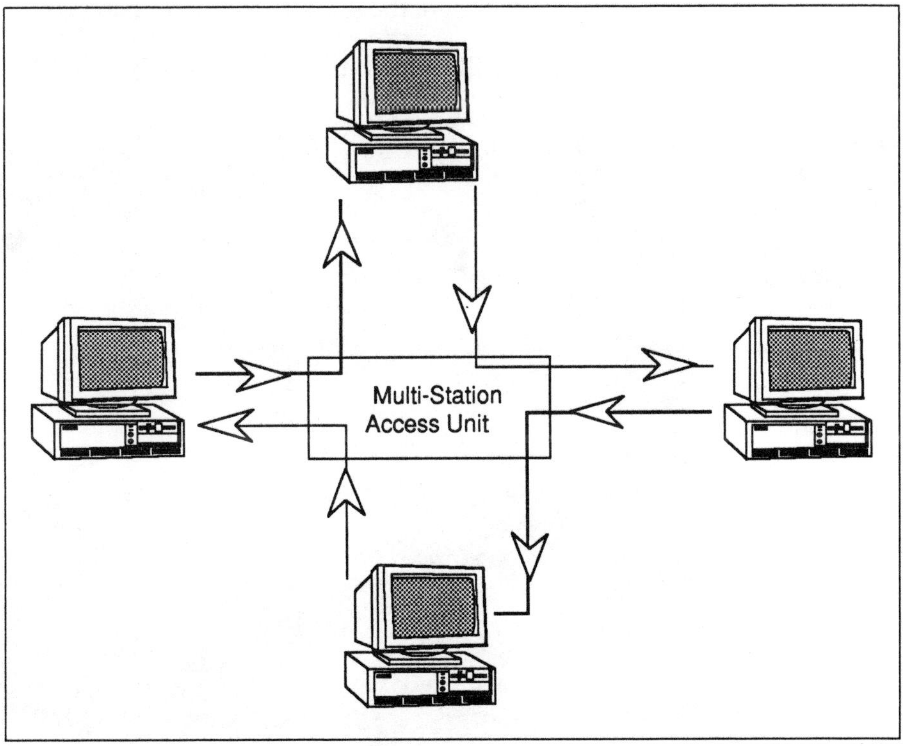

Fiber-optic wiring is great if you can afford it or your network environment absolutely requires it because of distance, security, or noise. Otherwise, it's not practical.

Hardware Required

To use a Token-Ring network, you need the following hardware (this assumes you're using the standard and not fiber-optic or unshielded twisted-pair wiring):

- IBM type 1, 2, or 6 shielded twisted-pair cable
- Token-Ring interface board that supports the cable selected
- Multistation Access Unit (MAU)
- Repeaters
- Patch cables (needed for large networks with more than one MAU or networks where the stations are more than eight feet from the MAU)

This hardware is illustrated in Figures 2.8, 2.9, and 2.10.

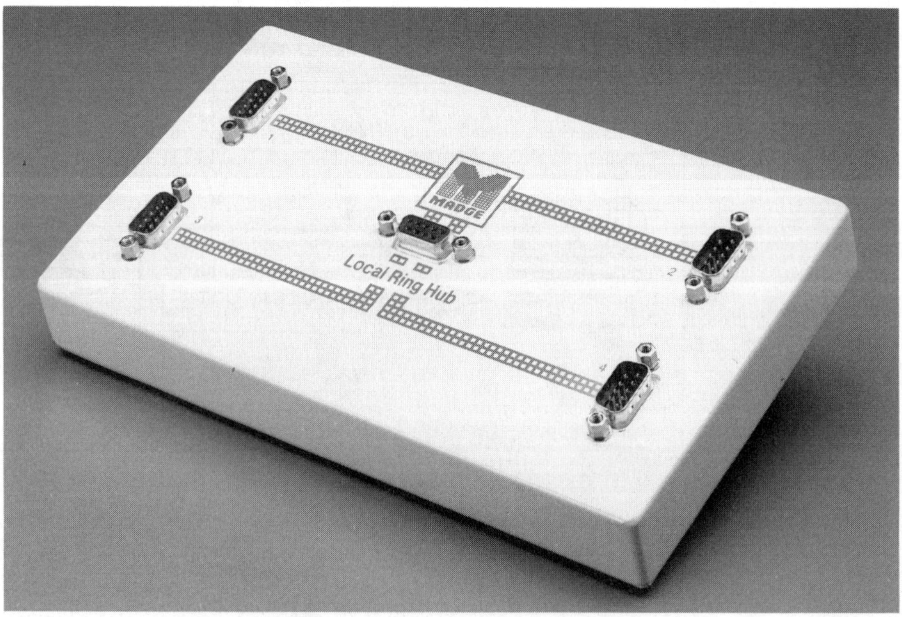

Figure 2.8. Four-Port Local Ring Hub (MAU) for Smaller Token-Ring Networks Courtesy of Madge Networks

Figure 2.9. Eight-Port Ring Hub (MAU) for Large Token-Ring Networks
Courtesy of Madge Networks

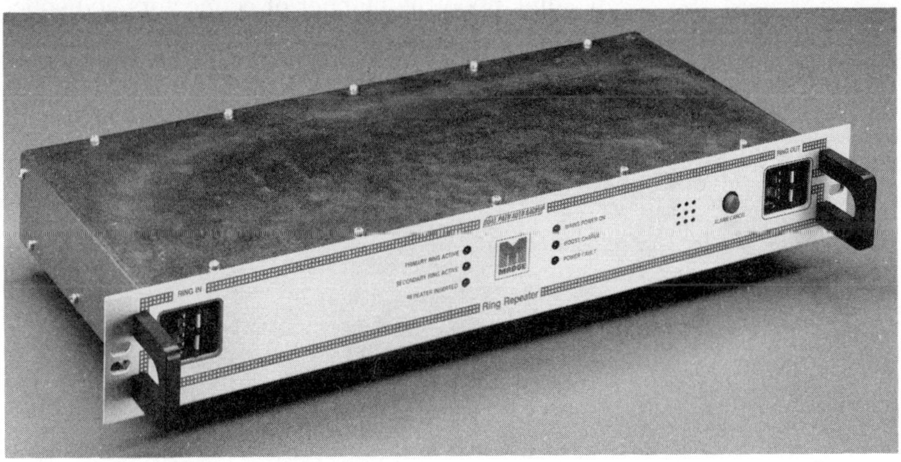

Figure 2.10. Ring Repeater
Courtesy of Madge Networks

CABLING RULES

The most important rule to remember is that 260 nodes are allowed on the network. Beyond that, a number of general rules pertain to all Token-Ring networks that use copper-based twisted-pair wiring (shielded or unshielded twisted-pair cable).

- The maximum number of copper segments in a series is three.
- Each end of each copper segment must be terminated.
- Each copper segment can be grounded at only one point.

Shielded Twisted-Pair Cable

These rules are in addition to the listed cabling rules.

- The longest lobe cable (which connects the PC to the ring) is less than 100 meters.
- The longest segment is less than 280 meters.
- A node can send a signal up to 380 meters (round trip).
- Each ring can have up to 33 IBM-compatible MAU (MAUs).

Fiber-Optic Wiring

- The maximum length of a fiber-optic segment is one kilometer, depending upon the number of connectors and splices.
- Fiber-optic wiring can be mixed with twisted-pair wiring to provide connectivity between buildings.

III

Boards

OVERVIEW

You can put a plethora of different boards into your computer: network interface boards, memory boards, disk controller boards, monitor boards, modem boards, and bridge boards.

However, the only boards that are considered in this book are boards that pertain to networking, and basically a small network at that. Bridges and routers, for example, are used to connect several networks together and are not discussed. Neither are monitor boards, memory boards, or the new, nifty internal modem boards: those are general computer issues, outside the focus of networking. This leaves only network interface boards and disk controller boards and a whole host of issues, many of which also apply to those boards that have been eliminated from this discussion.

In addition, there's even a plethora of names to call these two classes of boards: board, card, adapter, NIC. While they all mean the same thing, NIC stands for Network Interface Card and usually refers to a local area network board. Unless the manufacturer of the board specifically refers to it as a card or adapter, I refer to it as a board. Card has always sounded like a game to me and adapter like something that modifies something else.

Disk controller boards are being called host adapter boards as the more sophisticated of them change function. (Adapter belongs here.) The newer disk drives have their controllers built in; while they still need an interface board between themselves and the computer, the boards are otherwise free to take on a greater share of processing tasks from the computer's bus, speeding up throughput.

General incompatibility problems that face network interface boards and disk controller boards include:

- Idiosyncracies of computer hardware and software manufacturers,
- Bus and clock speed, and
- Bus mastering.

Specific issues affecting LAN boards and disk controller boards are discussed in the sections on network interface boards and disk controller boards.

IDIOSYNCRACIES

Taking idiosyncracies first, all hardware and software comes with bugs built in, usually inadvertently. A bug, which usually means a feature that doesn't work properly (or, perversely, an undesirable feature that insists on working to the detriment of something else), is frequently the price that manufacturers of hardware and software pay to make another feature work. With luck, the bug is of minor consequence to the manufacturer that created it; however, bugs can be disastrous to those who are struggling to offer compatible products. For one thing, the bug is often not immediately apparent; only the original manufacturer knows that it's there, and that may not be until somebody complains.

I know several instances in which hardware manufacturers sent recently released products to computer publications to be tested with the best in their class only to learn, in print, about a bug of such magnitude that their product couldn't complete the tests. The "in print" part, of course, assures manufacturers that nobody who has read the review will buy the product even after the bug is fixed.

In addition to bugs, there are differences in implementation, which means that different manufacturers work differently. When the manufacturers are done, their completed, supposedly compatible products may do the same things, but differently. If the differences in implementation are too great, then the products aren't really compatible.

Reputable manufacturers work with each other to ensure basic compatibility in spite of all the idiosyncracies. This is one reason why Novell offers its testing program; it gives everyone in the networking field a chance to make sure that the products being positioned as NetWare-compatible are in fact compatible. The testing program also gives Novell the opportunity to make sure NetWare is compatible with most hardware.

Several manufacturers, among them Madge Networks (Token-Ring products) and 3Com (LAN products), said that their firms spend a lot of time trying to solve any and all conflicts between their boards and any other hardware or software on the market. The reason behind this effort is simple: money. Madge, for example, did a study and determined that every time the technical support staff takes a call about a board, the profits received from the purchase of that board go down the drain.

To prevent future problems, Madge (along with most reputable firms) listens carefully to any complaints. If a customer complains that a particular board has a problem with a system, for example, the incompatibility is solved and the solution put on the board, even if it's just a problem facing one system; that way, that problem will never darken tech support's phone lines again.

3Com took a similar view, correcting every incompatibility, even if that incompatibility affects only one type of computer. The only lament is, because so many different computers are out there, 3Com just can't test everything for compatibility in advance. The firm has to wait for the complaints to come to it.

If you come across a bug or other idiosyncracy in either your hardware or software, let people know. Start by checking where you made your purchase, then move to the vendors themselves. If a product doesn't do what it is advertised to do, the vendor or reseller should fix it or give you your money back.

BUS/CLOCK SPEED

Computers are getting faster and faster; NetWare is getting faster, too. One of the ways that technology handles this speed is through the CPU/bus clock.

While some systems have two clocks, one to govern the CPU/memory and the other to control the bus (I/O address channels), others only have one. In either case, a definite formula exists: the CPU speed will be half the clock speed, and the bus will be one-third the clock speed. For example, a computer that has a clock speed of 24MHz typically will have a CPU speed of 12MH and a bus speed of 8MHz. There are systems out there today with a CPU speed of 33MHz and a bus speed of half that, 16.5MHz, but these are still rare.

Problems arise when the bus/clock speed formula is not followed. Novell itself, with an eye toward compatibility, once tried to market a 286 diskless workstation whose bus speed specification was same as the clock speed specification (12MHz). None of the boards tested with the machine would work at the higher bus speed, because they were aimed at the market standard of 8MHz. The machine had to be set at its slower speed (6MHz) in order for the boards to work—slowly. Even the manufacturer of the workstation, whose main business was disk controller boards, couldn't provide a disk controller board that would work at 12MHz. And, of course, since speed is the name of the game, everybody—board manufacturers, Novell, and most particularly the original manufacturer of the workstation—was unhappy.

BUS MASTERING

Bus Mastering is a fairly recent concept that is supported both by IBM's Micro Channel architecture and the new EISA technology. (EISA means Enhanced Industry Standard Architecture, as opposed to ISA, Industry Standard Architecture, which we've had all along, only without the fancy name. ISA used to be the plain old AT-compatible bus.) Bus mastering is not supported by any of the old AT-type computers you have lying around the office.

As a practical issue, bus mastering allows network interface boards to bypass the CPU and take over the bus. This enables the system throughput to be a *lot* faster, since the CPU no longer has to play the middleman, relaying commands from the board to the bus and from the bus to the board.

The difficulty comes in implementing this technology uniformly: bus mastering intelligence has to be on both the board and the computer. Since usually the board and the computer are made by different manufacturers and since bus mastering isn't a universally demanded feature yet, bugs are likely to pop up here.

Bus mastering is an irrelevant concept if you are looking for a board to put into an existing computer; in most cases, the computer may lack the bus mastering intelligence to take advantage of this advanced feature. On the other hand, if you are looking for a board to go with your brand new EISA or Micro Channel architecture computer, look for bus mastering capability on the board as well. Otherwise, you're paying for technology you're not using.

The next several sections will discuss LAN boards and disk controller boards in detail.

NETWORK INTERFACE BOARDS

Your network interface board, along with the cabling system, is the ultimate in connectivity. If either the board or the cabling system does not work, then you are not going to be networking with a computer.

Network type and boards go hand in hand; once you've made a decision about your networking type, as you did in Chapter II, you've basically made irrevocable decisions about your network interface boards. That's not to say you don't have plenty of leeway, but you have limited the number of boards that you are interested in. And, given the millions of boards and drivers (a driver contains the software that runs the board) out there, it's probably a good thing.

The issues discussed in the overview of this chapter are general compatibility issues facing all boards. Basically, after you decide on your network type/cabling, two other compatibility issues are left regarding the LAN boards:

- The configuration option
- Remote booting

You can multiply your compatibility problems by mixing and matching different brands of network interface boards, but that's kind of a masochistic approach. Minimize the pain by choosing a brand and sticking with it.

CONFIGURATION OPTION

The configuration option gives NetWare information about where it can find the board in terms of I/O and memory addresses and the interrupt request line (IRQ) setting. These settings must be unique, that is, no two boards in the same computer can have the same memory addresses or IRQs. (NetWare 386 has eased these restrictions, but until the hardware catches up with NetWare, the limitations remain.)

Board manufacturers give you tables to help you ensure the uniqueness of your board's configuration option; the nice thing is that the default configuration option (Option 0) usually works if you only have one board in the system, requiring no more effort on your part than double checking the manufacturer's settings.

Occasionally, computers and network interface boards don't work together, a situation that can sometimes (not always) be resolved by changing the configuration option on the board to something besides Option 0. If changing the configuration option doesn't work, talk to the board and computer manufacturers about different options. Better yet, talk to the resellers before you buy anything. Get guarantees. Manufacturers don't consider configuration option changes as being indicative of either a flaw in the board or a flaw in the computer. (Other compatibility problems between LAN boards and computers are discussed in Chapter V.)

Changing the configuration on your board is a two-step process unless you have a new-style board with no hardware settings. For a new-style board, just put the diskette that came with the board into your computer and make your changes. Otherwise, tell NetWare what the new settings are going to be, and then physically change the switches or jumpers on the board to match what you have told NetWare.

On a typical ISA interface board, such as the one illustrated in Figure 3.1, you'll have to change both switches and jumpers if the default setting can't be used. The switch block in the upper left-hand corner is where you change the memory and I/O addresses, and the 8-position jumper block in the center, labeled "IRQ," is used to change your IRQ setting. (The socket labeled "PROM" is for the remote boot PROM chip that is required if you put this board into a diskless workstation. Most manufacturers sell this chip separately.) Note that boards designed for use in Micro Channel and EISA machines will have no user settings on the board at all.

REMOTE BOOTING

One networking issue that affects network interface boards in diskless workstations is remote booting. Workstations, when turned on, go through self tests, load the drivers for the boards in the system, and then connect with the file server.

If the workstation is completely diskless, the LAN board in the workstation can complete the physical connection to the file server. The LAN board re-

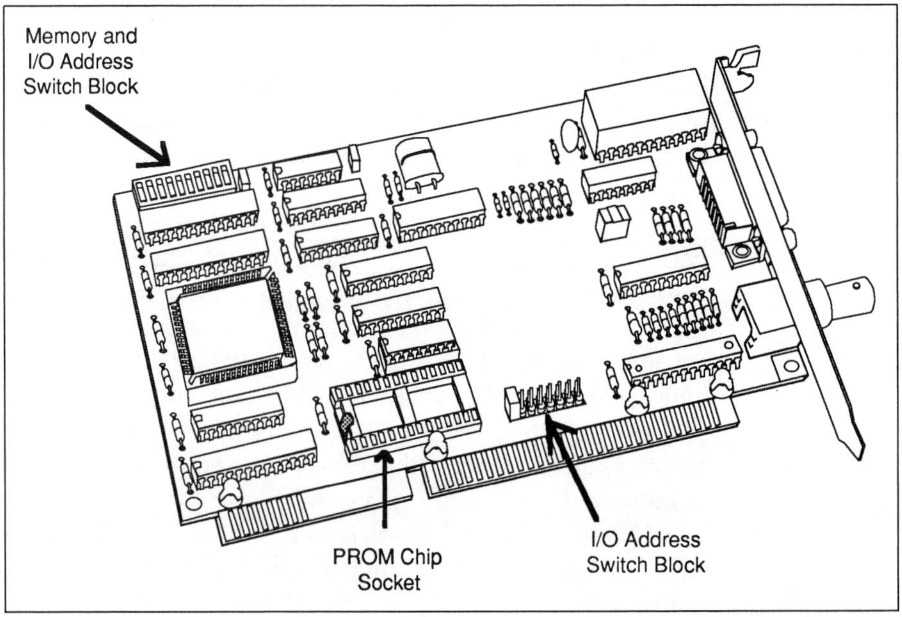

Figure 3.1. Typical ISA Ethernet Board, with Switches and Jumpers

quires an additional chip in order to support the remote boot option for a workstation.

Most LAN boards are sold without a remote boot PROM chip, allowing you to purchase one separately if you need it. (A file server has no need for a remote boot PROM; neither does a workstation with a hard or floppy disk drive.) Some boards, usually the really fast ones, are designed exclusively for use in file servers; they don't even come with a socket for a PROM chip.

Occasionally, the remote boot PROM on your board isn't supported by the workstation. This problem can possibly be resolved by buying somebody else's boot PROM, but then you have to figure out if the new boot PROM will work with the board you just put it on. A better idea is to check with the manufacturer and get some guarantees before you buy a workstation LAN board for a diskless machine.

NETWORK TYPES

There are a batch of network types in the industry today, but the only ones that are considered here are the same ones as in the previous section: ARCNET, Ethernet/StarLAN, and Token-Ring. IBM's PC LAN is also discussed briefly, but other network types, such as X.25, which is really for wide area networks (WANs), broadband, Macintosh, and proprietary network types are not covered here.

Proprietary network types may contain the greatest network cabling systems in the world today. However, if only one company supports it, then that's where you are going to buy your boards. Compatibility is no longer an issue, except maybe with NetWare. (Several vendors of proprietary network types, among them SageSoft Limited, went through Novell's IMSP program and passed with flying colors.)

I've come across a quibble that the LAN hardware isn't really tested when Novell tests the LAN boards; what is tested is the LAN board drivers, the software that runs the boards. However, since a LAN board does not work without its driver and a LAN board doesn't work outside of the networking environment, it does not matter. If the driver does not work with NetWare 386, for example, then the board doesn't either, not until somebody makes it work. This quibble does mean that an undetected hardware bug could be lurking, but as a general rule, if the driver works so will the board.

ARCNET

ARCNET board manufacturers are striving to keep up with the latest technological advances in the Ethernet and Token-Ring fields. They are adding a board that will run at 20 Mbps, as opposed to their current board of 2.5 Mbps, the slowest of the popular network types. This board, when available, should have faster throughput than either Token-Ring or Ethernet.

However, ARCNET has several critics, all of them proponents of other network types. Those critics of ARCNET say that the network type has three problems:

- Compatibility between two different-speed ARCNET boards
- Elimination of ARCNET's price advantage over Ethernet and Token-Ring
- Standardization

ARCNET answers the critics by saying that compatibility between the 2.5-Mbps board and the 20-Mbps board isn't going to be any more of a problem than between Token-Ring's 4-Mbps board and its 16-Mbps board. Thomas-Conrad, which makes both ARCNET and Token-Ring boards, says that its ARCNET driver supports both its 2.5-Mbps board and its 100-Mbps board, so compatibility is unlikely to be a problem. (The 100-Mbps board is aimed at really *high*-performance networks.)

Those who say that ARCNET will lose a price advantage with the new board are probably right. However, both Ethernet and Token-Ring manufacturers are coming out with technologically more advanced (and more expensive) boards themselves. If price is truly the deciding factor for you, compare the boards you want to buy and their attendant network types.

As far as standards go, ARCNET standards are now being controlled by the ARCNET Trade Association, and any member of the organization can propose revisions, working much the same way that the IEEE committees work with Token-Ring and Ethernet. Although Datapoint created the network type, it now has no larger a voice in ARCNET standards than any other ARCNET vendor, said a ARCNET Trade Association spokesman.

ETHERNET

Ethernet cable, as discussed earlier, comes in three flavors: twisted-pair cable, thin Ethernet cable, and thick Ethernet cable. Manufacturers usually handle the twisted-pair cabling option by providing a separate version of the board, although occasionally you can find a board with a hardware setting for twisted-pair wiring as well as for thick and thin Ethernet cable.

Thick/Thin Ethernet

The thick/thin option for Ethernet is handled through a setting on the board that is usually labeled "Ethernet" and "Cheapernet."

The word "Cheapernet" comes from the fact that when thin Ethernet cable was first introduced, it was (and still is) considerably cheaper than the standard, thicker Ethernet cable. The Ethernet label referred to the standard Ethernet cable at the time—thick coaxial cable. The two labels have stuck up to today, even though cable is more likely to be called thick and thin than Ethernet and Cheapernet.

Another odd label on many Ethernet boards is "DIX," which technically means DEC, Intel, Xerox, the three inventors of Ethernet. In actuality, it refers to the DB 15-pin connector for the thick Ethernet cable; the unlabeled round connector, meant for thin Ethernet cable, is known as the BNC connector.

Most manufacturers are no longer recommending thick coax cable. As mentioned earlier, it's fairly expensive and horrendously hard to use. Instead, they recommend thin-coax cable if you have a limited number of nodes to network (25 or so) or unshielded twisted-pair wiring if you have a network that will be expanding. Fiber-optic cable, everybody agrees, is about the best around—if you want to pay for it.

One thing you might want to consider is using the same manufacturer for both your Ethernet boards and your computers. That way you get around the problem of different manufacturers implementing the same thing differently. One note here, however, if you have an old computer and you want to add a new board by the same manufacturer, you have no guarantee that the manufacturer is doing things the same way now as then, although most manufacturers try to maintain compatibility with their own products.

Among the manufacturers who make both computers and Ethernet boards are:

- Acer
- AST Research, Inc.
- AT&T
- Everex
- Samsung Information Systems America
- TeleVideo Systems, Inc.
- Toshiba

- Wyse Technology

Twisted-Pair Cable

For twisted pair, two of the biggest manufacturers of computers and what used to be called StarLAN boards (but are now being built to the new 10-Mbps Ethernet-on-Twisted-Pair standard) are Hewlett-Packard and AT&T. (AT&T still makes the traditional StarLAN board, which runs at 1 Mbps, as opposed to its Ethernet-on-Twisted-Pair option that runs at 10 Mbps.)

Novell's Boards

Novell is still a major player in the Ethernet market. Before it got out of the hardware business, Novell manufactured Ethernet boards, among other products. Today, Novell still provides hardware engineering support for two boards (the NE1000 and NE2000, marketed by Anthem) and is co-developer of another (the NE3200, with Compaq). But most of its left-over Ethernet energy goes into writing NetWare drivers for other manufacturers' boards. Novell plans to turn the drivers back to their respective owners and find other outlets.

One interesting thing is that Novell's tests show that the NE2000 16-bit Ethernet board driver (which is updated frequently) passes all its tests with flying colors. However, many systems can't run this board (or can't run it well). (Systems that have difficulty with this board are in listed Appendix F.)

Novell explains the system difficulties by saying that some versions of the board have two problems. One is that the basic Ethernet chipset from National Semiconductor has a soon-to-be-corrected bug, and the other is that the chipset from Chips & Technologies has a problem that requires an additional workaround (if your computer also has a chipset from Chips & Technologies, you'll need to move a jumper on the board). (A chipset is a "building block" that gives computer manufacturers a head start in making a computer. Chipsets in computers and in boards provide a commonality and also provide a basis for compatibility, or incompatibility, as the case may be. This is the reason you need to get guarantees before you buy anything.)

3Com's Boards

Of course, Novell isn't the only player in the Ethernet market; there are lots of others. One of the biggest is 3Com, which is considered to set the industry's Ethernet standard. And there are good reasons for considering 3Com's Ethernet boards the industry standard. One is that some of its boards far exceed

IEEE standards; the EtherLink II (3C503) can transmit data more than twice as far as the IEEE specifies. All of the 3Com boards also come with RAM on the board, which speeds up the network throughput.

3Com has lots of Ethernet boards. (One is illustrated in Figure 3.2.) Since it's the standard in Ethernet and since Novell has been writing NetWare drivers for those boards, nearly every system sent to Novell for testing has been tested against them. The result can be predicted: No one board is going to work flawlessly in every one of the millions of computers on the market today.

Some of 3Com's boards work only if you fuss a little by changing the configuration option; 3Com does not consider this a problem. The main problem that was reported for 3Com's boards affects ELS users who want to run their file servers in non-dedicated mode; several systems do not work properly with some of 3Com's boards in that mode. (These computers are listed in Appendix F.)

Other 3Com problems are caused by the other traditional problems of computer technology:

- Old board, new computer (3C505)
- New computer (whose bugs aren't quite worked out yet) (3C503)

Figure 3.2. 3Com's EtherLink II TP Ethernet Board Courtesy of 3Com Corporation

- New board, newer computer (3C523 MC)

If the problem is merely technological catch-up, rest assured that the difficulty will be resolved as soon as anyone hears about it. If the board is at the end of its market cycle, it will probably never work right, but it will be replaced by a newer version that will work fine.

Before you buy an Ethernet board (anyone's, not just those discussed here), get guarantees from the seller that the board will work in the environment that you will be using it in. All of 3Com's boards, for example, worked flawlessly in many applications, including non-dedicated mode in many file servers.

TOKEN-RING

IBM is the standard in Token-Ring network interface boards. Although an IEEE standard exists that all manufacturers are supposed to follow, one Token-Ring manufacturer assured me that his firm was following the IBM standard rather than IEEE and that if IBM deviated from the IEEE standard then his firm would too. So far, IBM hasn't done that.

Although IBM is the standard, a large number of computers had difficulty running the board in Novell's systems testing. That's because the board is sensitive to problems in system timing and to hardware address incompatibilities.

The overall significance of the IBM Token-Ring sensitivity is that other Token-Ring manufacturers work to make themselves compatible with IBM and may work in this sensitivity inadvertently. Manufacturers aren't likely to try to emulate a flaw in a board, even if it is IBM's (and in fact those whom I talked to emphatically said that their boards aren't as timing/hardware address sensitive as the IBM board). However, test the boards in the destination system before you buy anything.

Again, before you buy a board, get guarantees from the seller that the board will work in the environment that you will be using it in.

Most of the computers that have difficulty with the Token-Ring board are the 80486-based 486 computers, which may mean that IBM has some unresolved issues with the latest technology. (Machines having difficulty with IBM boards are listed in Appendix F.) *Latest technology* is a moving target. Undoubtedly, by the time this book is published, IBM will have resolved any problems with 486 computers; latest technology then will refer to something else.

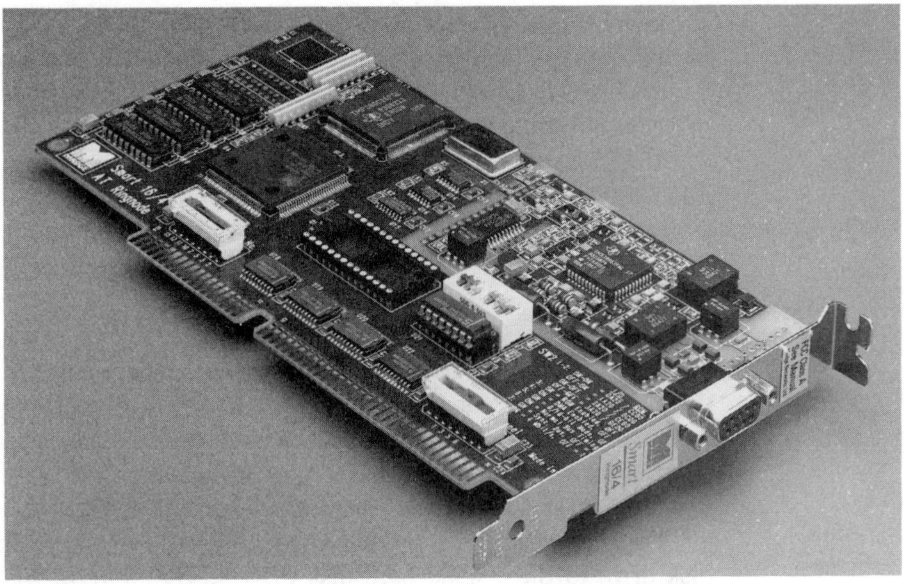

Figure 3.3. Madge's 16/4 Switchable Token-Ring Board Courtesy of Madge Networks

IBM PC LAN

If you're thinking about using the PC LAN Network II Adapter, think carefully. An awful lot of systems have difficulty running this board, and many of those system manufacturers said the "PC LAN" market wasn't one they cared about. (In fact, some asked *me* what network type the PC Network Adapter was meant for.) Check with any prospective systems' manufacturers to see if they know what they're supposed to do with the PC Network Adapter. (Systems that have had major problems with the PC LAN board are listed in Appendix F.)

DISK CONTROLLER BOARDS

Disk controller boards have traditionally provided the interface that allows the computer to talk to the hard disk drive. (Disk controller boards are included with the LAN boards in this section because of the issues they have in common—bus/clock speed, hardware/software idiosyncracies, bus mastering, and physical installation. These issues are discussed in detail in the overview of this chapter.)

With the advent of intelligent hard disk drives that can talk to the computer without help and modern computers with hard disk drive connectors on the motherboard, the term "disk controller boards", is dying. Not that all hard disk drives don't have a controller of sorts, but on today's more sophisticated hard disk drives, the controllers are built into the drive, freeing the regular controller board for other functions.

Disk controller boards are being replaced by host adapter boards, which allow the board to take over some processing tasks for the computer as well as provide the traditional interface between the computer and the hard disk drive. How much of the bus management the board takes on depends on the quality of the board. Some do almost nothing; others can take over a substantial amount.

The intelligent host adapter board not only plays a role in computer throughput by allowing disk duplexing and disk mirroring, but also plays a role in adding storage space to the system through disk subsystems that can be attached. (See Chapter IV for more information on hard disk drives, hard disk drive arrays, and disk subsystems.)

Disk mirroring is a method of duplicating data from the primary hard disk drive to the second hard disk drive in the system. Disk duplexing is a method of duplicating the same data into two different systems. Each of these backup methods is discussed in more detail in Chapter IV.

STANDARDIZATION

When Novell talks about disk controller boards, it specifically mentions Western Digital disk controller boards, saying that your file server board must either be a WD or compatible.

According to WD, it's easy to find a WD disk controller board, in spite of the waning interest in the plain old vanilla boards, because Western Digital has 80% of the disk controller board market. And even if you find a disk controller board made by someone else, the odds are very good that board is fully compatible with the Western Digital board, because Western Digital sells its chips to the other disk controller board manufacturers.

The Western Digital controller board is illustrated in Figure 3.4.

CHANNELS

One issue that affects disk controller boards is channels, and it's only important if you want to add as many hard disk drives to your computer as you can squeeze in. If you are happy with the one or two hard disks in your file server and don't have any large data storage needs, then this issue is irrelevant for the moment.

Figure 3.4. Western Digital Disk Controller Board
Courtesy of Western Digital Corporation

Channel, like disk controller board, is a dying term as far as Novell is concerned; NetWare only uses the term in NetWare 286. NetWare 386 doesn't mention channels, instead preferring to discuss shared I/O addresses and shared IRQs, looking ahead to a technology that really hasn't arrived. (Only Micro Channel architecture machines even support the concept of shared I/O addresses, but no disk controller boards or drivers have that feature.) One of the big selling points of NetWare 386 is that it has removed the software limitations from the network. This doesn't mean that there aren't performance limitations but only that the software isn't causing them. Today's hardware can't support shared I/O addresses and joint IRQs. Until the hardware does become a little more advanced, the discussion that follows applies equally to NetWare 286 and NetWare 386.

A channel, which is really a disk controller board's I/O address, is the pipeline from the computer to the drives managed by the controller board. The number of hard disk drives allowed on a channel depends on the controller: AT hard disk controllers allow up to two; SCSI hard disk controllers allow up to seven.

The number of channels allowed depends on your version of NetWare. If you have NetWare 286 (except Novell's Entry Level System), you can have up to four channels. (ELS only allows one channel.) If you have NetWare

386, you can put as many boards into your system as you have slots, as long as the boards don't conflict with any other board in your system.

Channels are designed to add disk storage to a system. They are also used for disk mirroring (where data are stored sequentially on two different hard disk drives attached to one disk controller board) and for disk duplexing (where the same data are stored simultaneously on two different hard disk drives attached to two different disk controller boards).

While hard disk controllers limit the number of hard disk drives attached to it, a hard disk controller does not limit the capacity of the hard disk drive; that is, you can find single hard disk drives up to 660MB or so and disk storage systems of many hundreds of gigabytes (if you take advantage of things like WORM optical disk drives and autochangers). You can attach as many of those drives (and disk subsystems) to the hard disk controller as the hard disk controller allows.

In practical terms in today's technology, one hard disk controller board equals one channel in the system. Technically, some SCSI host adapter boards have the hardware capability to support two channels or I/O addresses at once, but none have the software to support two different I/O addresses simultaneously.

The extra channels in a computer are utilized, if you need them, by adding hard disk controller boards, each with a different I/O address, to your computer. The way you handle the additional disk drives, since they aren't going to fit in your average computer, is through disk subsystems (discussed in more detail in Chapter IV).

ELS AND CHANNELS

Entry Level System (ELS), a closed architecture system designed for ease of installation, allows only one channel. Up until March 1990, that one channel had to be through an ISA-compatible hard disk controller. Now, if you have ELS II (but not ELS I), your one channel can also be through an IBM PS/2 (or compatible) SCSI host adapter board, allowing you to attach up to seven hard disk drives on your computer, daisy chained. Those seven drives, if they're large, will far exceed the total NetWare 286 data storage limits of 2GB. All these hard disk drives aren't going to fit into your computer, which brings up another problem: finding a suitable box with a power supply. They're often available at your local electronics store, if you want to "roll your own."

The significance of ELS only supporting one channel is that you can't attach disk subsystems. You are limited to the number of drives supported by the disk controller boards, either seven (for ELS II and IBM PS/2 SCSI drives) or two (for ELS I and ESDI or IDE drives). However, even limiting yourself to two ESDI drives, which is all you're permitted with ELS I, you can get more than 1GB of data storage.

Channels and ELS is a tricky subject; if you need to expand your memory storage above 1GB, talk to several vendors or find a consultant who may be able to advise ways to maximize your use of your channel.

Remember, however, there does come a time when you have irrevocably outgrown your ELS network. Incorporating all possible methods of adding disk storage to the network and still coming up short of your needs is a good indication of that growth. While workarounds of various forms exist, you'll be happier at that point if you upgrade.

CACHING

Caching (putting data that are frequently requested in a special bank of high-speed memory) has not traditionally been a function of disk controller boards. More typically it was a function of the RAM on the motherboard. Many of today's host adapter boards have cache memory on the board, which can speed up system throughput. If you also have a hard disk drive with memory caching, the two caches together will be a little faster than one cache alone. However, the two caches are not going to be so much faster that it's worthwhile financially to go out and get dual caches. (That doesn't mean that you should throw them out if they're already there; it just means that the extra performance isn't justified by the extra cost.)

NOVELL'S DISK COPROCESSOR BOARD

Novell's Disk Coprocessor Board (DCB) is a SCSI host adapter board that interfaces with NetWare rather than MS-DOS, thus increasing throughput. Although it's no longer new technology, being at least three years old, it is guaranteed by Novell to work with various versions of NetWare (except ELS, which only supports AT-compatible disk controller boards and IBM PS/2-compatible SCSI host adapter boards). This guarantee holds even though the DCB is no longer shipped by Novell. Since Novell departed from the hardware business, the AT version of the board has been licensed by Samsung Information Systems America and ADIC, while the PS/2 and enhanced versions of the board now belong to ADIC, in a codevelopment venture with Novell. (The enhanced DCB, called the EDCB, is aimed at the EISA and NetWare 386 market as well as the ISA market.)

The theoretical drawback to the DCB is that, unlike most SCSI host adapter boards, it only works with SCSI hard disk drives. Most SCSI host adapter boards are more versatile, working with optical drives, printers, plotters, and even tape media, as well as hard disk drives. (I say theoretical because very few applications require you to mix your SCSI devices. Mixing SCSI devices means the host adapter is going to work at the speed of the slowest SCSI device attached, which is definitely not desirable.)

Novell was the first to market a SCSI host adapter board that interfaced with NetWare, and for a long time it was the only SCSI board to do so because Novell was slow to release the developer's kit that made it easy for vendors to write appropriate drivers. However, the developer's kit has been released, and disk controller boards aimed at the NetWare market abound. Adaptec, for example, has just come out with an SCSI host adapter board for NetWare and the EISA market, in addition to the boards it has already had for AT-compatible and PS/2-type machines running with NetWare. Samsung, which licenses Novell's AT-compatible DCB, is said to be getting ready to come out with a board for the EISA market as well.

INSTALLING NETWORK INTERFACE BOARDS

Since you've investigated and purchased the perfect network interface or disk controller board, now you would like quick instructions on how to install them into your computer. (These instructions apply equally well to any board being placed into a computer.)

Hardware installation is just half of it; when you finish putting your hardware in your computer, you have to tell the operating system, whether it's MS-DOS or NetWare, that the board is there. So you need to find the software instructions and keep them handy.

Before you touch the board or your computer, rid yourself of any static electricity buildup by touching bare (unpainted) metal, or you use a grounding strap if you have one. You can destroy the add-on board or the computer's motherboard if you zap them just right with static electricity.

INSTALLATION PREPARATION

As the first step to installing the board in the system, make sure that your board's hardware settings are compatible with the computer and that the board doesn't conflict with any other board in your system. This procedure is a lot easier if it's one of the first boards in your computer. If it's not, hopefully you have a record of the other addresses and interrupt lines being used by any other boards. If you don't keep records, you should start.

Since manufacturers do think ahead (usually), the default hardware settings are frequently correct for the first board of each variety (network, disk controller, monitor, etc.), not conflicting with anything. On some of the newer boards and all EISA and PS/2 boards, all settings are done through the software, so no hardware settings need to be made on the board—but check. If nothing else, make sure that your manufacturer hasn't added something "special" to the board.

If you have a LAN board that you're putting in a diskless workstation, you also have to add a remote boot PROM chip (discussed in the next section). If you're adding a disk controller or host adapter board to your NetWare 286 file server, you'll need to check the board to be sure it has the appropriate channel number as discussed in the next section. This step isn't necessary if you're installing a NetWare 386 host adapter board. (For NetWare 386, you need to make sure that the board has no I/O or other address conflicts with any other board in the system.)

INSERTING THE REMOTE BOOT CHIP

If the board you're installing is a LAN interface board for a diskless workstation, you'll need to insert the remote boot PROM chip so that NetWare can talk to the computer. Remember that if you put the chip on the board backwards you'll ruin the chip; you'll probably also ruin the board. Which way is the right way? Why, the way all the other chips are installed, of course.

Actually, it is a little less complex than that. The sockets that the chips go in always have a marking—usually a notch, a circle, or the number 1—at one end of the socket. The chip also has a marking—a notch or circle—at one end. (This concept is illustrated in Figure 3.5.) Match the markings, and your chip is installed correctly. (Boards are always designed so that every chip on the board faces the same way; which way that is varies from board to board, but it never varies from chip to chip on the same board.)

Now, identify the socket on the board that is supposed to hold the remote boot chip. Usually, the socket that is supposed to hold the remote boot chip is the only empty socket on the board. Some vendors label the sockets on their boards, but all sockets are numbered, whether or not they have a label. If all else fails, check the documentation that came with the board for the number of the boot PROM socket.

To insert a chip, make sure that all prongs are straight and then gently push the chip into the socket (after checking its orientation, of course). If the prongs are bent or broken, the chip won't work.

Figure 3.5. Orienting a Remote Boot PROM Chip

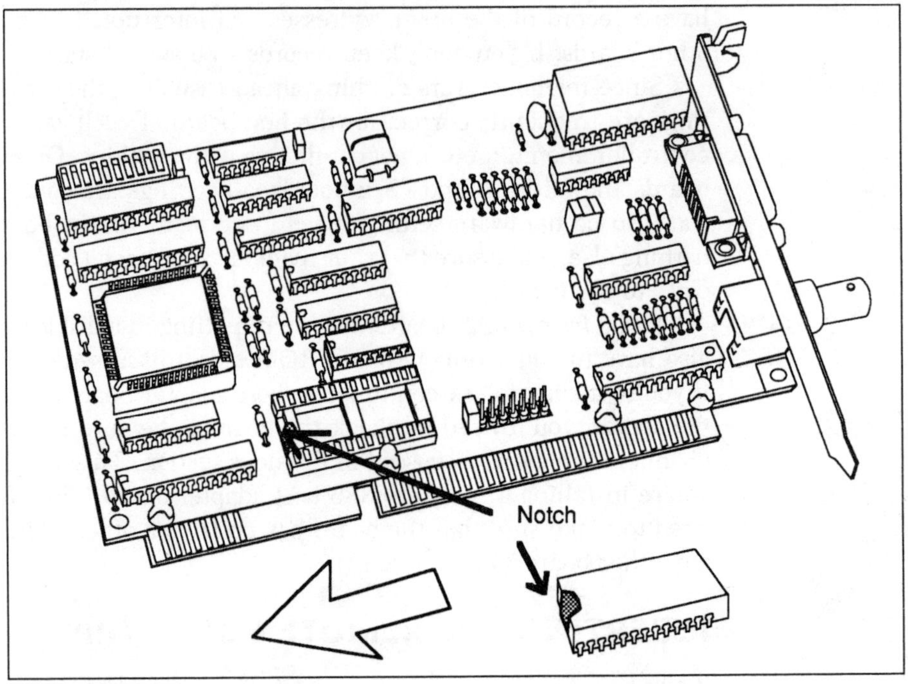

CHECKING THE DISK CONTROLLER BOARD SETTINGS

With a disk controller or host adapter board being installed in a NetWare 286 file server, check to be sure that the channel I/O address is correct by referring to the list of default settings that came with your board. If you have a NetWare 386 operating system, be sure that the board's I/O address does not conflict with anything else in the system. It's better to check board settings before you power up your system and find out that the board will not work because of a conflict.

If you are adding a second disk channel to NetWare 286, you must get another board that has the second I/O channel address on it. You can't add the chip to the existing board without changing the I/O address of that board.

You also need to tell the vendor in advance that you need a second (or third or whatever) channel. Channel 1 is the default setting with a particular I/O address on the chip; Channel 2 has a different default setting with a different I/O address on the chip. If you don't specify a different channel, you get Channel 1.

INSERTING THE BOARD

Once the remote boot chip (if needed) is on the board and/or you've checked the disk controller board settings, you can put the board into your file server or workstation.

The first step, logically, is to turn off and unplug your computer. Unplug the computer from the wall as well as turn it off, because electricity could still be going to the computer even though the computer is not on.

Next, remove the cover. Usually, you have to remove three or four screws from the back before lifting the cover up and out. Occasionally, manufacturers are afraid the cover is going to get away if it isn't really screwed down. Check the manufacturer's instructions if there seems to be a lot of screw attached to the back or bottom of the computer. One computer I saw had 16 screws and every single one of them had to be removed. And they weren't easy screws to remove, either.

Once the computer is open, locate the expansion slots, usually at the rear of the machine opposite the power supply, as illustrated in Figure 3.6. Remove the holding screw and expansion slot bracket from the appropriate empty slot (the farther from the power supply the better), placing the screw and bracket to one side.

Remember that you can't put a 16-bit board into either an 8-bit or a 32-bit slot—you'll destroy the 16-bit board.

Put your new board into the expansion slot, attaching it with the holding screw you just removed.

If you aren't installing any other boards, the final step in hardware installation is to replace the cover of the computer. If you are installing other boards, install them now before closing up the system. NetWare doesn't care how many boards you want to tell it about at once, as long as you give it the information it needs.

The way you tell NetWare about your new boards (network interface or disk controller) depends on the version of NetWare you have. For NetWare 386 v3.0, it's simple. The drivers for the various boards are called NetWare Loadable Modules (NLMs). Add your NLM to the ones that the NetWare in your system already recognizes, and you're done. (Refer to the NetWare 386 v3.0 installation manual for more information.)

For NetWare 286, copy your network interface board driver to the NetWare operating shell and then run the NETGEN program to configure the system again. Refer to Chapter 4 of the *SFT/Advanced NetWare 286 Installation Manual* for proper procedures. If you have ELS, refer to the section on file server installation in your main installation manual.

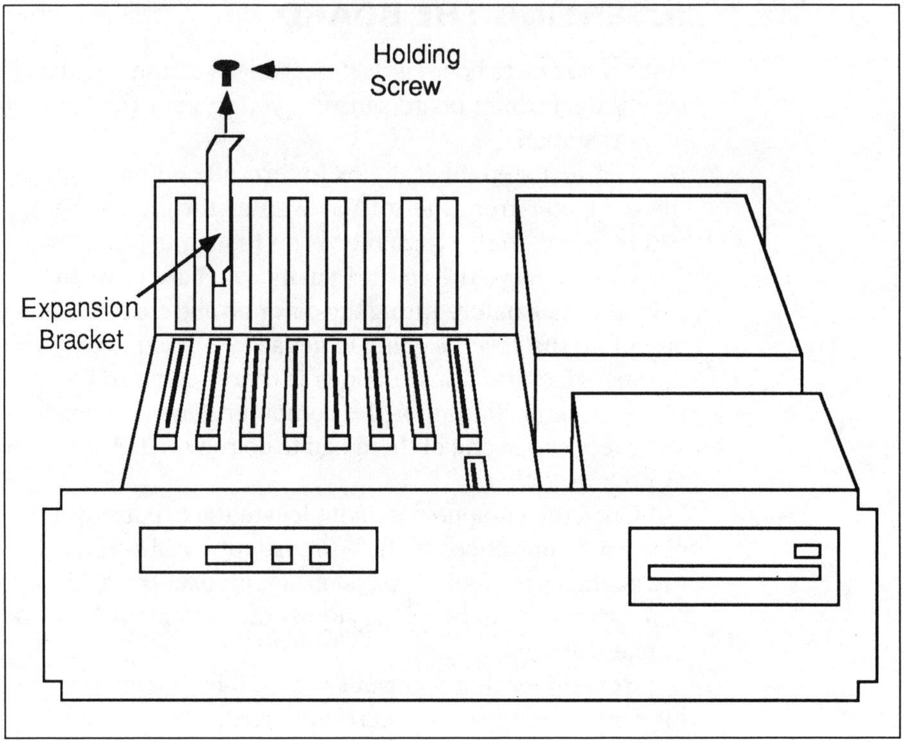

Figure 3.6. Locating the expansion slot, holding screw, and expansion bracket

If you're installing a disk controller board into a file server running any version of NetWare 286, you'll need to refer to Chapters 2 and 6 of the *SFT/ Advanced NetWare Installation Manual* to tell NetWare about your new board.

ELS assumes that you aren't going to install any disk drive controller boards into the system because it's not mentioned in the ELS installation manual. Instead, Novell, speaking of a generic add-on board, refers you to the documentation that comes with the hardware, after cautioning you to be sure that no settings on the new board conflict with the LAN board you're using. Since ELS supports only one channel, you can't add a second disk controller board. You can, however, remove the disk controller board that's in the system and replace it with a better one; just make sure it's compatible with your system and with ELS.

IV

Hard Disk Drives

OVERVIEW

When you talk to people about hard disk drives, you are involved in a discussion about alphabet soup. MFM, RLL, ESDI, SCSI, and IDE are all bandied about, and you're supposed to know their definitions, if nothing else. Either that, or you're talking with people who are as ignorant as you are, and are usually quick to admit it. The people who really know their hard disk drive terminology think that you are joking when you ask for definitions of such basic terms. It took weeks of talking to knowledgeable people who assumed I was either an idiot or a practical joker in order to get concise definitions of those alphabet soup terms. (The ones who assumed I was an idiot gave me more information in the long run. They were a lot less fun to deal with, though.)

Spelling out the alphabet soup turned out to be less enlightening than I had hoped when I first started asking these questions. This is very *technical*, technical terminology. And to me, what's really important is what they do. (As far as I can determine, these alphabet terms don't describe anything in real-world terms.) However, for the benefit of those who have always wondered (but not enough to look it up), following are the unabbreviated words that define hard disk drive terminology.

- MFM: Modified Frequency Modulated
- RLL: Run Length Limited
- ESDI: Enhanced Small Device Interface
- SCSI: Small Computer System Interface
- IDE: Integrated Device Electronics

What all these fancy terms boil down to is that MFM and RLL are encoding schemes for hard disk drives, and ESDI, SCSI, and IDE are ways that the hard disk drive interfaces with the computer. (At least ESDI and SCSI managed to get the word "interface" into their acronyms.) Furthermore, these aren't mutually exclusive terms: Although it wasn't this way at the beginning, most drives today are both an ESDI (or a SCSI or an IDE) *and* an MFM or RLL.

They're more likely to be RLL than MFM. RLL is a newer, faster technology that gets the maximum amount of data on the disk (50% more than MFM), and, with today's hard disk drives simultaneously getting larger in capacity and smaller in physical size, hard disk drive manufacturers are seizing every opportunity to give themselves a competitive edge.

The main difference among ESDI, SCSI, and IDE is not in the data transfer rate. SCSI and IDE host adapter boards are more intelligent than ESDI controller boards and handle blocks of data rather than dealing with the actual mechanics of moving data in and out. SCSI and IDE host adapter boards don't care how the data are moved. Controllers mounted on the SCSI and IDE drives deal with the actual performance of the disk.

In the beginning (or as far back as we're going), all drives were MFM. ESDI, SCSI, and IDE either didn't exist at all or didn't exist as far as personal computers went. Then someone came up with RLL, which was a way of doubling the capacity on a hard disk drive without changing the MFM standard.

For a long time after RLL was created, the industry stayed away from that technology because of questions about the product's reliability. Once the technology allowed RLL to be as reliable as MFM, RLL took off. At that point drives were either MFM or RLL, each with a data transfer rate of about 5 megabits per second (Mbps). The next technological advance combined RLL with a faster data transfer rate (10 Mbps) and called it ESDI.

ESDI also has an even faster data transfer rate (15 Mbps) in the works. ESDI, with a current maximum disk drive capacity of about 660 MB (a figure that constantly grows larger) is technology exclusive to hard disk drives, unlike SCSI, and can only be used with MS-DOS machines, also unlike SCSI.

SCSI can be used in Apple products as well as MS-DOS machines, and the technology is not even exclusive to hard disk drives. Printers, for example, can have a SCSI interface and can be connected to the same SCSI host adapter board as a hard disk drive with good results. Benchmark tests by NCR on its SCSI printer show that it prints graphics-intensive documents up to seven times faster than with a parallel port and up to 100 times faster than with a serial port. (It also costs $8,000.)

SCSI I technology has a data transfer rate of 5 Mbps, and the new SCSI II technology has a data transfer rate of 10 Mbps, spurred no doubt by the need to match ESDI's 10 Mbps data transfer rate. Since SCSI II is brand new, practically all SCSI devices out there are SCSI I. For the next year or so, be careful when you purchase SCSIs and SCSI interfaces; SCSI II technology isn't going to do a thing for existing SCSI I devices.

IDE drives are the newcomers. They are 3.5-inch hard disk drives developed by Conner Peripherals for Compaq with an interface that was designed exclusively for hard disk drives (unlike SCSI). Vendors think that these drives, even though they are functionally comparable to SCSI, will have a long-run advantage over a SCSI interface. That's because SCSI, which takes a generic approach that allows it to work with all sorts of devices, also works at the lowest, slowest common denominator of the computer peripheral attached, which is usually a printer.

These drives are also gaining popularity in the industry because of lower prices than other hard disk drives and because of good performance (the built-in RAM buffer feature, which is a method of putting the most frequently requested data in a special place for fast retrieval). IDE is increasingly being integrated into some computers, allowing IDE drives to be connected without requiring a host adapter board. A typical IDE drive is illustrated in Figure 4.1. (This drive is the type used in Compaq's disk drive array technology.)

With all this new technology, don't forget that MFM and RLL (without any disk drive interface technology) haven't gone away. My eighteen-month-old 80 MB drive is an MFM. You wouldn't want it in a network's file server, but it's fine for word processing applications. (Or it was fine, before it got so full; now it's a little slow. Even with good computer habits, more data gets written to hard disks than deleted from them.)

Before you buy a hard disk, make sure that the computer will support the hard disk drive. (I can think of several instances where widely selling computers don't support all of the three popular types of hard disk drives, and not because of any hard disk drive limitations, either.) Sometimes products get put on the market before they're completely ready, with vendors thinking they'll fix them when they get a chance or when somebody complains. It's a lot easier for you to purchase a compatible product to begin with than to spend your time complaining to the vendor because the product wasn't made the way it was supposed to have been made.

NETWORKING ISSUES

Networking is concerned with hard disk drive capacity and performance. Right now ESDI and SCSI I drives are the main players in 286 and 386

Figure 4.1. Conner's CP3200F 3.5-inch, 212 MB Hard Disk Drive Courtesy of Conner Peripherals, Inc.

computers and in NetWare 286 and 386, with IDE drives trailing a bit. IDE drives are much newer than ESDI or SCSI and haven't had the opportunity to make as much of a market impact as the other two. They also have a smaller disk capacity, which makes them less desirable for use as a file server hard disk drive, and they have some incompatibilities with other older drives.

SCSI HARD DISK DRIVES

SCSI hard disk drives are flexible and easy to install and more compatible with other hard disk drives because so many manufacturers make them. Right now, their data transfer rate is also twice as slow as ESDI drives and will be until SCSI II drives are being sold in volume.

SCSI drives are often used in disk drive subsystems because the SCSI interface allows the drives to be hooked up easily to the file server. A few manufacturers have come out with disk drive subsystems that do use ESDI drives, mainly as a workaround for ELS II networks.

Optical disks are also SCSI hard disk drives. Three kinds of optical drives are in the market today: CD-ROM, WORM (Write Once, Read Many), and erasable. These drives feature highly reliable media, and two of them feature non-erasable disks. The main drawback to most optical drives is the cost, easily several thousand dollars more than a conventional hard disk drive of comparable size. Also, in the case of non-erasable disk drives, when the disks are full, they're full forever. (All three kinds of optical disks are discussed in "Alternative Hard Disk Options" later in this chapter.)

As far as networking goes, SCSI hard disk drives (either I or II) are not supported by ELS I or ELS II NetWare, unless the SCSI drive in question is an IBM PS/2 SCSI (or fully compatible, of course). SCSI drives are supported by all other versions of NetWare. Optical drives are supported by NetWare v2.15 and up *if* the driver supports NetWare. The CD-ROM file format is supported by NetWare 386, v3.1, but no drives have been certified by Novell for use with NetWare 386.

ESDI HARD DISK DRIVES

ESDI drives are more difficult to install (because of the difficulty of formatting them) and are less flexible than SCSI, as well as not being as intelligent. If the intelligence isn't on a built-in controller board, then the disk controller board must concern itself with how the drive functions as well as how it sees the computer. Intelligent host adapter boards take on more of the functions of the CPU, thus increasing throughput; this means that the transfer rate figures for ESDI, SCSI, and IDE are closer than the actual numbers indicate.

However, ESDI drives are faster than SCSI I drives (10-Mbps as compared to 5-Mbps data transfer rate), and manufacturers are planning on implementing technological improvements that will make ESDI drives faster than SCSI II (15 Mbps as opposed to 10).

Because of their faster data transfer rate, ESDI drives are used most often in larger networks, in spite of the difficulty of installing and formatting them. (Hassles during installation should be expected, even if installation is supposed to be easy.)

ESDI technology is more popular than SCSI when flexibility and ease of installation don't count for much; when the network is large, you don't want a hard disk drive with a seriously low data transfer rate. This is even more true if the hard disk drive in question has a high capacity, which means that it will take longer to find the data it's looking for.

SCSI II drives may change this equation; they are as fast as ESDI drives, at least until ESDI puts out its next version; they interface with more devices with more flexibility than ESDI drives; and they are easier to install. If SCSI II lives up to its promise, ESDI may not be able to regain a competitive edge. All versions of NetWare support ESDI drives, although ELS supports only two ESDI hard disk drives in the system.

IDE HARD DISK DRIVES

IDE hard disk drives may be the wave of the future. Designed by Conner Peripherals and Compaq, they are used in Compaq's disk arrays in its top-of-the-line EISA 386 and 486 computers. Disk drive arrays, which is a way of making multiple hard disk drives share the load in a file server, speed up file server throughput considerably by allowing faster access to the data on the disks. With multiple hard disk drives in a disk array, the file server isn't limited to writing or reading one thing at a time. (Disk arrays are discussed later in this chapter.)

Beyond disk arrays, IDE drives are also being used in ISA-type computers as standalone hard disk drives. Syntrex, for example, is shipping a 386SX using IDE drives. (Syntrex built the hard and floppy disk controllers into the motherboard so that none of its six expansion slots need to be used for a hard disk drive controller board, which is a nice feature.)

For all the good things about IDE drives, a couple of problems exist. One drawback to IDE drives is their incompatibility with older technology. Since they use the same address as the AT-compatible disk controller board, IDE drives cannot coexist with the older MFM and RLL hard disk drives. (SCSI and ESDI drives don't have this problem.)

Another drawback with the current 210 MB drives is that (Compaq's disk arrays excepted) only two drives and one controller can be in the system. This means that the maximum total hard disk capacity for any system that runs IDE drives is 420 MB. (SCSI, by contrast, can have up to six host adapter boards, with seven drives attached to each one, for a total maximum hard disk capacity of 42GB, or thereabouts.)

IDE technology is still new enough that these technical problems will be resolved very quickly. Hard disk capacity is already increasing with several manufacturers including Conner Peripherals (a 510 MB version), and Plus Development and Quantum Corporation (330 MB versions). This is still smaller than the current 660MB maximum of ESDI or SCSI drives, but it's in the ballpark.

The other problems (incompatibility with older technology and inability to support more than two disk drives in a system) will also be resolved, although probably in different ways. Sometimes, if you ignore old technology, it goes away. On the other hand, limited system support is a major obstacle to becoming the pre-eminent hard disk drive technology of today; ignoring this limitation might be the end of IDE technology.

Most versions of NetWare support IDE hard disk drives, but if you want to use IDE drives with your ELS network, be careful. Some IDE drives have a hard disk driver problem that precludes them from being used with ELS NetWare. Remember that ELS is old technology and IDE is new; it's very difficult for software to be compatible with hardware products that didn't exist when the software was created. It's easier for products, software and hardware, to be compatible with older technology, but it doesn't always happen.

As a general rule, not just for hard disk drives, make sure the peripheral will work in your system, with your software, before you buy anything.

What kind of disks you have in a file server isn't the whole story, of course. Other things can be done to hard disks to increase performance of a file server: using a RAM buffer to store most-frequently requested data, duplexing, and mirroring, along with disk subsystems and disk arrays, can play a role in making the file server and the network fast or slow. Each of these subjects is discussed in the following sections.

CACHE BUFFERS, MIRRORING, AND DUPLEXING

In hard disk drives, performance is the only end result that matters. It doesn't matter if the disks are MFM, RLL, ESDI, SCSI, IDE, or TTC (Technology To Come). The only major concern, especially on a file server, is how quickly a hard disk can write (save) information to disk and read (retrieve) the information from the disk. Tied to this is the seek time: how quickly a hard disk can find the information it's looking for. While important, this has been referred to as "checking the tires on the car," meaning that nobody wants to hear about this stuff.

So, just for reference (and I'll never mention it again), here are the statistics for SCSI, ESDI, and IDE drives, with MFM, RLL, and optical drives thrown in for good measure. (Remember that as far as data transfer rate goes, the larger the figure, the better; for seek time range, the smaller the figure, the better.)

Drive Type	Data Transfer Rate	Seek Time Range
MFM	5 Mbps	26-65 ms
RLL	5 Mbps	25-65 ms
SCSI I	5 Mbps	16-30 ms
Optical (SCSI)	7 Mbps	65 ms
SCSI II	10 Mbps	16-30 ms
ESDI	10 Mbps	16-30 ms
IDE	10 Mbps	16-30 ms

Remember two things about these figures:

- They represent the rosy picture that manufacturers were able to find after putting their hard disks through benchmark tests. Real-world figures are going to be lower. The figures not only vary from hard disk drive vendor to hard disk vendor, but they vary depending on the application being used and the number of users trying to access the hard disk drive.
- All numbers connected with hard disk drives are constantly moving targets: disk capacity, data transfer rate, and disk seek time, not to mention industry price, are all subject to change, sometimes daily, depending on when vendors make announcements of their "latest and greatest."

No matter how quickly or slowly the disk writes and reads data, more data gets written to the disk than deleted from the disk; this means you can't overlook the importance of the capacity of the disk. Today, the biggest individual disks are around 600 MB. Tomorrow, that figure will be higher; soon, 1GB drives will be common. Although manufacturers are struggling to minimize it, the larger the capacity, the longer it's going to take for the appropriate data to be retrieved.

As a related issue, somewhere along the line some good computer habits must be developed by network users. Disks are not infinitely expandable; data that should be archived should be archived someplace else besides the primary hard disk drive on a file server. Besides, a hard disk drive that is nearly full is a hard disk drive that is slow, so it's in everyone's best interests to keep the hard disk drive as empty as possible.

While both ESDI and SCSI hard disk drives have a disk capacity of about 600 MB, IDE, which is a 3.5-inch drive, currently has a disk capacity of 210 MB or so. (ESDI and SCSI hard disks are both 5.25-inch, giving them more room than IDE.) Quantum and its wholly-owned subsidiary Plus Development have each announced plans to ship a 330 MB drive, meaning that they have come up with a way around the size limitation. (The new maximum IDE disk capacity is 425 MB.) Once manufacturers are routinely shipping 330 MB and 425 MB IDE drives, the next version of the IDE drive will undoubtedly be as large as the ESDI and SCSI drives.

Several ways exist to increase hard disk drive performance, among them using a cache buffer, disk mirroring, and disk duplexing, all discussed in the following sections. Disk arrays and disk subsystems also increase system throughput, but they do it differently and are discussed later in this chapter.

CACHE BUFFERS

Of the disk performance issues discussed, using a cache buffer is the only one that can be done without purchasing additional hardware. That's because it's built into the drive.

When you use a cache buffer, data that are requested frequently are placed in a special location for quick retrieval. When data are requested, the hard disk drive checks the special location first. If the data are there, they are retrieved much more quickly than the data stored in the main hard disk drive.

This idea has taken some time to catch on, but now all SCSI drives ship with a RAM buffer built in, along with the better-quality ESDI and IDE drives.

In addition to using a cache buffer with hard disk drives, hard disk controllers (or host adapter boards) also frequently have buffers. (It's a special feature for which you pay a little more.) The two buffers are complementary to each other, usually a little faster than one of them would be if alone. However, the two buffers are not twice as fast, and it is a waste of money to pay extra for a controller board with a cache buffer if you already have a hard disk drive with that feature unless you need that particular host adapter board for another reason.

DISK MIRRORING AND DUPLEXING

Disk mirroring and duplexing are two ways of saving data so that if one hard disk crashes, the other can take over with a minimum of downtime. As a qualified statement, data retrieval is faster with mirrored or duplexed hard disk drives because the data can be retrieved from the hard disk drive that is closest to the information.

The qualification that data can be retrieved faster with mirrored or duplexed hard disks is true as long as the software doesn't designate one drive primary and one drive secondary. (NetWare designates primary and secondary drives when mirroring, but not duplexing.) If a drive is designated primary or secondary, drive throughput will probably be no faster than with non-mirrored and non-duplexed hard disk drives. However, keep in mind that disk mirroring and duplexing were developed primarily to back up the main hard disk in case it failed, for whatever reason. The fact that mirroring and duplexing can speed up file server performance under the right conditions is a bonus, not the main point.

Disk Mirroring

Disk mirroring is the cheaper of the two methods, and it works by saving data sequentially to two different hard disks on the same channel; that is, if you have two hard disks in your file server, using one disk controller board, the same data can be saved to each drive. The data are not saved simultaneously; the primary disk receives the information first, then blocks of data are copied to the second disk. (This concept is illustrated in Figure 4.2.)

This gives you protection if the first hard disk fails for some reason. If the *file server* fails for some reason, however, the fact that data have been saved to two different disks won't do you any good. You can't access the data on either disk until you get the file server working again.

NetWare and Disk Mirroring. If you are using System Fault Tolerant (SFT) NetWare 286 or 386, the disk mirroring feature is built into the software, and all you need is an additional hard disk drive. If you have Advanced NetWare 286 and don't want to upgrade, you'll have to find a hardware solution.

Figure 4.2. Mirroring Disks

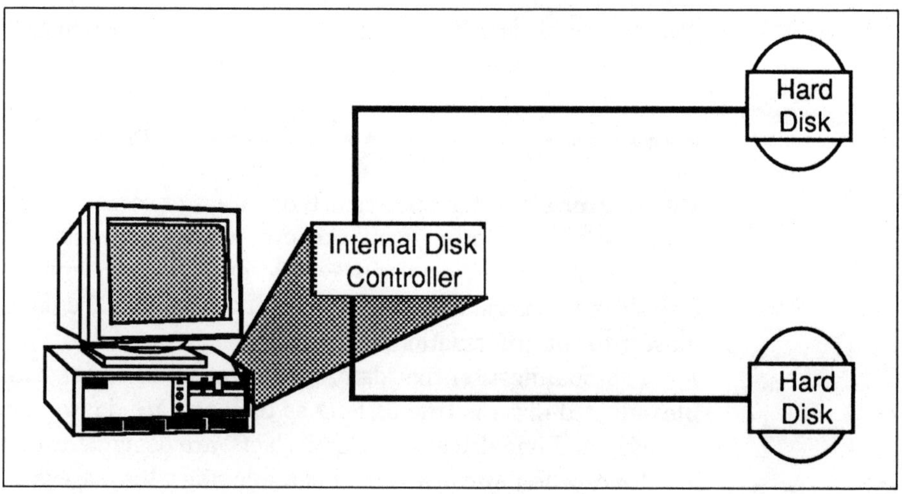

Upgrading to SFT is an option that should not be overlooked if you are struggling to add what techies call redundancy to your network. SFT not only offers disk mirroring but disk duplexing as well. It also offers something called Transaction Tracking System (TTS), which keeps databases from scrambling data in the case of a power failure. (The example that was given to me was of an accounts payable database; you have entered one transaction but haven't changed its paired transaction when the power goes out. TTS doesn't save the half of the transaction you changed, which means that you have to manually re-enter it. This is better than trying to figure out just what figures go with what transactions.) If you're planning on spending money anyway, find out how much an upgrade to SFT will cost before you choose a different option.

However, if you only want disk mirroring and you want to keep Advanced NetWare, look into the hard disk controllers and host adapter boards that offer disk mirroring. Since NetWare designates primary and secondary drives with disk mirroring, the hardware solution to mirroring will likely be faster.

ELS and Disk Mirroring. If you have ELS, you can't mirror your disks, although you might want to check around before you give up on the idea. Novell spokesmen say that ELS Level II, v2.15, doesn't support disk mirroring either through hardware or software, but it makes sense to me that an intelligent disk controller board with the mirroring feature might be able to fool NetWare, especially if the board is compatible with either the Western Digital or IBM PS/2 SCSI disk controller boards that ELS does support.

Also, ELS II is a restricted version of SFT NetWare, which does support mirroring in the software. Check with your NetWare dealer.

ELS I is a version of NetWare v2.12, which doesn't support disk mirroring in the software; you can't expect a restricted version of NetWare to do more than the full-fledged version. However, it certainly does not hurt to ask third-party vendors if their hardware mirroring products support ELS I.

Beyond NetWare, you must be sure that the computer that you want to use to mirror disks will support that option. In some instances, the computer does not support mirroring as a software solution (i.e., NetWare) but supports it as a hardware solution (i.e., a board). If you know you want to mirror disks before you purchase hardware, make sure that all of the hardware supports mirroring.

Disk Duplexing

If keeping the network up and running is of paramount importance (that is, you can afford *no* downtime), disk duplexing is a possible solution. Disk duplexing saves data simultaneously to two different hard disks on two different channels; that is, if you have two file servers connected to each other, the same data can be saved to one disk in each system (as shown in Figure 4.3). Then, if one disk fails, the other is unaffected and can take over the duties of the working file server.

Keep in mind that you don't have to duplex data to another file server; you can also duplex data to an attached disk subsystem, which may be a more economical business decision, especially if your mass storage needs are such that you already have a disk subsystem.

Disk duplexing is obviously more effective than disk mirroring, because the data are in two separate locations, with separate hardware. Disk duplexing with another file server is obviously much more expensive than disk mirroring, though, and you need to decide if buying an additional file server (of the same quality as the first one) is an economical business decision.

I have been told that the cost of an extra file server is negligible—and it is—when you compare it to the millions of dollars that America's big business loses each year through computer downtime. I just don't know if it's negligible when you compare it to an individual firm's financial losses through computer downtime annually. In many cases, I'd be inclined to doubt it.

When I've been on a network that crashed, it was usually due to power outages, and the whole company was indeed brought to a standstill. However, it was brought to a standstill because no lights were on in the building, not because the network was down. Even in companies where networking is the main business, you don't spend all your time on your computer; however, there's not much you can do at work when you can't see your desk. It's not really fair to count power outages as part of computer downtime; that's company downtime, a different line item.

NetWare and Disk Duplexing. Disk duplexing can be done through software if you have SFT NetWare 286 or NetWare 386. If you have Advanced

Figure 4.3. Disk Duplexing

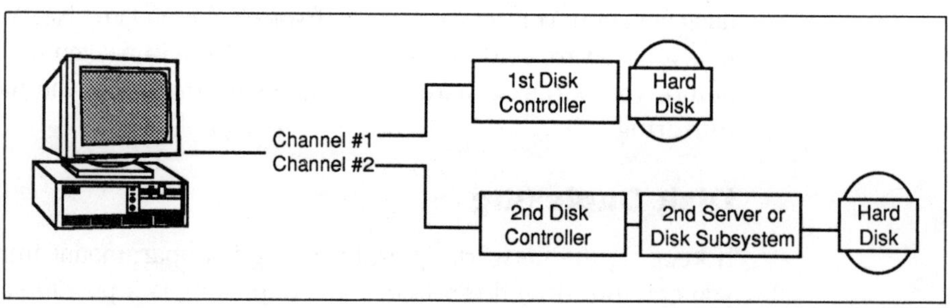

NetWare, you will have to find a hardware solution; that is, some disk controller boards will provide a disk duplexing feature that is transparent to the user.

Before you commit yourself to a hardware solution for Advanced NetWare, look into the option of upgrading to SFT. SFT offers disk duplexing, disk mirroring, and Transaction Tracking System (TTS), which is still another way of protecting valuable data in case of a power or system failure (see the discussion in the disk mirroring section.)

No matter which version of NetWare you use, you still have to purchase the extra hardware (hard disk drives, disk controller boards, file server, or disk drive subsystem) that you are going to use for duplexing.

ELS and Disk Duplexing. If you have ELS, you cannot duplex your hard disks. While everything about ELS is subject to change as ELS strives for compatibility with today's technology, for ELS to support duplexing of hard disks would require the reversal of three or four existing conditions.

ELS is a closed architecture, meaning that Novell doesn't want the industry to find ways to enhance ELS performance; Novell really wants you to become frustrated with ELS limitations and go buy a version of NetWare that can do what NetWare is advertised to do. And truly, if you have a real need to duplex your hard disk drives, you probably have outgrown your ELS network and should investigate the other options that NetWare offers.

DISK DRIVE SUBSYSTEMS, DISK ARRAYS

Disk drive subsystems and disk arrays are file server issues. A workstation does not need the additional storage provided by disk drive subsystems or disk drive arrays, and it does not need the extra performance that these two options can give.

DISK SUBSYSTEMS

Disk subsystems, basically, are really big hard disk drives in a box that is attached to a file server's host adapter board. The box usually has a power supply (or two) attached for a source of power. Whether it is a disk subsystem or just a box with external drives in it depends on whether it has its own disk controller board or is attached to the same disk controller board as the drives already seated in the system.

Disk subsystems are used to provide additional data storage for a file server when the primary hard disk drive in the system isn't enough. And the hard disk drives in the system probably are not enough if you have a large-ish network, especially if your hard disk drives are older, with a smaller hard disk capacity than today's monsters. No matter how well trained the network users are, more data are going to be written to the hard disks in the system than deleted from them. Although you should try to make your network users learn good computer habits by keeping less-current data *off* the network, you're always going to have an increasing need for data storage. (Data always expands to fill the available space to hold it.)

Disk subsystems are not designed as backup units that save a copy of the most current file; instead they are designed to provide additional data storage, which means they need to be backed up themselves. (This is less true if you are using your disk subsystem for duplexing or mirroring, which does provide a form of backup.) Backup units, including those labeled erasable optical subsystems, are discussed in Chapter VI.

Disk subsystems can be as simple as one external drive or as complex as a box with four or more hard disk drives. And, of course, each drive can have the maximum capacity on the market today, so disk subsystems can range from about 100 MB to more than 2 GB each. You aren't limited to one hard disk drive subsystem. You can have as many disk subsystems as your computer and NetWare allow.

Disk controller/host adapter boards are required if you want to use disk subsystems. Each host adapter or disk controller board can handle up to a certain number of hard disk drives or disk subsystems; after that, you must get another disk controller/host adapter board.

Each disk controller/host adapter board has its own I/O address, and each version of NetWare has its own limit as to how many disk controller/host adapter board I/O addresses it supports. NetWare 286 supports four disk controller board I/O addresses (called channels), which means that you can have four host adapter boards in the system; ELS NetWare, always a special case, only supports one channel in the file server; and NetWare 386 supports as many host adapter boards in the system as you have slots to hold them.

NetWare 386 has eliminated the term "channels"; the key instead is in avoiding conflicts, such as I/O and DMA address conflicts and IRQ lines, when you insert boards. As long as you have open I/O and DMA addresses and IRQs, you can insert as many boards (of whatever variety) as you want. This means that NetWare 386 has removed software limitations to performance. (Hardware technology hasn't caught up with the software, so some limitations remain.)

NetWare 386 has a total data storage limitation of 32TB (terabytes). Again, NetWare has removed the software limitations on performance; 32TB is the equivalent of 32,000 1GB disk drives. Today's technology has no way of attaching that many hard disk drives or disk drive subsystems, and even if you could attach that many drives today, it would take roughly three years to install them all (said one person with nothing better to do than figure it out).

On the other hand, NetWare 286 (all versions) has a total data storage limitation of 2GB (2,000 MB), which means that the maximum capacity of today's biggest hard disk drives has long since outstripped the older NetWare technology, and you have to be careful not to exceed the NetWare limitations.

Mainstream NetWare and Disk Subsystems

Disk subsystems is one area where the stickers from Novell's IMSP (see Chapter 1) are really significant. Several firms, most recently ADIC, have co-developed disk subsystems with Novell. These co-developed subsystems are guaranteed to work with NetWare. In addition, the drives in the co-developed subsystems are frequently shipped "NetWare Ready," as well as with all the bad blocks (flaws in the hard disk that every disk has) mapped and with NetWare Ready diagnostic software included. These features save you hours and hours of work. (NetWare Ready is a guarantee from the vendor that NetWare will recognize the subsystem when it's installed.)

Most disk subsystems come with either two or four drives installed, and all the drives in the system must be identical to each other in both type and capacity. You can't have a 330 MB ESDI drive and a 651 MB SCSI hard disk drive in the same subsystem, for example; every drive must be either an ESDI or a SCSI and each must have the same capacity.

Remember that, as far as NetWare 286 goes, two 512 MB drives in the file server plus a disk subsystem containing two 512 MB drives exceeds the data storage limitations of the operating system.

If one disk subsystem isn't sufficient and you haven't hit your NetWare 286 data storage limit, you can attach other disk subsystems to other host adapter boards in your system or you can daisy chain the disk subsystems to each other (if the manufacturer provides that option) up to the memory limits of your version of NetWare.

Besides adding data storage capacity to the file server, disk subsystems can be used for duplexing and mirroring, providing redundancy. Keep in mind that while a disk subsystem can provide both redundancy in the form of additional storage and duplexing/mirroring, you will probably need more data storage or even more than one disk subsystem if you choose the duplexing/

mirroring option. (Duplexing and mirroring are in essence, duplicate disks, halving data storage space.) A disk subsystem is illustrated in Figure 4.4.

ELS and Disk Subsystems

Disk subsystems are almost out of the question for ELS. For starters, a disk subsystem usually requires a second channel, which ELS does not support. However, given the maximum data storage limitation that NetWare 286 supports (2GB) and the maximum size of today's hard disk drives (600 MB or so), a disk subsystem is not going to be a real necessity. By the time you hit your data storage limitations and are looking around for a way to use a disk subsystem, you will need to upgrade to a different version of NetWare for other reasons. (Too many users, for example.)

Several firms, among them Storage Dimensions, have come up with large-capacity hard disk drives compatible with and certified for use with ELS NetWare. In the Storage Dimensions example, two ESDI hard disk drives, each with a capacity of 512 MB, can be inserted into the ELS file server; putting two of those drives into an ELS network gives you more than 50% of the total data storage capacity allowed by NetWare 286.

If you really do want to install a disk subsystem, keep in mind the ELS rules regarding hard disk drives, disk controller/host adapter boards, and disk subsystems:

- Only one channel is supported (each hard disk controller/host adapter board equals only one channel in practical terms).

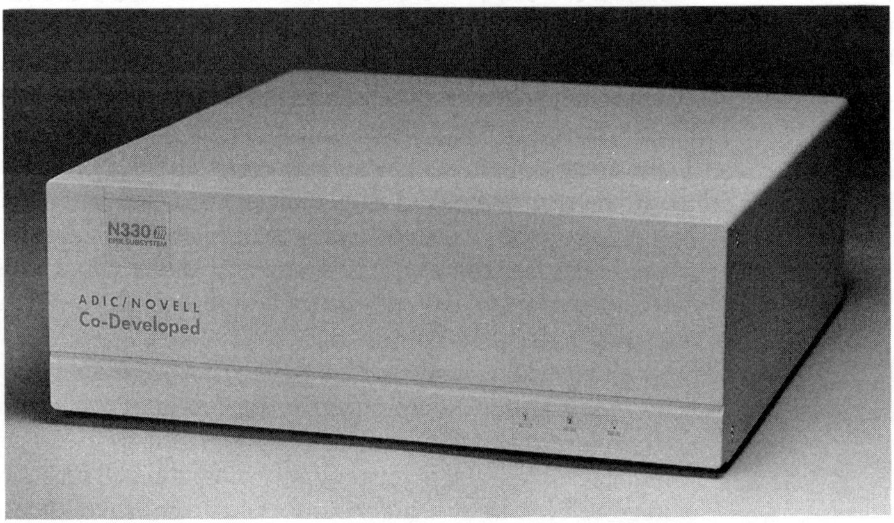

Figure 4.4. ADIC N330 Disk Subsystem Courtesy of Advanced Digital Information Corporation (ADIC)

- Only one ISA-compatible disk controller board (which supports two hard disk drives) can be inserted into the system.
- Or, only one IBM PS/2 SCSI host adapter board (which supports up to seven hard disk drives) can be inserted into the system.

If you have ELS I, you are limited to the number of drives that the AT-compatible disk controller board supports, because ELS I doesn't support the SCSI interface. And no one has come up with a workaround that allows you to attach disk subsystems.

For ELS II, on the other hand, there is at least one workaround that allows that NetWare version to support a formal disk subsystem; however, ELS II also supports both the AT-compatible and the IBM PS/2 SCSI-compatible host adapter boards (but only one host adapter board can be in the system at a time), and a disk subsystem would be needed only under rare circumstances. If you have ELS II and an IBM PS/2 SCSI host adapter board, the network operating system can support up to seven hard disk drives: the two or so within the file server and up to five in an external box. (Those hard disks could come to more than 3GB, which exceeds the data storage limitations of ELS and NetWare 286.)

The five external hard disk drives must remain in the same channel (attached to the same host adapter board) as the two within the file server, which means that you have to daisy chain the drives. (Daisy chaining physically connects each hard disk drive to the previous hard disk drive, unlike a formal disk subsystem where the box is connected to its own host adapter board.) With seven high-capacity drives, you are in danger of exceeding the limits set by NetWare 286 for data storage. Be careful not to buy more data storage than you can use.

However, if you just have to have a disk subsystem, look into the ELS II Conversion Kit by Plus Development. This kit substitutes its drivers (with Novell's blessing) for the drivers that Novell ships, allowing up to eight ESDI drives to be connected into a subsystem. A Plus Development spokesman said that the ELS II Conversion Kit hasn't been a big seller, partly because ELS users have discovered that the Hardcard II, a hard disk drive on a host adapter board that is also manufactured by Plus Development, works very well in ELS file servers. (Be advised that this kit has a major drawback in that you are limited to the Plus Development hard disk drives supported by the kit. You can't use any existing, non–Plus Development hard disk drives already in the machine, even if they worked with ELS before you installed the conversion kit.)

All these extra drives that you can now attach to an ELS file server do not mean that ELS can support either mirroring or disk duplexing. According to the Novell spokesmen, ELS does not support mirroring or duplexing through either the hardware or the software. Double check with some third-party hardware vendors before giving up on the idea of mirroring those extra drives, but disk duplexing is definitely out until a second disk controller board (with its attendant third-party device driver) is supported in an ELS file server.

ELS doesn't support third-party device drivers now, which is the basic reason that it has so much difficulty with hard disk drives and disk controller/host adapter boards.

DISK DRIVE ARRAYS

Disk drive arrays are found only on EISA machines; right now they're only found on the 386 and 486 models of the Compaq SystemPro, although Dell Computers has announced (but not shipped) a file server with a disk array. A disk drive array is a way of making multiple hard disk drives share the load of the file server. With multiple hard disks, the array can handle simultaneous multiple requests, which speeds up the server throughput tremendously.

In disk drive arrays, as in practically everything in the computer industry, two approaches are used: hardware and software. The software is much the cheaper, sending the request load across the network and all drives in a bell curve.

The hardware approach, used by Compaq and Dell, is more expensive and allows the disk drives to appear as one to the user or the network. This approach has several advantages:

- Assurance that load will be spread evenly
- Higher performance

A hard disk drive array, as set up by Compaq, uses four paired drives of 210 MB IDE hard disk drives controlled by one special host adapter board. Compaq also supports a fifth pair of devices, for a maximum of 1.68GB, which is a lot of storage for one computer, but bigger networks could go through that much fairly quickly. However, the hard disk drive throughput on a disk array is much faster than other drives with a similar disk capacity because of the simultaneous multiple request feature that the host adapter board supports.

But not everyone is enamored with disk drive arrays. One data storage expert said that he thought disk arrays were mismarketed with performance being touted when they were primarily designed for fault tolerance (duplexing). (That's what they said about duplexing and mirroring in the beginning, too, but in many instances duplexing/mirroring does speed up system throughput.)

This same expert said that he could take the same number of SCSI drives as used by the disk array technology and "blow the disk array out of the water" in terms of performance, probably because the disks he would use would be higher capacity. (IDE drives are only shipping in a maximum capacity of 210MB, although a 510MB drive has been announced by Conner Peripherals, and other manufacturers are also planning larger drives.)

Disk array technology is new technology from Compaq. The hardware solution is designed for EISA machines and NetWare 386 and requires, in addition to the appropriate disk drives, the Compaq disk array host adapter board in order to work. You positively can't install a disk drive array in your 286 workstation, or for that matter your 386.

As a general rule, it's better not to try to attach new technology to old. While it may work, it wasn't designed that way; you're likely to find bugs popping up, or key features disabled, and you're likely to have to struggle the whole time the new technology is in place. If the new technology provides a quantum jump for you, it's better to throw out the old technology and start over than try to blend the two.

ALTERNATIVE HARD DISK OPTIONS

Although ESDI, SCSI, and IDE hard disk drives are currently the mainstream hard disk drives types, they aren't the only options. SCSI provides an alternative to the traditional hard disks—non-magnetic optical, which uses light (laser) to write its data. However, the most popular alternative hard disk options are for people who don't have any room left in their computers but who need or want another hard disk anyway.

Popular hard disk alternatives include:

- Removable hard disk drives
- Hard disk on an interface board
- Optical drives

None of these options is suitable for placement in a file server, with the exception of the optical drives (under certain circumstances). You emphatically do not want a hard disk, for example, that you can easily remove from the system. It would ruin all of your previous efforts at security. You also do not want a hard disk in a file server if you can't re-use the disk. (Accounting and legal applications might like an optical disk, because of the need for a permanent history, but the optical disk would not be the primary disk in the system. See WORMs, later in this section, for more information on using these non-erasable hard disk drives in file servers.)

Removable Hard Disk Drives and Hard Disks on a Board

If you have several computers and work on each of them, you might want a removable hard disk drive for your workstation, assuming that your computers are each compatible with the removable hard disk drive. Vendors selling this option say that you can increase the security of your workstation because you can take the hard disk drive with you. These disks are also built to take more abuse than traditional hard disk drives, making them easy to pop into your briefcase and take home. (Traditional hard disk drives aren't built to take *any* abuse. Treat a removable hard disk drive with the greatest of care.)

If you have no drive bays left in your workstation but you just have to have another hard disk drive, you can try inserting a hard disk on a controller board into one of the expansion slots. Many manufacturers are selling this popular option, frequently in 20MB and 40MB capacities.

Some smarter ELS II customers tried the hard disk on a controller board in their own servers and have discovered that it works. (ELS I doesn't support SCSI drives, and most hard disks on a board are SCSI.) Without something like Plus Development's Hardcard II, ELS supports only one or two internal disk drives, although ELS II can have up to seven hard disk drives daisy-chained off the IBM PS/2 SCSI disk controller board. (Plus Development has also come up with a workaround to give ELS II users a disk subsystem, but customers are more interested in the Hardcard II.)

You aren't going to get a super-large capacity hard disk drive with either a removable hard disk or a disk on a card, but maybe these alternatives will hold you until you can upgrade either your primary hard disk or your primary computer. Or, in the case of ELS users, your primary network.

Another option is an external hard disk drive, which can be as plain as one hard disk or as fancy as a formal disk drive subsystem, which means the capacity ranges from 20MB or 40MB to gigabytes of extra storage.

Since they're placed on the workstation, these options (external hard disk drive, removable hard disk drive, or disk drive on a board) do not affect NetWare in any way at all, any more than using the A: drive of your workstation affects NetWare. Your workstation BIOS will have to be told of the additional drives if you want to use them. (Your workstation BIOS will also have to support these drives. Check before you purchase.)

Optical Hard Disks

Optical hard disks come in three varieties, and contrary to public opinion, not all of them are non-erasable. The three types are:

- CD-ROM
- WORMS
- Erasable

CD-ROM and WORM drives are better known than the erasable optical drive. CD-ROM drives usually contain data, such as an encyclopedia, programmed somewhere else. All you can do is read them.

WORM drives, so-called because of their function (Write Once, Read Many), allow you to write data to them until they're full—once. You can then read them as often as you like.

Erasable optical disks can be used just like traditional magnetic hard disk drives, as long as you don't mind paying several thousand dollars more for the privilege.

In fact, the biggest drawback to any of these optical drives is the cost. Buying one of them (for example, an erasable drive) can set you back the amount of a cheapish file server ($5,000 or so). A WORM isn't quite as expensive, but it's still easily $2,000 more than a SCSI drive with the same capacity. The cost of a CD-ROM drive is going to depend on what is on it.

One of the biggest advantages of optical drives over magnetic hard disks is that all optical disks use removable cartridges to store their data, much like traditional magnetic floppy disk drives. The disk capacity of optical drives is unlimited, because you can just pop in another cartridge when the first one is full. And the cartridges are cheaper than the optical disk. (This advantage becomes a disadvantage if you're using the optical disk as the primary drive on the system; if you put an application on a removable cartridge, you'll have to re-install that application every time you insert a new cartridge.)

Another advantage to optical drives over traditional hard disk drives is the reliability of the media used in the drive, which is guaranteed to last between 10 and 100 years, depending on who you're talking to. Even in archival storage you don't need to refresh the media every few years by calling it up and re-saving it, as you do with magnetic media.

A third advantage is in the reliability of the drive itself. Magnetic hard disks can crash, but optical drives use a different technology, laser, and the drives themselves don't contain any traditional heads.

These drives usually fit into an existing PC with an empty full-height disk drive bay; they can also be rack mounted, and some are designed as standalone units. The standalone units probably are the best idea. Not many working computers are going to have a free full-height disk drive bay. (A few half-height optical disks exist, but they are rare.)

Optical read/write disks are supported by NetWare servers, with the possible exception of ELS. ELS supports an optical disk as long as the interface is IBM PS/2 SCSI (or compatible) or ISA compatible (by which ELS means MFM, RLL, or ESDI, and sometimes IDE). Note that CD-ROM drives are not considered read/write; pre-programmed, you can only read these disks, and not with NetWare, not yet.

NetWare 386, v3.1, does provide file format support for CD-ROM drives, which means, of course that no prior version does. However, Novell says that no CD-ROM drive has been certified for use with NetWare, and while some CD-ROM manufacturers can make their drives work with NetWare, it's a struggle because no NetWare specifications have been printed by Novell to make the job easier. That will come with the v3.11 release of NetWare 386, in mid 1991. Each of these drive types is discussed in more detail in the following sections.

CD-ROM. CD-ROM drives fill the need for library-type functions. Dictionaries, for example, are often put on a CD-ROM drive, and several publishers (*PCWeek* among them) put their entire publication on disk. You get to the stories of interest much more quickly than by leafing through the paper copy page by page. (That's because you can search for a particular key word.)

WORM Drives. WORM hard disk drives are mainly used to provide a history for sensitive data. You can write data to these disks, but you can never erase the data. And when the disk is full, it's full; you have to get another cartridge (at $150 or so).

Like any other hard disk drive, WORMs require a specially written driver to work successfully with NetWare. Several firms have filled that niche, including Corel Systems Corporation, the same people who bring you CorelDRAW! While they will sell you the drive and host adapter board (or you can get the drive someplace else), Corel's specialty is in writing the networking software.

The software guarantees optical disk compatibility with a specified version of NetWare (v2.15 and up) while using the same host adapter board as your magnetic hard disk drives, a truly great feature. Corel's software, called OptiStar, allows the WORM to act like a standard hard disk transparently to the user, who will never know that the hard disk on the file server is saving a new version of the file each time, rather than writing over the previously saved version.

While that may be a blessing for some applications, such as accounting or legal, where you need a clearly defined history, WORMs should not be put transparently on file servers with word processing network users, and you should not tell people who do a lot of word processing how to get to the optical disk.

For example, I save my files frequently. If the network administrator had me saving my work by default to an optical disk, the disk would end up with 17 versions of the same file—each day. Each file would be different by only two or three words, or at best two or three paragraphs. (If I had been staring at it for awhile, the file might very well be saved with *no* new information at all.) That 651 MB optical disk would be full in no time.

A better word processing use would be to deliberately save the final, and only the final, version of a document to a WORM disk. Then, when the document is inevitably updated, you have an unchangeable version of the previous document, even if you forgot to give the document an updated name. It's very easy (dumb, but easy), when updating a document, to save the changes as you go and not realize until it's too late that you have changed the original rather than creating a new document.

Archiving, not just leaving a paper trail but storing data that are not currently needed, is another function of WORM drives. Backup systems that use optical media to archive data are described in more detail later in Chapter VI.

WORMS come in external standalone form as well as internal forms. In addition, you can use library units (technically called autochangers, informally called jukeboxes) that will hold WORMS and CD-ROM drives (although not at the same time). The library units are known as jukeboxes, because you can punch out your selection as you would with a real jukebox. These massive libraries can hold hundreds of gigabytes of storage, so they're meant to hold all the data that's ever been or ever will be generated by your company.

As noted earlier, NetWare doesn't really support CD-ROM drives yet, in or out of jukeboxes; also, drivers that have been written for WORMS and NetWare only support SFT NetWare, v2.15, and above. If you have Advanced

NetWare 286 or ELS, it will be difficult to use a WORM on your system. You will have to find a driver for the optical drive and your version of NetWare.

Erasable Optical Disks. Erasable optical disks have been around for several years. Traditionally, they've always been slower than mainstream hard disk drives, and they've always been extremely expensive. While they are still extremely expensive, to the point that of some non-optical vendors are telling me that these drives still aren't commercially available, the data transfer rate are now comparable to the larger ESDI and SCSI drives. Only the drive seek time lags behind, comparable to pure MFM and RLL drives.

However, the main virtue of an erasable optical hard disk drive is its reliability. The data integrity under repeated recording conditions is far superior to that of traditional hard disk drives.

Erasable optical disks can be re-used just like regular magnetic hard disk drives. In this way, erasable optical disks are more like traditional magnetic hard disk drives than other optical disks. However, since these drives also use removable media, the ultimate storage capacity of the drive is as unlimited as with other optical disk drives.

A common use of erasable optical drives is for users with big files—video animation, simulations, and CAD-type drawings. Users say that the ability to put complete CAD drawings on a disk saves design costs because previous drawings are easily located and copied, meaning that you don't have to recreate earlier work.

However, if you don't need the media to be reliable for 10 years or longer, with an exceptional low data error rate, and if you don't need to store images of up to 1GB, then you probably don't need these erasable optical disks, at least not until the prices come down.

If you do need extremely reliable disk drive media, look into these drives. The cost, while high, gets lower as you take into consideration the fact that the capacity of the disk is unlimited through the use of cartridges.

HARDWARE INSTALLATION

The hardware discussed in this section includes hard disk drives, disk subsystems, and disk arrays. Simplified installation instructions for hard disk drives and disk subsystems follow. Disk arrays, which usually consist of four hard disk drives and a special disk controller board, would be installed the same way as a disk subsystem, but right now I recommend against putting disk arrays into a system that doesn't already come with them.

INSTALLATION PREPARATION

When you install a hard disk or a disk subsystem, remember that hardware installation is just half of it; after you put it in your computer, you have to tell the computer (and NetWare, if in a server) that it's there. So find the software instructions and keep them handy.

Before you touch your electronic add-ons or your computer, rid yourself of any static electricity buildup by touching bare (unpainted) metal or by using a grounding strap. You can destroy electronic components if you zap them just right with static electricity.

The first step is to turn off and unplug your computer.

Next, remove the cover. Usually, you'll find three or four screws in the back that you must remove before lifting the cover up and out. Occasionally, manufacturers are afraid the cover is going to get away if it isn't really screwed down. Check the manufacturer's instructions if there seem to be a lot of screws attached to the back or bottom of the computer.

If you are installing a hard disk drive, continue with the next heading; if you are installing a disk subsystem, skip to the next page.

INSTALLING A HARD DISK DRIVE

Once the computer is open, locate the hard disk drive bays, usually at the front of the machine next to the floppy disk drive bays. Then remove the holding screw and bracket.

Before you attempt to slide the hard disk drive into the system, you will probably have to add rails to the hard disk drive. Rails, always shipped with the hard disk drive, are used to add extra width to the hard disk drive, making them fit in the hard disk drive bay; they aren't always needed. The rails are labeled right and left or top and bottom; they only work if they are fit properly.

Once the rails are attached, take the cable shipped with the hard disk drive and attach it to the appropriate connector on the back of the drive. Remember the pin-1-to-pin-1 orientation. Pin 1 on the cable is marked with the colored strip; pin 1 on the hard disk drive connector is marked usually by a "one" or a notch. The hard disk drive will not function if the pin-1-to-pin-1 orientation is ignored.

The drive bay in the front of the machine will handle one full-height or two half-height 5.25-inch hard disk drives. Handling the drive by its edges (and not the circuit board), slide it into the computer with the circuit board down. The hard disk drive is now resting on the rails, not the circuit board.

Take the free end of the cable attached to the hard disk drive and connect it to the appropriate connector on the hard disk drive controller or adapter board, again remembering the pin-1-to-pin-1 orientation. Pin 1 on the controller board is indicated by a "one" or a notch.

Next, take the 4-pin power supply cable and attach it to the appropriate connector on the hard disk drive. The power supply cable is keyed and only fits one way. It also doesn't matter which power supply cable you use; each will work.

The final step in hardware installation is to replace the holding screw and bracket on the front of the hard disk drive and then close up the cover, repeating the steps at the beginning of this procedure.

To make your hard disk work, partition it and format it according to the manufacturer's directions. After that, the first step in software installation is to tell the computer that a new hard disk is resident. Enter the system's setup procedure and identify the drive so that the computer can access it. To do this, you need the documentation that came with the hard disk drive, labeling the number of heads, cylinders, and sectors and giving the precomp value.

You don't need to tell NetWare about the drive if it's being installed in a workstation. If it's being installed in a file server, you need to partition the drive differently, and you should refer to your main NetWare 286 or 386 installation manual before you start.

INSTALLING A DISK SUBSYSTEM

To install a disk subsystem, you'll have to install a second host adapter board into the computer, cable the board to the disk subsystem, and let NetWare know of the existence of the subsystem.

Before you install the board in the file server, make sure that the board will not conflict with previous boards already in the system.

If you have NetWare 286, be sure that the channel I/O address is correct by referring to the list of default settings that came with your board. Since this is the second host adapter board in the system, the board should be set for the second I/O channel address. (As a matter of fact, you should check this before you buy the board. The first I/O channel address is the default; if you don't specify the correct channel address and the vendor forgets to ask, you'll get the default, which won't do you any good.)

If you have NetWare 386, the channel limitations have been removed. Instead, you can install any board as long as the board doesn't conflict (I/O and DMA addresses and IRQ lines) with other boards in your system.

Inserting the Board

Once you've checked the disk controller board settings, you can put the board into your file server. With the computer open, locate the expansion slots, usually at the rear of the machine opposite the power supply, as illustrated in Figure 4.5. Remove the holding screw and expansion slot bracket from the appropriate empty slot (the farther from the power supply the better), placing the screw and bracket to one side. Put your new board into the expansion slot, attaching it with the holding screw you just removed, and replace the cover of the computer. Remember that you can't put a 16-bit board into either an 8-bit or a 32-bit slot.

Attaching the Disk Subsystem

Taking the cable that was shipped with the disk subsystem, attach one end to the port on the back of the host adapter board you have just installed. The cable is keyed so that it will fit into the port only one way. Then connect the other end of the cable to the port on the disk subsystem.

Some of the better disk subsystems come "NetWare Ready," meaning that the software installation has been done for you. This is a feature I would seek out; subsystems with this feature will usually have a sticker from Novell that says "NetWare Ready" on it. If not, refer to the manufacturer's instructions as to what you should do to make the subsystem recognizable to NetWare.

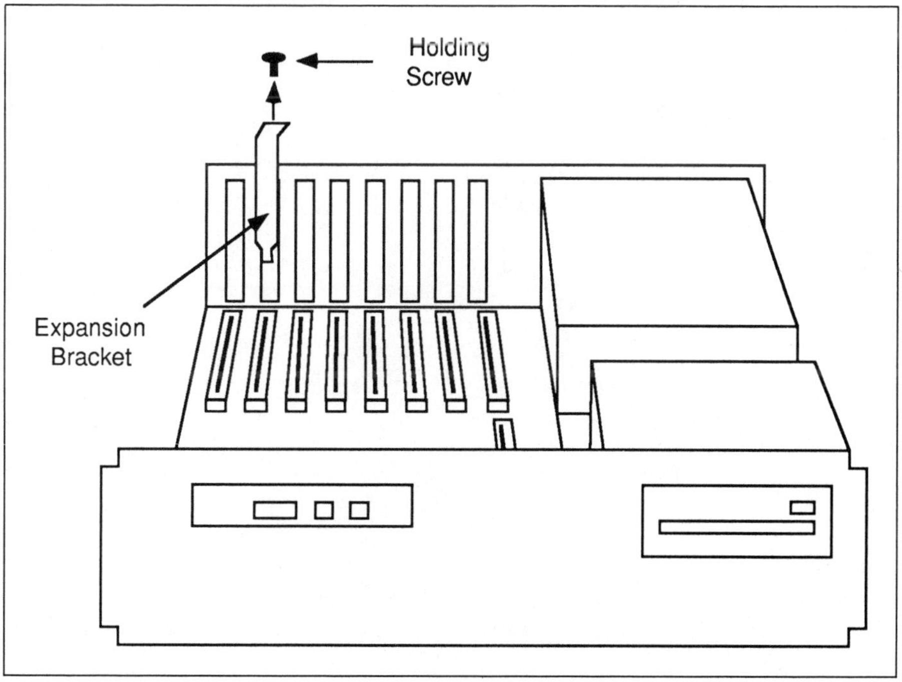

Figure 4.5. Locating the expansion slot, holding screw, and expansion bracket

If you have NetWare 286, v2.15, you will have to load the Value-Added Device Drivers (VADDs); if you have NetWare 386, you'll have to add the NetWare Loadable Modules (NLMs).

V

Personal Computers

OVERVIEW

As you know by now, there are millions of personal computers and every one of them earnestly claims to work successfully at whatever purpose you want. Actually, computer is a misnomer—at least if you listen to the old timers. Real computers, they say, are those monsters that run NASA spaceships; what we have here are personal systems or *personal* computers. However, and in spite of what the old-time programmers say, we're going to consider a computer to be the machine on your desk that does word processing, spread sheets, and databases and receives electronic mail. Just be aware that every so often you'll come across someone who takes exception to your terminology. But otherwise they're usually nice people.

Sorting through the claims of these millions of computers takes patience, planning, and knowledge. To get the best computer for your purposes, you have to know exactly what your purposes are, what hardware requirements must be met to fulfill your purposes, and how to read the advertisements.

Weird as it may seem, reading the advertisements correctly is just as important as knowing what you want. Almost every computer ad, for example, shows a picture of a complete system and says that you can have this for only x-number of dollars. You have to read the fine print to realize that the monitor and the hard disk are not usually included. You add the cost of a monitor and a hard disk and you've just added $1500 or so to the "low, low" cost of getting a complete system. The rationale is that all the vendors do it, high-quality monitors and high-capacity hard disks are expensive, the end-user's application may not call for a monitor (for a file server) or hard disk (for a workstation), or many customers want to install their own peripherals rather than use those provided with the system. And sometimes, peripherals do clash with the software, such as with NetWare Access and VGA monitors, so it makes sense to let customers buy everything piecemeal. (See Chapter I for a discussion of NetWare Access and the VGA problem.)

Sometimes this rationale backfires on the vendors, as it has for IBM and one of IBM's computers that is positioned for the home-use market, the 286-based PS/1. The PS/1 is priced lower than many of IBM's office machines, it isn't sold with a hard disk, and a number of people have decided that it is just fine as a diskless workstation.

IBM is trying to prevent this; they're going to their bigger corporate clients and telling them that the warranty is void on any PS/1 that is found with a network interface board inside it. The reason for this, assuming that IBM isn't trying to cover up a terrible design flaw that causes the PS/1 to destroy itself if you put expansion boards in it, is money. The small computer, by taking over a spot in the networking market, is eliminating the market for some of IBM's more costly machines.

If IBM has difficulty with (its own) ads that imply a complete system but don't actually provide a hard disk drive, imagine the poor user. If you're a beginning network administrator, all you are trying to do is put together the best possible network for the lowest possible price. Why wouldn't a small 286 machine sold without a hard disk by one of America's best-known and respected computer manufacturers serve as a diskless workstation? Or, why should you have to go buy a standard PC for use as a workstation and then find you have to buy a monitor as well?

Anyway, to read the ads correctly you have to know your needs (not to mention IBM's). Leaving aside IBM's problems, your needs can be defined four or five different ways. For example, which version of NetWare are these computers going to work with? Is the computer going to be a file server? A non-dedicated file server? A workstation? Is the person getting the workstation a power user (basically, someone very experienced with computers)? Is the system you want to buy compatible with the systems you already have and the network cabling you want to install?

BACKGROUND

All these questions have taken us a long way from the beginning of the computer, when the first question probably was, "How many rooms is it going to take up?"

Working computers have been around longer than a generation, starting with Remington-Rand's UNIVAC I in 1950, which used vacuum tubes (just like our older television sets). The UNIVAC only took up one room, but it was a large one. However, it wasn't until the 1970s that technology brought computers to our desks. It was at that point that the electronic chip came into being and with it, the microprocessor. It was also at that point that the public (non–computer literate) became aware of the computer as something that was real instead of abstract.

It was then that spreadsheets and word processing began, although they probably weren't any fun at all for the public to use. I'll bet the techies loved them, though. I can remember an old (he was 36 in 1989) computer techie talking about how he had to manually set the address bits on the front of his computer in order for the machine to boot, because the BIOS hadn't really been invented. (He wasn't complaining, though; he thought it was fun. I think he built that computer himself, too.) Until the BIOS came into being, computer acceptance was slow. (Not too many people are interested in throwing eight or 16 switches to turn on a computer, especially if you don't know what to do with the machine once it's on.)

The first personal computer to be marketed was the Xerox Alto computer, but it was Apple Computer, Radio Shack, and Commodore who (separately) got the ball rolling in 1977 by introducing computers that were actually sold in stores.

Notice that IBM isn't on this list. Although IBM is frequently thought of as the founding father of computers, especially by people who are fairly indifferent to computers, IBM didn't show up until 1980, when it introduced the 8088 PC, which used Microsoft's disk operating system (MS-DOS). The 286-based AT from IBM appeared in 1983, at the same time as Apple introduced its short-lived Lisa. From the Lisa sprang the Macintosh, one of the most popular computers on the market today.

In 1986, Compaq shipped the first 386-based AT, followed by every computer manufacturer in the world. In 1987, IBM introduced a machine with a different bus than the 286- or 386-based AT—the Personal System/2, which also has its own non-compatible operating system. And now, on the cusp of the 90s, we're up to the 486-based machines, with probably a 586 soon to follow.

Where next? One of the underlying goals of computing is artificial intelligence, whereby the computer can talk to you, telling you things you need to know without you giving the computer the information first. However, no less an esteemed person than Isaac Asimov says that he thinks artificial intelligence is a long way away. The author of *2001* no longer thinks that we will achieve meaningful communication with our computers by that year; instead, he's holding out for the year 2100. However, the rapid history of the computer indicates that it's a mistake to underestimate man's ability to make tremendous strides with these machines. And besides, we have the computers to help.

Leaving aside tomorrow's wonders, today the computer world is divided into three incompatible camps: UNIX, IBM-compatible, and Macintosh. You know where IBM and Macintosh came from. UNIX is an operating system originally developed by AT&T for the precursor of today's VAX systems. It is flexible enough, thanks to the C programming language, that programs designed for it can run on many different kinds of computers.

The problem arises when you try to talk to people who have taken up residence in the various camps. Of all of them, only some in the IBM camp have historically been willing to discuss the merits of other operating systems. Macintosh and UNIX people are willing to discuss the demerits of MS-DOS and the superiority of their own operating system. They aren't interested in learning *anything* about IBM compatibles. (Proving that I belong in the MS-DOS camp, I think a computer is a tool; different jobs call for different tools, and there is a place in the world for all of these operating systems and others besides. I have used Macintosh and, briefly, UNIX.)

However, people are now acknowledging that even if you don't like an operating system you still need to communicate with the people using it. Hardware hasn't made much headway in making it possible to talk to non-compatibles. One of the firms that's filling this void is Novell, which has created Portable NetWare, a version of NetWare 386. Novell is wisely sticking to its mainstream product, but it is allowing others to move (port) NetWare to their own hardware platforms and operating systems. This means that anyone using this version of NetWare will very likely be able to talk to anyone else on this version of NetWare, no matter which desktop operating system they are using. Novell also has NetWare v2.15c, which allows MS-DOS and Macintosh computer users to talk to one another. (Portable NetWare is discussed in more detail in Chapter VIII.)

The next few sections discuss compatibility issues that workstations and file servers face with their network interface boards. (Compatibility is what Novell tests when it tests computers and boards against the various versions of NetWare, and the next few sections discuss the results of some of that compatibility testing.) The sections also discuss how to choose the best workstation and file server for your needs, as well as listing some commonsense techniques for installing your network.

BOARD COMPATIBILITY ISSUES

Compatibility, between the boards and the personal computers in the marketplace, is one of the biggest problems facing manufacturers of workstations and computers. (Compatibility issues facing the boards themselves are discussed in Chapter III.)

Although defining the test suite is a moving target because the lab has to keep up with the latest technology, Novell breaks its system testing down into three parts:

- LAN boards and disks that are shipped with the system
- Shells (software that establishes network communications) shipped with the system
- Drivers (Value-Added Device Drivers or NetWare Loadable Modules)

After testing everything individually, the lab then puts everything together and tests the computer as a complete system. Also tested against the computer are the drivers that ship with the version of NetWare that the vendor hopes the system can run. Soon, fewer drivers will be shipping in Novell's "red box," because Novell wants to turn over driver creation to the participating vendors. Novell is finding that it's difficult to keep up with the revised versions of other companies' products, especially when, as in IBM's case, Novell isn't notified that the version is going to be revised.

As a contrast, the computer trade magazine *InfoWorld* also runs a testing lab for hardware and software (it publishes results weekly) and always tests its file servers and workstations with the following very sensitive peripherals:

- Hayes Smartmodem 2400B (internal)
- Paradise VGA Plus 16 video board
- 3Com Etherlink II (3C503) board
- IBM Token-Ring board

The 3Com and IBM boards are substituted for each other.

InfoWorld then gives computers that can run all the listed peripherals without a problem an excellent score, which tells you that it isn't that easy to do.

As a note, let me add here that every manufacturer contacted about the compatibility issues with their own machines claimed that either:

- The problem didn't exist in *their* own testing.
- The problem wasn't as major as was stated in the test bulletin published by Novell.
- The problem had been corrected.

That may be true. Remember, however, that the Novell lab employees are expert computer users. If they got confused and installed everything completely backwards, causing all the compatibility problems themselves, it's easy to do.

There's a fourth point that some marketing people, after acknowledging themselves as the only expert in the building on that particular product, brought up: "I don't know nuthin' about it," stated firmly. Then all further comment is referred to Novell, which knows nothing beyond what's on the test bulletin.

IBM went a step farther, saying indignantly, "*We* didn't do the testing! It's not *our* problem." 3Com said the same thing, but phrased it more diplomatically. After asking to see the test bulletins and then reviewing them for a week, it said that it hadn't seen these problems before and someone would get back to me with the answers after checking with Novell. And maybe someone will.

And then there was Club American Technologies, which said that it hadn't been able to duplicate the problem I had discussed with them, although they had tried. It also said that the machine in question had been selling for a year without anyone complaining about that problem. (And it turned out it was right; I had confused its product with another with similar-sounding name.) Just to be on the safe side though, it gave me a solution in case the problem turned out to be a problem for someone else. Very few other firms took the time to explain themselves or provide possible solutions for problems that were not theirs.

The incompatibility problems that are described in the following paragraphs are historical; that is, many of these issues are likely to have already been resolved one way or another (the bug fixed or the product withdrawn, for example). These compatibility problems are illustrative of the kinds of things you should discuss when purchasing a computer, not necessarily illustrative of problems that are current with the computer in question. The computer industry changes very quickly.

Reputable manufacturers make every effort to correct compatibility problems that are brought to their attention. Many of these machines were tested in late 1989 and early 1990. If the computer is still on the market, it will undoubtedly work with the peripheral products that the manufacturer feels it should work with; i.e., not a whole lot of manufacturers care about IBM's PC Network II board, but all of them care about IBM's industry-standard Token-Ring board. The systems that couldn't run the Token-Ring board with NetWare will be able to run it now, or else they won't be on the market.

Some systems don't work with some boards because the system is technologically more advanced than the board. A number of 486 computers are simply too fast for most of the boards out there.

Novell's testing has found one solution to fast computers and slow (relatively speaking) LAN boards: Slow down the computer by disabling the internal cache. This, of course, defeats the purpose in buying the machine, but at least the board works.

A happier solution all around, albeit one that doesn't help compatibility *now*, is to speed the boards up. This solution is being implemented now, since the Intel 80486 chip has been out for more than a year, and the new, faster board revisions should start showing up any time.

IBM's Boards

Many computers can't handle every network interface board out there, but not because the computers are technologically behind. Novell's testing showed that generally if a computer can't handle a board, the board it can't handle belongs to IBM. Specifically, the PC Network Adapter II (PCNII) and the Token-Ring interface boards.

PCNII. The (PCNII) is a network interface board for a proprietary Ethernet-like network type. The design is IBM's, but IBM has basically abandoned this network type in favor of Token-Ring. The board lives on, however, confounding a number of systems being tested against it.

When pressed for an explanation of why computers were having difficulty supporting this board, IBM eventually said that the PCNII board had been revised, with some software being taken off the board and put in the computer, so manufacturers who hadn't put the same software into their own computers were naturally going to have a compatibility problem.

Other manufacturers cited the facts that this board is old, technologically speaking, and that no one tests for compatibility. Novell tests this board with all systems sent to it because it writes the NetWare drivers for it and because the PC LAN network type, which uses the PCNII, is one of three that can be used if you have ELS Level I, v2.0a (no longer shipping as of mid-1990).

One interesting point is that some systems could support the board in either workstation mode *or* in file server mode; just because a computer won't support one mode doesn't mean that it won't support the other mode.

Computer/PCNII board problems fell into three categories:

- The computers were too fast for the board.

- The computers could run the board in file server mode but not in workstation mode (a variation on the previous point).
- The computers could not run the board at all.

Most of the machines involved are 486 computers, another sign that the technology has moved away from the technology of four or five years ago. The computers that had these problems as late as June 1990 are listed in Appendix F. Remember that computers are always being updated; from the lack of vendor concern, I doubt that any compatibility problems with the PCNII have been resolved, but you can always ask.

One interesting thing is that a couple of IBM's own model 70s and 80s had difficulties with the board in workstation mode. They would work, but only if the shell driver for the board was produced after a certain date. This is only a problem for you if you plan to use IBM's most powerful computers as "lowly" workstations on a slow network, sort of like killing a fly with a cannon.

Token-Ring. IBM didn't have a good explanation for the failure of computers to run the industry-standard Token-Ring board. What IBM said was that it hadn't done the testing and therefore couldn't comment; I should ask whoever did do the testing what the problems were. IBM does say that all of its products are tested for compatibility with each other, but that it can't test the products of smaller companies for compatibility. (There's a company bigger than IBM? Does General Motors make computers?)

I think that IBM should be more concerned about systems that can't run its boards, especially since IBM has positioned Token-Ring as the network type for today and tomorrow and wants smaller companies to be able to use the board; others take IBM's point of view. *InfoWorld*, for example, deducts points for systems that can't run the standard. And the standard in Token-Ring is IBM.

The problems with computers and Token-Ring boards fall into two categories:

- Computers that couldn't run the Token-Ring board at all, either in workstation or file server mode, or couldn't run it without disabling the memory cache
- Computers that could run the Token-Ring board only in file server mode

A number of machines on this list are some of the most powerful and technologically advanced on the market today. It's highly likely that either

IBM or the computer manufacturer had some difficulties with the newest technology that caused the two products not to work with each other. The difficulties may have indeed been resolved. I would check. (Machines with Token-Ring problems as late as June 1990 are listed in Appendix F.)

Novell does not test computers in conjunction with Token-Ring boards made by other manufacturers. Novell tests the boards shipped to them with the machine, and they test the machine against boards whose drivers are shipping with the NetWare version that the machine is being certified with; that is, Novell tests computers with boards if Novell wrote drivers for those boards.

This gives other Token-Ring manufacturers two strikes as far as Novell's testing goes: Novell currently writes a Token-Ring driver for IBM—no one else. And most system manufacturers, if they send a Token-Ring board to be tested with their systems, will send the standard, IBM.

This is not to say that other Token-Ring manufacturers do not have a good product. Most manufacturers, as discussed in Chapter III, design their board to two standards—IEEE and IBM—and, they say, exceed them both. It's just that everyone agrees that *first* you achieve compatibility with the industry standard—then you can worry about achieving compatibility with others.

This is also not to say that IBM has a bad Token-Ring product. If other Token-Ring boards were tested with as many systems as the IBM board was, problems would undoubtedly crop up with them and probably the same kinds of problems.

However, IBM products (including its Token-Ring boards) are best suited to environments where the other computer-related products are also IBM. As a general recommendation, it's better to either stick completely with IBM's products or to avoid *all* IBM products and stick with the clones and compatibles.

Sticking with the clones is considerably cheaper, and because most manufacturers in the field use good quality assurance procedure, the end products are no less reliable than that of the biggest industry giant.

Novell's Boards

A number of computers couldn't support Novell's 16-bit Ethernet board (NE2000), although the board did better than IBM boards. Novell blames the NE2000 problems on a bug in the National Semiconductor chipset, saying that currently the high-end (386/33 and 486) systems work best with the board if caching is disabled. (A powerful computer's most powerful selling point is likely to be its internal cache, which allows the most-used data to be stored for fast retrieval.) Novell also said that it would take National Semiconductor five or six months to bring out a new revision of the chip, at which time the high-end systems should be able to run the NE2000 board without a problem.

Most of the systems that had difficulties with Novell's NE2000 board could run the board by changing jumpers, making sure the driver was created after a certain date, changing the board's default configuration, or not running the board in AppleTalk networks. (Manufacturers with problems are listed in Appendix F.)

Novell's Disk Coprocessor Board also gave a few manufacturers problems; since this board is found in file servers and never in workstations, the compatibility problems are discussed with file servers later in this chapter.

3Com's Boards

3Com had problems, but 3Com has a lot of boards aimed at various segments of the market. (3Com's Ethernet boards are the standard in Ethernet networking.) However, only one or two computers had difficulty with each board, difficulty that was usually surmounted by changing the default configuration option to another setting.

3Com says that a board that works if you fuss a little is a board that works, and it remains unconcerned about problems with the default configuration option—as long as one of the 10 or so options work. When none of the configurations work, 3Com wants to know about it, saying that all incompatibilities are fixed as soon as they are brought to 3Com's attention. Unfortunately, there are so many machines that 3Com can't test *everything* before shipping the product.

3Com likes to give its boards similar names. 3C501, 3C503, and 3C505 are 8- and 16-bit Ethernet interface boards, plus an Ethernet board for the PS/2 (3C523).

Discussing generalities, a 3Com spokesman said that while the 3C505 board had several problems, at least in Novell's testing, it is basically obsolete; it says it has lots of better products on the market now. The 3C503 board, continued the 3Com spokesman, is one of 3Com's most popular boards. Between 20,000 and 30,000 boards are shipped a month. Being the Ethernet standard, this board was tested with many computers; it's not surprising that not all of them could run the board flawlessly.

Most of the 3Com board problems were found in trying to run a file server in non-dedicated mode, a difficulty of importance only to ELS I and II users who may try to get questionable double-duty out of their file servers. (The machines with difficulties with 3Com boards are listed in Appendix F.)

WORKSTATIONS

A workstation is a computer that hooks up to the file server running the network operating system. Although workstations come in many forms, the workstation described here is one in an MS-DOS environment positioned for a small network. (I'm eliminating workstations that run in a UNIX environment, such as the Sun workstation, and I'm eliminating those workstations that are usually called engineering workstations.) While you can generally use any PC that meets the memory requirements for NetWare as a workstation, the machines described here are the workstations that you can find on the market today.

In these workstations, a hard disk drive (or even a floppy disk drive) is not required, since the software the workstation uses is stored in the file server and since the file server uses its own hard disk to store the material generated on the workstation. (One note of caution: Don't try to give a power user—someone very experienced with and comfortable around computers—a diskless workstation. A power user always *needs* a hard disk drive.)

A workstation without a hard disk is a computer that is probably not going to be as costly to maintain as a computer with a hard disk, since disks are among the computer components most likely to fail. In addition, most workstations usually have four or fewer expansion slots, which is only logical because the options are provided by the file server, so the workstation doesn't need to allow extra space. Computers that are designed as workstations, as opposed to those that are designed as desktop computers, are more likely to have a small "footprint," that is, they are designed to be as small as possible. They'll fit on a desk a lot better than computers designed as file servers with large footprints.

Your ideal workstation is a 286 or 386, depending on your processing needs, such as the machine illustrated in Figure 5.1.

Several advantages are touted for "diskless" workstations, a slight misnomer since a computer that doesn't have a hard disk drive will almost always ship with at least one floppy disk drive. (Completely diskless computers are available, but they are so unpopular that most manufacturers don't ship them.) One advantage is that these systems are cheaper than systems with a hard disk. Another is that with the real diskless workstations, network security is

Figure 5.1. GoldStar 230
Courtesy of GoldStar Technology, Inc.

enhanced. (There's no simple way to load files onto or unload files from the network if you don't have a disk.)

Frequently, a workstation without a hard disk drive is all that most people need if the network is complete with the software for their jobs. People come in to work, turn on the computer, work with the software, and turn off the computer at the end of the day. The data generated are stored on the file server, which is usually backed up at least several times a week. (Daily is even better. See Chapter VI for a discussion on backing up the file server.)

The drawback to a workstation without a hard disk drive is that if the network is down (which usually happens at least once a month), you can't use the computer. (Except for the power user, who probably wasn't on the network at that time anyway.)

It takes a great deal of effort to make a workstation without a hard disk drive serve as a standalone computer. In order to use your hard diskless workstation when the network is down, you must have two floppy disk drives on the system. Then you need an MS-DOS disk, a copy of the software you're going to use, *and* a current copy of the file you want to modify, as well as a place to save the file after modifying it. (The person who demands all that, rather than waiting for the network to go back on line, is a closet power user who needs a hard disk drive.)

Once you have decided about the disk drives for your workstation, you need to determine the amount of memory on the motherboard and whether you want to add memory to the system, a poor idea unless the system comes with sockets for SIMM modules, or buy a different system. (SIMM modules

Figure 5.2. The Closet Power User

are printed circuit boards with memory chips on them, placed into sockets on the motherboard. SIMM modules are much cheaper than buying memory chips individually.)

If you'll be running NetWare 386, each and every workstation on the network will have to have 512KB on the motherboard before you start counting the memory for the applications that you will be running from the workstation. If you are running NetWare 286, the memory requirement for each workstation is only 384KB (not counting whatever memory you need for your applications). Remember that some of the oldest computers cannot be upgraded to 512KB on the motherboard, which means that they can't, even as standalones, run a lot of the newer software packages.

One more thing to keep in mind is that some workstations, with and without hard disk drives, come with a built-in network adapter. (Most built-in adapters are Ethernet, but more Token-Ring connectors are being built in as Token-Ring gains in popularity.) As long as you are going to use that kind of networking topology anyway, it's a good deal, saving you the cost of a board.

Another advantage to a built-in network adapter is that you don't have to worry about compatibility issues between the board and the computer. The disadvantage is that if the port supports Ethernet, it's not going to support Token-Ring, and you'll have paid money for technology you're not going to use.

No matter what you buy, it makes sense not to buy more than you need. IBM says its model 70s and 80s can be used as workstations. This is true; however, they are computers that IBM has positioned as top-of-the-line file servers, fast and powerful. You usually don't need that kind of power in a workstation, unless you have that previously mentioned closet power user, and even then you have to draw the line someplace. Top-of-the-line file servers are expensive, no matter what they're being used for. The top-of-the-line Compaq costs at least $30,000 fully configured.

As I said at the beginning, millions of computers are out there that will fit your qualifications, whatever they are, for a workstation. Any equipment that you want that isn't offered standard will definitely be offered as an option, either from that manufacturer or from someone else. Just be sure the options are compatible with what you've already got.

FILE SERVERS

A file server is usually the fastest, most powerful computer you have around. It has more memory on the motherboard, more expansion slots so that more options can be supported, and more and larger hard disk drives than any workstation would need. Usually, it also has two floppy disk drives and a switch on the back to change the wait state of the system for fast or slow software.

While at the beginning of networking, any big PC would do for the file server, nowadays a class of machines exists that is meant for file server use exclusively. These machines, including the Compaq Systempro, Everex Stepserver, Storage Dimensions' FileMaster, and the Novell/Samsung 386AE, not to mention the IBM Model 80s and 90s, simply don't function well as workstations. (It is also a tremendous waste of money and power to use them that way, even if these vendors did have Novell test them for compatibility as workstations.)

These systems, because their manufacturers are focused on the NetWare marketplace, are frequently shipped with NetWare decisions already made: that is, the hard disk drives are pre-configured for NetWare (you have no idea how many hours you have just been saved—Compsurfing takes forever), and the amount of memory and caching on the motherboard is designed with NetWare in mind. (As a design note, file servers are often "tower" units, rather than desktop models. You can get more into them.)

File servers that are designed as file servers are going to work better than machines that were designed as PCs. In networking, a PC is a workstation. While I think that you can use all the computers in your office as workstations, I do recommend that you go out and buy a file server. You'll be happier if the computer that interfaces with NetWare is not old technology. Old, as far as computer technology goes, is a couple of years. A new file server is going to offer more reliability and more security than a computer that could be used for a workstation, and it's going to offer more reliability and more security than *old* file servers.

The Compaq Systempro is currently being touted as the example all others should emulate (or purchase) in terms of file server design. The Systempro has 11 expansion slots, giving you lots of options if you need them and allowing you to upgrade motherboard RAM from 4MB to 256MB; it features disk drive arrays, which is a way of making NetWare think that a number of drives are only one (this speeds up throughput); it allows up to 11 internal storage devices for a total internal capacity of 1.68GB; it also has an external keylock to protect internal components and a power-on password and keyboard password to prevent someone from turning the machine on or off without permission. The Compaq Systempro also supports multiple system processors, which makes it more than a little ahead of its time. The software currently does not exist that can take full advantage of the machine as a NetWare server. (Multi-processor support is one of NetWare 386's "VaporWare" options to be incorporated in the future.)

According to Novell, your basic NetWare 386 file server must be either a Compaq 386/20 (the Compaq Systempro is a 386/33 or a 486/33) with 2MB memory on the motherboard, an IBM model 65, 70, or 80 that runs OS/2, or something fully compatible. (Remember that 100% compatible is not the same as functionally compatible, although IBM and Compaq may try to tell you so. Remember too about top-of-the-line costs for these top-of-the-line file servers.)

I would recommend either a 486 computer that was designed as a file server, (if you have an OS/2 computer) such as the machine illustrated in Figure 5.3 or an IBM model 80 PS/2 system for NetWare 386.

As an interesting note, *InfoWorld*, the previously mentioned computer trade magazine, did a July 1990 product comparison of several systems that have positioned themselves as file servers and found that one of IBM's PS/2 Model 80s crashed when 24 workstations were on the network. (IBM has three or four Model 80s, but only one was tested by *InfoWorld*.) The comparison ended with *InfoWorld* saying that "at this time we can not recommend the PS/2 Model 80 386-A31 as a file server for NetWare 386 installations."

Figure 5.3. TeleVideo Tele486Te Courtesy of TeleVideo Systems, Inc.

Novell took some time to comment on this product comparison; among many points made was that NetWare 386 v3.1 corrects the problems that the PS/2 Model 80 had in running NetWare 386 v3.0 and that Model 80 users should send for their upgrade to v3.1 immediately. Novell also said that IBM had not sent that particular model through Novell's testing program for certification and that IBM was therefore taking a gamble on compatibility.

Your NetWare 286 file server should be an IBM PC AT or compatible or an IBM Personal System/2 Model 30 286, 50Z, 65, 70, or 80 with at least 1MB or 1.5MB of memory on the motherboard (depending on the environment you will use). (Models 50 and 60 are also supported; they're no longer being shipped by IBM.)

You can use either a 286 or a 386 computer as a file server for NetWare 286, such as the one illustrated in Figure 5.4. However, I recommend that you use a 386 that was designed as a file server and save the 286 machines for use as workstations. A 386 is generally more powerful than a 286. Your file server should have more punch than your workstations; a file server should be able to handle the network operating system easily. If your computer is

Figure 5.4 Memorex Telex 7075
Courtesy of Memorex Telex Corporation

strained to capacity, as 286 computers are likely to be, your file server will be slow, which means that your workstations will be slow, which means that the whole thing is no fun at all.

The 286 and 386 computers are used in two NetWare environments—dedicated and non-dedicated. Dedicated, which is the norm, means that the file server does not handle any non–file server jobs. Non-dedicated means that the file server can also be used (slowly) as a workstation.

NON-DEDICATED NETWARE

Non-dedicated NetWare, which only comes as an option for Entry Level System (ELS) for NetWare 286, requires more memory than other versions of NetWare 286 (2MB as opposed to 1MB).

A file server that does nothing else but run NetWare doesn't have to have a fast keyboard (in terms of how long it takes for the computer to recognize typed commands) because only brief commands will be entered from the keyboard. However, a file server that is going to double as a file server and occasional workstation needs a keyboard that is really functional. Novell's tests showed a surprising number of computers whose slow keyboard input speed practically disqualified them as non-dedicated servers. (A couple of machines, listed in Appendix F, *did* get disqualified as a non-dedicated servers in Novell's 1990 tests because they were so slow.) This is not entirely the problem of the keyboard or keyboard chip on the computer.

In fact, Novell says that it's a three-way problem with NetWare, the keyboard, and the keyboard chip involved, but also says that as far as a solution goes, Novell is out of the loop. The solution, according to Novell, is to replace the keyboard or get a modified version of the keyboard chip.

An easier solution, if you're going to use non-dedicated NetWare, is to be particularly careful not to handicap yourself with a file server that's going to basically refuse to do double duty. If you are going to require your file server to run in non-dedicated mode, get guarantees from the seller that the keyboard is functional.

Some manufacturers I spoke with downplayed this problem, saying their keyboard was as functional as it needed to be. (I think that means that those manufacturers don't have a financial reason to speed things up.)

Some other systems' manufacturers, listed in Appendix F, have already provided a solution to the slow keyboard problem, which is to require that you use their special keyboard to function properly in non-dedicated mode.

But a whole slew of computers, also listed in Appendix F, are just going to be unavoidably *slow* if you insist on running them as non-dedicated file servers, according to Novell's 1989/1990 testing.

With each version of NetWare, Novell provides patch files as "workarounds" for minor bugs reported by customers. For example, patch files in 1989/1990 included one to help overcome slow keyboard input for several Zenith Data Systems computers and one aimed at the Philips Electronics and Intel computers. Each year, the patch files are consolidated into the NetWare version for which they were created. These patch files are usually created for specific customers.

The moral of this is to not bite the bullet too long and assume that it's your fault that you can't merge your hardware and software properly. Patch files may exist for your difficulty already, Novell may recognize your problem as a NetWare bug and be happy to create a patch file, or your dealer may know of a solution (either from Novell or your systems manufacturer).

Remember the squeaky wheel! Better yet, don't run non-dedicated file servers!

BOARD INCOMPATIBILITY ISSUES

Once you've mastered the dedicated/non-dedicated problem, you still have to face compatibility issues between the file server and the network interface boards. This is the same compatibility issue that you faced when you were trying to decide among workstations. But remember that just because a system couldn't support a board as a workstation does not mean that it can't support it as a file server. Or vice versa.

In a file server though, you will always have at least one other board to contend with in addition to the network interface boards, and that is the disk controller board, which manages the interface between the hard disk drive and the computer. The file server disk controller board is usually not interchangeable with a disk controller board in a workstation. For one thing, it's going to be more powerful.

In NetWare 286 terminology (but not NetWare 386) the I/O address on a host adapter board is called a channel. Channels are the pipeline from the computer to the drives managed by the controller. In its simplest form, the hard disks in your computer would be on one channel; a disk subsystem connected to another disk controller board in your system would be on a second channel; and so on.

NetWare 286 ELS supports one channel; NetWare 286, Advanced and SFT, support four channels, and NetWare 386, dispensing with the term channels, supports as many disk controller boards as you can jam into the file server. (Refer to Chapter III for a more extensive discussion of disk controller boards and channels and I/O addresses.)

If you have more than one disk controller board in your system, you're going to have a conflict until you change the default configuration option on one of them. This is to be expected and does not indicate a flaw on the part of either the boards or the system.

Novell doesn't test a lot of these disk controller boards, mainly its own (or what used to be its own before it got out of the hardware business). Its own board, the Novell Disk Coprocessor Board (DCB), which has an SCSI interface, has the advantage of being able to bypass MS-DOS and talk directly to NetWare, which made it faster than other disk controller boards when it was just released. After a time, Novell released the developer's kit for disk controller boards, which allowed other SCSI disk controller board manufacturers the same advantage. Now that EISA boards are here, that speedy NetWare performance from ISA host adapter boards does not look so fast anymore. Novell's DCB also has the disadvantage of being a touchy board and difficult to use.

Most of the problems with this board and various computers came in the form of not supporting the four I/O addresses/channels supported by the DCB itself. If the ability to use channels in your NetWare 286 file server is important, ask the vendors about the channel support on other disk controller boards.

The support of channels is only important if you are adding hard disk drives, in the form of disk subsystems, to your NetWare 286 file server. It is not important if you have ELS, because ELS basically does not support anything that requires a second disk controller board. (The first disk controller board/channel is to the hard disks in the system.) ELS also does not universally support SCSI host adapter boards, being limited to the IBM PS/2 (or compatible) SCSI host adapter board and then only with ELS II. This is, of course, a qualified statement in that ELS may be updated or that third-party vendors, with or without Novell's blessing, will find workarounds for the problem. In fact, at least one (with Novell's blessing) has found at least one way to provide disk subsystems for ELS, which usually requires a second channel.

NETWARE INCOMPATIBILITY ISSUES

When tested several systems had trouble with various features of NetWare 386. IBM was one, although representatives swore that IBM was not at fault.

The DOS partition in several IBM file servers becomes inaccessible after the IBMSCSI.DSK driver is loaded.

When I checked with IBM, I received a highly irritated statement from someone who said something to the effect that IBM had nothing to do with the creation of that driver, that it was created by Novell. And then Novell had gone and listed the problem as being IBM's in all the test bulletins and IBM was getting all sorts of calls about this driver that they knew nothing about.

Novell says that NetWare 386 v3.1 has a new IBMSCSI.DSK driver that corrects this problem, along with the related NetWare 386 auto boot difficulty, and wants IBM users to upgrade to v3.1 immediately. In the meantime, if you still have NetWare 386 v3.0, remember that a number of IBM systems (listed in Appendix F) have a serious DOS problem with the IBMSCSI.DSK driver (every time the server is rebooted the drivers have to be reloaded).

A few other problems occurred with several systems: mirroring (where the same data are copied to different disks on the same disk controller board) and internal bridging (connecting between two networks, done from inside the file server) were the main difficulties that were reported through Novell's testing.

In a small network, an incompatibility problem may not bother you too much because there are so few computers and you may not be using all the features anyway, such as bridging or mirroring. In a larger network, and especially in a network where bridges can be used to form a *big* network, incompatibilities may be extremely bothersome. The larger the network, the more likely that you're going to have incompatibility problems, especially if you aren't careful at the beginning. If you start out with a homogenous network now, you'll have fewer problems later.

Remember that a computer is not a rotten system just because it doesn't work with one peripheral. A lot of systems, for example, show up in Appendix F on the list of machines that have difficulty with IBM. If you're not using IBM peripherals, it's irrelevant if the system can run them. If you are running IBM peripherals, ask questions. Most of these problems have probably been resolved; if not, IBM will have workarounds for you.

A computer may also be suited more for one kind of NetWare than another. For example, a file server that is going to be running any kind of dedicated NetWare (that is, everything but non-dedicated ELS), doesn't need to have blazing speed in terms of how quickly the computer can recognize commands from the keyboard. Blazing speed in the system memory is a lot more important. It's only if you are installing ELS and want a file server that can also be used as a workstation that the issue of a slow keyboard input becomes important.

In that case, as in all other cases where you have a compatibility issue, check with the vendor, and get guarantees that everything will work together before you buy it.

INSTALLATION OF FILE SERVERS AND WORKSTATIONS

Installation of networked file servers and workstations, and various other peripherals, must follow the cabling rules for the network type you have chosen. For example, if you are using thin Ethernet cable, the nodes must be no closer together than half a meter, you must use BNC connectors to connect the nodes to the backbone, and you can only have 30 nodes on a segment (including repeaters, which count as one node on each segment they connect). (Remember that a node is any device—printer, workstation, modem, file server—that occupies a physical place on the network.)

Beyond that, some commonsense rules also prevail. For example, you should put your printer in a central location so that the walk to the printer from the workstation is minimized for everyone.

Although it is not of crucial importance in small networks, file servers on larger networks most typically have their own dedicated power line, with only the file server on it. This dedicated power line will prevent power surges caused by network users turning their machines on and off. Dedicated power lines do not do anything for surges from outside the building, but every little bit helps. (This, by the way, is definitely the point where you call in the professionals. Managing electricity can be a dangerous business.)

It is also a very good idea to follow the traditional advice and place your file server in a locked room that can be accessed only by qualified personnel. Too many people are power users, knowledgeable about not only hardware but NetWare as well, and they are capable of doing all sorts of things to a network, with the very best intentions, that the administrator probably doesn't want done. If nothing else, a file server that is in a locked room can't be turned off by somebody who is tired of the network being on line. (It happens.)

VI

Backups and Power Supply Units

OVERVIEW

Once the network is up and running, the most important thing you can do is keep the network up and running. Unfortunately, no matter how hard you work at it, the network is going to crash. For one thing, you have no control over your power company. For another, things wear out; hard disk drives, for example, are more likely than any other peripheral to give up the ghost. Fortunately, if you have a little extra cash and can establish some good networking habits, you can minimize the downtime and damage from power outages and weary peripherals.

The cash is needed for purchasing two more peripherals, one to back up your network and one to prevent power surges and spikes from shutting down your network before you're ready. The good habits are needed if you're going to use the backup and uninterruptible power supply units.

Most computer people develop good habits, right after the need has been demonstrated to them in real-world terms, on their very own computer. I, for example, back up my files daily and have been doing so faithfully since the time my hard disk drive crashed, causing me to spend literally days frantically re-creating the 80-page manual that I had almost finished. Days, I might add, that I wasn't paid for. Many things on that crashed hard disk drive couldn't be re-created at all, like memos, proposals, and lists of prospective clients, things I had put on the disk and then forgotten. After that demonstration, I have had no difficulty finding two minutes a day to back up the files I'm currently using.

When you're talking about a network, however, you're not talking about one person's files. You are talking about all the files that all the people on the network have stored on the file server's hard disk drive—or drives—or disk subsystems. In other words, you're talking about a disaster that can shut down your company for days, or even put it out of business.

A formal backup, which can be done with all versions of NetWare, can prevent a lot of grief. Duplexing or mirroring is a possible alternative solution—if your version of NetWare supports either option or if you a find a hardware solution. (A Novell spokesman says that ELS software won't even support a hardware solution for disk mirroring.) Users should also be performing their own backups of their own files, if they have the hard disk drive or access to extra floppies and if they remember.

But even with duplexing and mirroring, and especially with user backups, you still need a formal backup, especially of critical files or files that have reached a permanent form. You need a regular backup of all files that have changed since the last backup.

A backup of some sort is the solution for minimizing downtime caused by weary peripherals and forgetful users, but what do you do about the power company? Or lightning strikes? A power surge suppressor, which is a long strip that holds electrical cords and smoothes out some of the spikes that go through any electrical line before they get to your electronic equipment, belongs on every computer, networked or not. A power surge suppressor does not belong on your file server because the surge suppressor can't do anything about the power going out.

An uninterruptible power supply (UPS) unit cannot only smooth out electrical spikes before they get to your file server, but it can do something about the power going out. Equipped with a battery, the UPS can keep power going to the network long enough to notify the users to save their work and exit and long enough for the network to shut itself down in an orderly manner. Shutting down in an orderly manner, as opposed to being shut off because there's no power, means that the network will be fully functional as soon as the power comes back on and the file server rebooted. Shutting down because there is no power means that all previously unsaved data are lost, and it may mean that your file server is damaged.

A UPS can shut the file server down in an orderly fashion when no one is there, too, which is a great blessing at three in the morning when the computer is doing an automated month-end accounts payable billing and the power goes out.

These two peripherals are not the only things you can add to your network to prevent or mitigate disasters—there are various troubleshooting devices, such as network analyzers and cable break detectors, for example—but the UPS and the backup units are the most essential and prevent the greatest number of problems with the least amount of effort. Neither one of them is exclusive to networks. If you can afford it, they would both be a nice touch for your very own PC.

The next few sections discuss these two peripherals in detail.

BACKUP UNITS

To back up your valuable data, NetWare offers disk mirroring as an option on SFT (System Fault Tolerant) NetWare 286 and NetWare 386. Note that this excludes Advanced NetWare 286 and ELS. Disk mirroring, and an even fancier option called disk duplexing (also only offered for SFT NetWare 286 and NetWare 386), copies the files as they are being saved to either another disk controlled by the same hard disk controller board (mirroring) or to another disk controlled by a different hard disk controller board (duplexing). (Using disk duplexing and disk mirroring, both through hardware and through software, are discussed in Chapter IV.)

Disk duplexing is a lot more expensive in up-front costs than disk mirroring. It is also a safer option—the information is in two different locations rather than just one.

I was told by a fellow in the disk subsystem business that a lot of the bigger firms like to get a second file server and duplex all information to the hard disk on it. He said that then, when a file server failure occurs, the second file server can just take over with very minimal downtime involved, assuming that the second file server isn't affected by whatever brought the first server down. When I said something deprecating about the expense of a file-server capable machine being used basically as a backup, he said that network downtime costs big business millions of dollars a year and that the cost of a file server is minuscule compared to that. Sometimes, he said, the extra file server is the difference between staying in business and going out of business.

This may be true, but those of us with ELS or Advanced NetWare, or without the extra cash to buy the disk duplexing software/hardware and a file-server capable backup (Compaq's top-of-the-line file server costs around $30,000 fully configured, a fact that never ceases to amaze me), might have to consider other truly safe options besides duplexing, in spite of the urgency of the situation. (Unlike Advanced NetWare 286, ELS can't use disk duplexing hardware because ELS only supports one disk drive controller; disk duplexing would require a second at least.)

If, for whatever reason, you are not interested in disk mirroring or disk duplexing, your only other choice is backup units.

TAPE BACKUP UNITS

Backup units have been around forever; strictly speaking, they haven't historically been aimed at networking, but more at the minicomputer and mainframe markets. One vendor's recent announcement of its top-of-the-line product to the company's resellers listed all the advantages of selling in the LAN market and suggested that the resellers identify Novell's resellers, indicating that this had not been done before.

Of course, that company had never had such a powerful backup unit before. Tape backups, so called because they use tape as the storage medium, now range in capacity from 60MB to 125GB, although the top capacity of most backup units is currently about 15GB on a single tape cartridge. This is considerably more than the 500MB maximum storage backup that is required by most applications. A single user has absolutely no need for more than 100GB of day-to-day storage, or for that matter, 1.2GB, one of the standard sizes in the tape backup industry (shown in Figure 6.1). The network that does need 100GB of backup storage daily is going to be a very large one.

Some older large backup units have all the storage a network needs but come with a built-in problem. There are not enough hours in the night to back up a network that requires massive backup storage, and the backup may spill over into business hours. Although you can sometimes work on a network that is being backed up, you have to work slowly; the keyboard input speed (how long it takes the computer to recognize that you've typed something) is much slower than what you're used to, and retrieving files from and storing files to the file server takes forever.

Fortunately for the larger network, technology has come up with a solution in the form of a new standard that allows data transfer at about 11MB per minute and 1.3GB in a couple of hours, depending, of course, on the processor speed, disk controller board, and disk access speed of your own computer.

Called Digital Audio Tape (DAT), this technology utilizes helical-scan recording, which puts data diagonally on the tape (as opposed to traditional longitudinal recording, which puts data straight across the width of a single-track tape, wasting up to one-third of the tape). Figure 6.2 illustrates the difference in recording methods.

This technology allows 15GB of data storage backed up in 12 hours. However, I think it would be a rare network that would actually need that much daily backup, especially with NetWare 286's 2GB limitations.

Figure 6.1. FileSECURE 1300 Tape Backup Unit Courtesy of Tallgrass Technologies

Most networks aren't totally backed up every day, anyway. Most are backed up every so often, say when the network is created and then every couple of weeks; on a day-to-day basis, only files that have changed or applications that have been added are backed up. Today's backup units are built with that kind of backup in mind, allowing for automatic backup of those files that have changed since the last time the backup was performed.

One historical problem with tape backup units was the inability to *find* a file after you saved it. It used to be that you had to serially scan the contents of every tape that the file could possibly be on before you found it on the last one. Now, in today's top-of-the-line products, individual files are organized in a hierarchical structure through the software, making it easier to locate a particular file.

In fact, today's backup units almost universally come with software that allow you to specify which files and hard disks should be backed up and how often to do it. You can also back up multiple file servers without being in attendance. You choose the options, provide enough cartridges for the backup to work, and then leave it alone.

Figure 6.2. DAT Technology Versus Longitudinal Technology

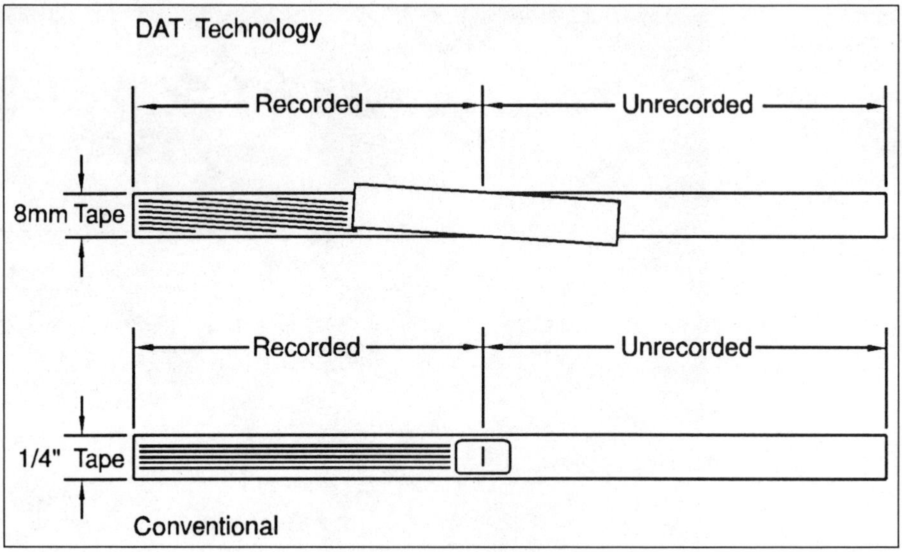

The fanciest of the these systems, working alone late at night, also provides extra security in the form of a network logout if anyone attempts to access the network through the backup workstation.

Some tape backup software will even allow you to rotate cartridges; that is, it allows you to write over the cartridge that was used for backup a week ago (or a month, or last year), allowing you to save the costs of buying an infinite number of cartridges.

A word of caution: Do not keep the most recent backup on site. It will not do you a bit of good to back up your network if the backup is still on the premises when the premises and the backup are destroyed by fire.

OPTICAL BACKUP UNITS

While tape is the historical option for backup units, optical disk drives are becoming more popular for backing up file servers. The most practical optical drive used for backups are the Write Once, Read Many (WORM) drives that allow you to maintain a permanent record. Many of these drives also feature removable cartridges, which means that the drives truly have an unlimited capacity. WORM cartridges frequently come in 1.3GB or 650MB formats, although other cartridge capacities are available.

These optical backup systems can feature the same kind of software, including scheduling options and unattended backups, as tape backup units, especially if they are made by the same firm that makes the tape backup units. ADIC is a good example of a firm that makes optical and traditional tape backup units; it provides the same software for both.

The kind of backup unit that is better for you depends on what kind of backup you're looking for. If you want a permanent record, WORMS are the best because you can't ever write over the data that is on the disk. When one cartridge is full, you can get another cartridge. (And then take that cartridge off site, so that you're protected in case of disaster.)

If you want to recycle your tape backups after keeping them for a period of time, traditional tape backup units will probably fit your needs best. Erasable optical drives are also available for use as backup units, but they are going to be more expensive than traditional tape drives without providing any measurable additional benefit.

Increasingly, today's backup units (both tape and optical drive) fit in autochangers (more commonly known as jukeboxes) that provide a directory structure and make it possible to find that file you're looking for. (In the future, as hard disk drives continue their never-ending march toward bigger and bigger disk capacities, nearly all drives will be compatible with these jukebox machines. A Novell spokesman says that they are beginning to see them already in the IMSP testing program.)

NETWARE AND BACKUP UNITS

Backup units, whether tape or optical, usually run from a workstation. Since the backup isn't attached to the file server, NetWare doesn't know about it, which means that NetWare doesn't care. All versions of NetWare support backups. Backups can run on any PC, and many standalone systems benefit from having an automated backup attached to them. (ADIC's backup units claim to work with MS-DOS 2.x or higher and NetWare, v2.0a or higher, which means it works with all MS-DOS machines running today, not to mention all versions of NetWare.)

POWER SURGE SUPPRESSORS AND UPS UNITS

People do not think of power as a necessity. Power is something that is "just there." It is only when the power is not there (because of an earthquake or thunderstorm, for example) that they realize that there was even something to miss.

However, the wise network administrator will devote a lot of thought to power and the lack thereof. Unfortunately, administrators of electronic equipment not only have to worry about the power but also about the quality of the power. Too much or too little or too much delivered at once are all causes of electronic equipment being damaged and networks collapsing.

Two solutions to keep the power running (or to at least minimize the harmful effects of the power not running) will be considered here—power surge suppressors and uninterruptible power supply (UPS) units. Power surge suppressors are more commonly called power surge protectors, but as Martha Graham of SCI/DataShield points out, this device is supposed to protect the electronics, not the power surge itself.

Power surge suppressors are usually a strip or box that connects between the electrical outlet and the electronic component in question. They are meant to smooth out the power when too much or too little power is sent to the electrical outlet. Power surge suppressors can't keep workstations or file servers running after the power goes out, but they can smooth out the quality of the power being delivered when it is on.

The UPS, which also attaches between the electrical outlet and the electronic component, is meant to not only smooth out the power when too much or too little is sent but also keep the electronic component (workstation or server) running long enough in the event of a power outage for the component to be shut down properly, preventing damage and preserving data.

Of course, power surge suppression vendors and UPS vendors (at least those who don't manufacture both) disagree on the importance of the other's products. UPS vendors say, for example, that most computer downtime isn't caused by power surges but by brownouts and blackouts, and that since surge suppressors can't handle those problems, you're wasting your money by buying a product that takes care of such a small percentage of the power problems. What they want you to do is buy a UPS that can handle the quality of power being delivered and can also handle brownouts and blackouts by shutting down the workstation in a manner that prevents data from being lost.

Power surge suppression vendors say that power surges are a larger component of power problems than UPS vendors claim. They also say that they can indeed prevent equipment damage due to brownouts and blackouts, although if you have chronic power problems you may indeed want a UPS. These vendors say that there is room in the marketplace for both of them.

I agree with the power surge suppressor people. There's room in the market for both products. The problem is that power surge suppressors are relatively inexpensive and a UPS is not inexpensive by any calculation, unless you go by the intangible "time not lost, files not corrupted" criteria. (With that criteria in mind, one UPS manufacturer ran an ad saying that a $80 power surge suppressor is a lot more expensive than a $600 UPS.)

In tangible dollars, a bottom-of-the-line UPS can cost almost as much as a bottom-of-the-line workstation. From that perspective, you need to decide if it would not just be better to buy a power surge suppressor for each of your workstations and then convince your network users to back up their data often, so that in the case of the inevitable network crash they wouldn't lose much. (This is one of those good habits that computers users need to develop anyway.)

UPS vendors are willing to concede that it's really too expensive to buy every workstation a UPS unit. (In an ideal networking environment run by UPS vendors, of course, you would get a UPS for every system.) As an alternative to buying every workstation its own UPS, UPS vendors recommend that one UPS be shared among four or five workstations.

The difficulty in sharing is in the rule of thumb that vendors use in determining the size of the UPS you need. They suggest that the total wattage used by the computers connected to the UPS be less than the wattage of the UPS. If you have a 286 computer and a monitor, for example, the wattage consumed is about 300. The bottom-of-the-line UPS that will support 300 watts is rated at about 400 watts. This means that you can't realistically connect more than one PC to one small UPS. In order to connect several workstations to a UPS, the UPS has to be a big one, which will cost more than $1000, and in some cases, a lot more. And there is no reason to put a UPS on a workstation that is used only sporadically. (Your typical file server is hardly ever shut off.) A power surge suppressor will be more than adequate for the average network user who maintains backups of current files.

To be thorough, you need to protect more than just the workstations and file servers on a network. If you are trying to do a good job and protect everything on your network, do not forget the network hardware: repeaters, transceivers, hubs, and the like, not to mention printers and modems. However, I would think twice about putting printers and modems on a UPS; they are receiving and/or transmitting data, data that are saved elsewhere. While it is an inconvenience to have to retransmit data, it is not usually a disaster if the equipment is only protected with a surge suppressor. Losing previously unsaved files can be a disaster.

POWER SURGE SUPPRESSORS

Do not use a plain (or fancy) power surge suppressor for a file server. The file server *absolutely* has to have an uninterruptible power supply. For one thing, the file server is the (very complex) heart of the network; if it is not working, the network is not either. For another, a file server has a lot more data stored on it than the typical workstation. The downtime will cost a lot more and will be a lot longer if the file server is destroyed by the power surge and loses its data than if the workstation is destroyed and loses its one or two opened files. If you have already paid big bucks for your file server, it does not make sense not to spend a thousand or two more to protect your investment.

However, you can use plain old power surge suppressors for your workstations, printers, modems, and associated network hardware.

The illustration in Figure 6.3 shows three of SCI/DataShield's line of power surge suppressors. These are called box power surge suppressors; many suppressors also come as a strip or bar. The shape is irrelevant. The quality of the workmanship inside and the features offered are what matter, just like anything else.

Remember that there are power surge suppressors and power surge suppressors, and you need to know the difference in order to buy the one that will do a good job for your installation.

Power surge suppressors range from fancy-looking extension cords to sophisticated technology that only lacks a backup power supply to be called a UPS. Electronics definitely fall under the heading of sophisticated, and you need sophisticated power surge suppressors. (Some power surge suppressors, according to an old report by *PC Magazine*, earn the name of "power surge *protector*" because they amplify power surges rather than diffuse them.)

Perhaps the most important thing to remember when buying a power surge suppressor is the volt/amp rating; just as you cannot exceed the wattage limitations of a UPS and expect it to do its job, you can't exceed the volt/amp rating of a power surge suppressor and expect it to protect your equip-

Figure 6.3. Power Surge Suppressors
Courtesy of SCI/DataShield

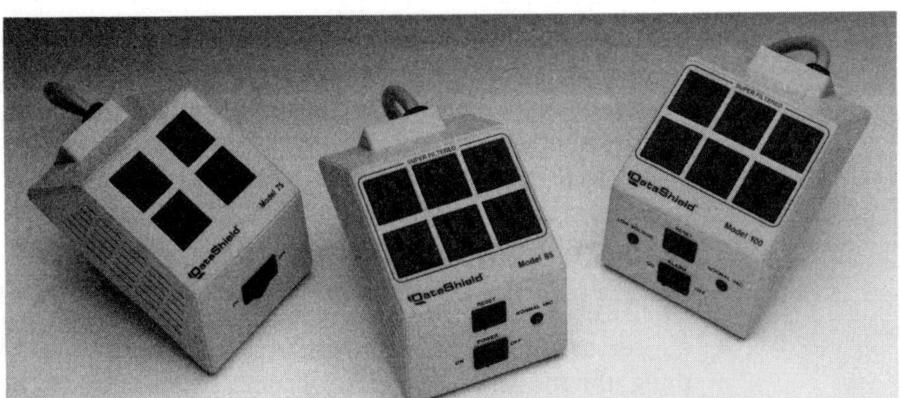

ment. As a rough estimate, according to a white paper done by Martha Graham of SCI/DataShield, one power surge suppressor can adequately protect one computer and its associated peripherals—monitor, hard disk, printer. (If you want to be precise, take the wattage rating on your electronic equipment, divide by .8, and divide that by 120 volts to get the number of amps generated by the equipment.) What this means is that you probably aren't going to be able to use every one of the six or eight outlets provided on the suppressor, and you shouldn't spend any extra money buying a suppressor with more outlets than you can use.

What a top-of-the-line power surge suppressor has that some models not aimed at computers lack is something called dropout protection that prevents the computer's hard disk drive(s) from crashing in the event of a power outage. According to Ms. Graham, a suppressor with dropout protection will shut off the power when the voltage drops below 60 volts, half of normal; some suppressors notify you when the power drops below 102 volts (just like a UPS unit) so that files can be saved before the power goes off. The power on these models will not come back on until *you* reset the suppressor; this avoids the problem of the suppressor coming back on before the power situation has normalized.

You need dropout protection for your hard disk drives. Above and beyond that, when you're looking for a power surge suppressor, look for ones with the shortest response or clamping time, the lowest clamping and suppression voltage levels, and the highest total power dissipation (watts and energy, expressed as joules).

Some of the nicer power surge suppressors have noise filtering, although that feature is not as critical to computers as the other points because computers are tolerant of electronic noise, as are printers. (However, unshielded cabling, such as unshielded twisted-pair wiring for Ethernet and ARCNET networks, is not tolerant at all. The less electronic noise bouncing around a network, the better.) The label that power surge suppressor manufacturers give this feature is noise attenuation. The wider the range, the better.

Power surge suppressors, for all the good they do, usually only have a very few components on the inside. (The more expensive the surge suppressor, the more complex the internal circuitry.) Unfortunately, an article in *LAN TIMES* ("Surge Protection Revisited," May 1990) linked power surge suppressors to unexplained network crashes. The article tied metal oxide varistors (MOVs), silicon avalanche diodes (SADs), and gas discharge tubes (GDTs), which all return surges to ground, to otherwise unexplained network crashes. The article said that if your network crashes a lot but is otherwise exemplary (your software is appropriate for the types of computers, you have protected your file server and workstations from power problems, and you're sure that static electricity plays no part in the problem), then you might want to check into your power surge suppressor being at fault.

Unfortunately, almost all power surge suppressors (and UPS units, for that matter) use MOVs, SADs, or GDTs to function. (And they usually use them together, to provide more protection than each component can provide standing alone.) I spoke to several people (UPS manufacturers as well as power surge suppressor vendors) and while no one said the article was not true, each said that he or she was unaware of any instance in which a UPS or power surge suppressor was to blame for a network crashing.

If you do have a lot of unexplained network crashes, you might look into this as a possibility. However, you need surge suppressors or a UPS; if surge suppressors and UPS units are only made with MOVs, SADs, or GDTs, then your other options are limited. Faith alone has never kept a network running, not when you are relying on your power company for 100% reliability.

The only measure you can take to prevent power problems caused by surge suppressors is to make sure that your surge suppressor is indeed listed by Underwriter's Laboratories for use as a surge suppressor. Beyond that, be aware that MOVs wear out fairly quickly and that a surge suppressor using them may need to be replaced when the MOVs lose their effectiveness. Ask the vendor about this potential problem. (The better surge suppressors have a lifetime warranty; if you are concerned about components wearing out, buy a good surge suppressor and send in your warranty card.)

UPS

The UPS unit is an absolute necessity for a file server, but statistics show that almost 80% of networks do not have one, probably because a UPS currently costs roughly one dollar per watt, and UPS manufacturers recommend that the wattage on the UPS exceed (by just a little) the total amount of wattage being consumed by everything that is attached to it. For example, a 386 computer with a monitor and standard hard disk drive draws about 375 watts; a file server will also run other peripherals, such as a disk subsystem and tape backup, that can draw several hundred more watts. A file server with a backup unit and a disk subsystem may require a UPS with more than 1,000 watts. If it is a truly top-of-the-line network with duplexed file servers, you may need truly a top-of-the-line UPS with more than 2,000 watts.

In other words, it may come down to choosing between another workstation (or two) and choosing a UPS. You get a more visible return for your money if you choose the workstation. However, at the risk of sounding like an advertisement, the UPS is a wiser investment.

If it is true that a business loses millions of dollars annually because of computer and network downtime, then that business is losing a lot of those millions unnecessarily if the cause of the downtime is power outages. If you have a UPS, your file server is basically shut down without harm when the power goes off and then automatically rebooted when the power comes back on. The only loss is the period of time that the power is out, a period when you can't do any other work that requires the use of electricity. With a UPS with automatic shutdown, at least no file server data are lost and the equipment isn't damaged.

A UPS comes with a battery pack to provide this backup power. However, no UPS unit, unless it is attached to a generator, is going to be able to power the file server indefinitely, and UPS units are not meant to do that, although you can have UPS units custom-designed to your specifications. The battery packs, depending on the number of watts attached to it, usually last 10 minutes or so, long enough for people to save their files and exit. Remember that if the file server is protected by a UPS unit and the workstation is not, only the file server will be on line for 10 minutes. The workstation will go down at the same time as all the other electrical devices hit by a power outage and not connected to a UPS. The open files, even if they are being saved to the network file server, will not be saved after the electrical connection is cut.

If you do not have a UPS on your file server, the file server loses all unsaved data in the opened files on the file server and may itself be damaged when the power goes off. At the very best, the file server has to be rebooted, which means that the network is dead until the network administrator appears on the scene. (This is assuming that you followed the traditional advice and put the file server in a secure location where only the network administrator can access it.) At the very worst, files and/or electronic components are damaged; downtime will last until the damage is repaired. If you balance the millions of dollars of losses because of downtime against the thousand or so for each UPS, the answer is obvious.

UPS units have evolved over the years, gaining in intelligence just as the other hardware in the computer industry have. Today, some of the better UPS units have software that allows them to talk to logged-in users in the event of a power failure, telling them how long they have until the file server will be shut down. These units can also shut down the file server without intervention and reboot the file server when the power returns, keeping a log of all power interventions. (Rebooting a file server without user intervention is a blessing if you have locked the file server away, so that the network doesn't have to wait for you to appear.)

When you buy a UPS, be on the lookout for the following things:

- Total amount of wattage supported
- Power surge (over/under voltage, spikes, electronic noise) suppression
- Notification of abnormal power situation
- Notification of power failure
- Notification of time before the file server shuts down (battery power left)

Figure 6.4. Elgar LANSafe UPS with LANSafe AI, the First Power Protection Software with Artificial Intelligence Courtesy of Elgar Corporation

Novell certifies UPS units for use with NetWare; since I think that *the* market for UPS units is in networked machines, I would be very wary of any firm that didn't care enough about its primary market to ensure compatibility with NetWare.

UPS manufacturers, like hard disk drive manufacturers, are very concerned with their mean time between failure (MTBF) rate; since they are, I think we should be also. The longer the better is the rule, and check several brands to find out exactly what the range is.

When you are looking for UPS units, do not overlook the importance of a small size and a long power cord, if these things are essential to UPS use on your network. These are little things, but you may find them to be show-stoppers.

The photo in Figure 6.4 is from Elgar Corporation, and it is demonstrating that, with Elgar's artificial intelligence software, you no longer need the UPS interface board that used to be required for UPS units with NetWare 286. That board took up an expansion slot that you can now use for something else. Today, most UPS units, like the ones from Elgar, can use the mouse port on a file server.

VII

Printers

OVERVIEW

You've spent days and weeks selecting your computers and your cabling, you've spent what seems like forever installing your computers and cabling them into a cohesive network, and now you're ready to choose and attach your printer.

Printers, by and large, are network indifferent; they print anything that comes to them from the computer to which they are attached and do not care where that computer got the file. This eliminates networking compatibility problems as a major issue in choosing printers, unless you are using a printer definition language system (board and software) to trick your printer into being more than it was created to be. The Hewlett-Packard LaserJet III user's manual, for example, does not even mention the word "networking," and this is a printer whose capabilities and price almost demand networking in order to be cost-effective.

This is not to say that printing is not a networking issue—it is. The software concerns in getting a document from a workstation to a file server/print server and then to the printer are enormous. It is just that from the printer industries view, compatibility with a network operating system is not the problem that compatibility with Hewlett-Packard is.

Printers are generally divided into two categories, those meant for standalone use and those designed for network use, and a whole industry has sprung up around them. Software programs exist to make your standalone dot matrix or inkjet printer capable of printing PostScript (slowly, under the best of circumstances); on the same order, several vendors make products (a combination of hardware and software) that make any networked printer capable of printing in several different printer languages. (PostScript is a printer language.) Several other vendors have created print servers (also a combination of hardware and software) that take over printing duties from the file server.

It is a waste of good effort and money to put a dot matrix-type printer on your network: Too many people need output good enough to represent the company, and a dot matrix printer is not meant to do that. Instead, dot matrix printers, by virtue of their price and output quality, have found a niche as a deskside printer, used for drafts where a letter-quality look is not important.

The next section discusses what to look for in a printer, networked or not. Networking concerns (why it takes longer to print on the network than off it, printer emulation packages, and print servers) are discussed in a later section.

WHAT TO LOOK FOR IN A PRINTER

When you're buying a printer for a network (or standalone, for that matter), you need to track the following items:

- Speed
- Paper handling capabilities
- Consumables (toner, print drum)
- Output quality
- Fonts available
- Memory (for graphics)
- Compatibility with HP

Do not forget price. The machine that best fits your needs does not necessarily have every extra ever created, and it does not necessarily have to be the most expensive printer out there. Like any other purchase, decide what printer features are important to you and pay for them, ignoring those state-of-the-art technological advances that do not mean anything to you.

Speed. HP laser printers work at eight pages per minute, at least if they have a Canon engine. (All HP printers currently have a Canon engine; most other laser printers do as well.) Eight pages per minute is optimum; if you print graphics, speed will be much lower. How important speed is depends on how much traffic you have on the network.

Paper Handling Capabilities. The ideal printer prints labels, envelopes, both sides of the paper, and different weights of paper, as well as understanding five different printer languages. However, if you do not need all that capability, you shouldn't pay for it.

Consumables. Consumables are the parts of the printer that have to be replaced every so often—the toner, the drum, the corona wire. Every printer has consumables. When you are looking for a printer, look for one that allows you to replace the consumables easily.

Some printers out there, for example, want you to tip the toner into the machine, being careful not to spill any toner onto the drum. And it is hard to avoid spilling a little toner. (The penalty for carelessness is hours of fussing inside the printer as you remove the spilled toner, all the while keeping in mind the manufacturer's edict that some parts will have to be replaced if they are exposed to more than five minutes of light.) The printer you are looking for allows you to slide the toner cartridge into position, with no possibility of spillage. I've had both, and I will never again buy a printer without making sure that the toner can be replaced without a mess.

Also, while all consumables are expensive, some consumables are more expensive than others. Learn the number of copies before consumables must be replaced, and compare them with other printers. Some consumables can go to 2,000 copies before they must be replaced, others can go to 10,000—longer is better.

Output Quality. Output quality should be geared to the use. If graphics are a major component of printing jobs (Gantt charts, presentations), look for graphics capabilities before you buy. If letter-quality text is more important, check for that and ignore graphics capabilities.

Fonts Available. Fonts go along with output quality, and more is better, of course. However, on the networks I used, almost everyone printed the documents in the printer's default (Courier) and ignored the vast array of other fonts, probably because they weren't sure of how to use them, what the fonts looked like, or what difference it made.

It is true that all sorts of firms are providing more and more fonts to use in your printer. However, be sure that purchased fonts will be used; fonts are expensive, and the money will be wasted if you cannot convince employees to use the different typefaces provided.

Memory. Memory goes along with fonts and output quality; the bigger the job and the more fonts used, the more memory it takes to print. Graphics are always big jobs, requiring considerably more memory than letter-quality letters. If you will not be printing graphics or PostScript, you don't need as much memory as you would if you attached a PostScript cartridge to your laser printer.

Memory has become more important as printers have acquired the capability to print graphics and other big jobs using a variety of fonts. Make sure the printer you choose has an expansion slot to add memory, so that you can add memory if you change applications.

Compatibility with HP. Compatibility with HP is important because HP is the standard, the printers that vendors work with, and most manufacturers try to match the features of HP printers with their own products. Font cartridges, for example, are usually aimed at HP-or-compatible printers; if yours is neither, you are a captive audience for the font cartridges produced by your printer manufacturer—if your printer manufacturer produces font cartridges. For some, that is spreading their resources too thin.

NETWORKING CONCERNS

Hardware printer issues are insignificant on a network as long as the printer has the capabilities, including memory, to print output from your applications. However, the printing issues on a network that ultimately affect the printers are many. One of the biggest is NetWare, but others include printer emulation packages and print servers. Each of these is discussed in the following sections.

NETWARE PRINTING CONCERNS

Printing from a network-attached printer is slower than printing directly from your workstation to an attached printer. That's because you have added a middleman—the file server—and because that middleman places the lowest possible priority on printing a job. Printing is a shared resource on a network, designed to allow a number of people to print; it is not designed to allow a number of people to print *quickly*.

In addition to the low priority, a printing job isn't started by the file server until the whole job is present. This means that if your document is 27 pages long, all 27 pages have to be sent to the print spooler (temporary storage area on the file server) before the first page prints. This is to keep another job from appearing in the middle of yours. If a 25-page document is sent to the file server at the same time as your 27-page document and finishes spooling first, it prints first, meaning that the wait for your printed document is even longer.

NetWare does have commands that allow you to move up or delete jobs in the print queue, but network administrators, who control the NetWare documentation, do not usually tell people that these commands exist; as a practical matter, you usually have to wait your turn for your document to be printed.

Two other printer network common problems exist: the printer refuses to print your job until you exit the software application, and the printer refuses to reset itself to the default after printing a different document. The first can usually be resolved by resetting NetWare's *timeout* or *endcap* commands, and the second can be resolved by using the *printdef* command, which creates a database that stores print device definitions.

The next few sections discuss ways to make your network printing operations more efficient and to make your printers capable of printing different printer languages.

PRINT SERVERS

Print servers are machines (usually a big PC or a small file server) that take over the printing duties from the file server by taking print jobs and sending them to the printer. Depending on your network traffic, this can slow down or speed up operations. If you have light network traffic, you can probably print efficiently without adding another middleman. However, since a print job is the lowest-priority file, heavy network traffic keeps the print job from being printed quickly. In this case, a print server can request the file (print job) from the file server and direct it to a printer more quickly. (File servers handle file requests quickly and efficiently; they just do not handle print requests quickly.)

Print servers use up a node space on the network; however, the hardware involved isn't necessarily the traditional PC. Instead, like the self-contained machine illustrated in Figure 7.1, print servers can be a dedicated box without even a monitor, hard disk drive, or keyboard that can request the print files from the file server and direct the files to the appropriate printer.

Figure 7.1. LANpress Print Server
Courtesy of Castelle, Inc.

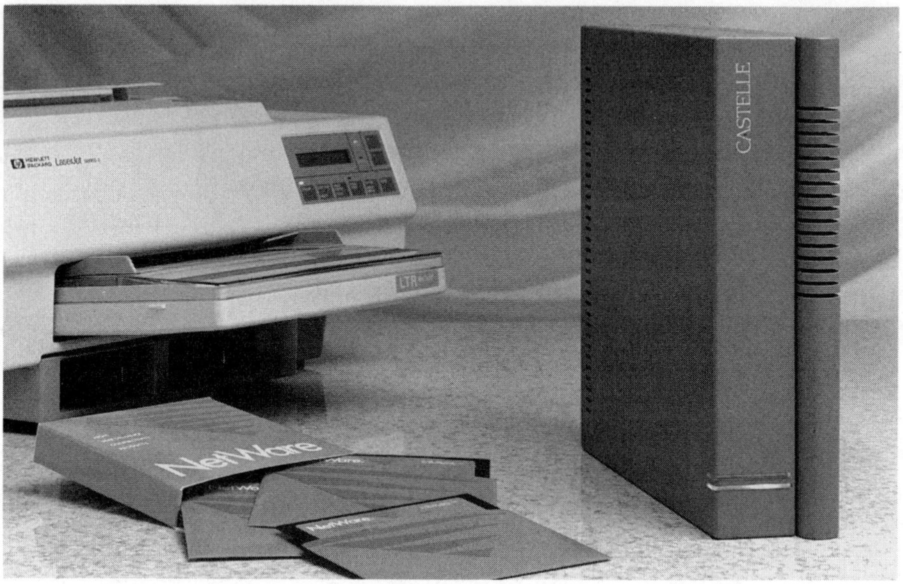

The big selling point of these print servers is that they are cheaper than a PC that you have pressed into service as a print server; also, since they were designed as a print server and not as a computer, they are likely to function better in the print-server environment. Many of these print servers can serve multiple print queues, so they are suitable for even large networks.

These print servers come with their own software that is also compatible with NetWare. Unlike the printer emulation packages, these machines, having more of a networking function and interfacing with the file servers and the workstations on the LAN, also come with security that prevents unauthorized users from accessing, changing, or deleting any files.

While you're checking features, check to see if the print server can be configured to your networking type—ARCNET, Ethernet, or Token-Ring. You would think that a machine designed for a network would support the standard networking types, but you will have to request the proper configuration for your installation.

As long as you are checking out print servers, also check out some of the software spooling packages that can be run from non-dedicated workstations to any networked printer. Of course, these packages do come with a price—you have to be sure that the printer to which you are sending your output is actually on line, and you may face the wrath of the person who considers the printer private property, but these TSRs (software packages that sit in memory until needed) give you another alternative.

PRINTER DEFINITION LANGUAGE SYSTEMS

Printer definition language systems (sometimes inaccurately referred to as printer emulation packages) overcome the technical limitations of your printer by giving you the capability to print on any printer attached to the network and using any typeface supported by the printer package. These systems usually work through a board placed in the file or print server. Be advised, however, that these systems require certain levels of technology, such as a 286 or 386 computer, and will not work properly if you ignore those requirements.

These systems also need memory, lots of it, and not only in the computer that's running the software. Any printer being used in a non-native mode will also require additional memory, depending on the printer language being used and the length of the page. (However, some of these systems provide their own memory.) Depending on the package's software, this is also one place where it is important that your printer be an HP or compatible.

Once you meet the requirements for these printer language packages, you will find that your printers are considerably faster than they used to be and that you can print to any printer on the network. As an example, LanQuest Group's LAN*script* High-Speed PDL Server prints up to 25 times faster than the Apple LaserWriter IINT and up to four times faster than the HP LaserJet III.

While these packages can be very valuable, get guarantees that they'll work with NetWare. Software-to-software compatibility (as in NetWare to a printer definition language package) is a bit trickier than software-to-hardware compatibility.

VIII

Portable NetWare

OVERVIEW

Although Novell's NetWare is the biggest network operating system in local area networking, Novell is just a bit player in the overall data processing field, which includes mini- and mainframe computers tied together in various nonhomogenous hardware and software platforms.

You can connect IBM-compatible local area networks to many other platforms, although to do so is a time-consuming, technically complicated, and hair-pulling task. In order to make NetWare more easily connected and thus more valuable to administrators with other platforms, Novell has created Portable NetWare, a version of NetWare 386. Most simply put, Novell makes available to selected vendors a portion of NetWare's basic source code; these firms, in turn, move (port) NetWare to their own hardware platforms and operating systems, allowing significant gains in integration of computing resources.

Portable NetWare is about interconnecting networks with different kinds of network operating systems (UNIX, for example). If you are just starting out in networking, the concept of Portable NetWare, while interesting, is hardly relevant. If, on the other hand, you have IBM-type mainframes, UNIX workstations, and MS-DOS–type personal computers in your organization, Portable NetWare may give you the capability of exchanging information among those disparate machines in a seamless manner.

If you've ever run around the building trying to convert a DOS file to a Macintosh file or vice versa, you understand the difficulty. Lots of hardware solutions exist now for that very common problem (I use the Deluxe Option Board from Central Point Software); however, the solutions involve copying the appropriate file to the appropriate size diskette (Macs can't use a 5.25-inch diskette and a lot of DOS machines don't have a 3.5-inch floppy disk drive), moving the diskette to a machine that has a conversion utility, converting the file, and moving the diskette to a machine that can read the file in its new form. (Run-around networking is known as SneakerWare.)

NetWare v2.15 with the Macintosh Value-Added Process provided a solution for the Mac/DOS conversion problem, allowing network users to skip all those steps, as long as the file in question was formatted in something basic, like ASCII. And that's what Portable NetWare does for those who want to move files among different networking platforms.

DIFFERENT LEVELS OF NETWARE

Novell, almost from the very beginning, has moved toward Portable NetWare, designing its various versions of NetWare for different levels of processing. In Novell's view, three levels of data processing exist:

- Desktop computing
- Server computing
- Host computing

Desktop computing, as we know it, is primarily done on PCs. The typical programs run on PCs, such as word processing, spreadsheet, desktop publishing, and other personal productivity programs, are all screen- and CPU-intensive applications.

Server computing, which allows the sharing of data and program files and printer files, is where Novell originally made its name in the data processing industry.

Host computing, which utilizes general purpose operating systems, most frequently is used for large database warehousing.

Novell has designed its product line with these three levels in mind, as illustrated in Figure 8.1. NetWare 286 is Novell's server solution for small business, workgroups, and departmental computing, and it has a feature set that matches the needs of that market segment well. NetWare 386 possesses the features and levels of sophistication that are needed by large corporate environments.

Novell is now moving its product development towards the host computing level with Portable NetWare, with the goal of providing a common set of data access protocols across differing hardware and software platforms.

Figure 8.1. Levels of NetWare

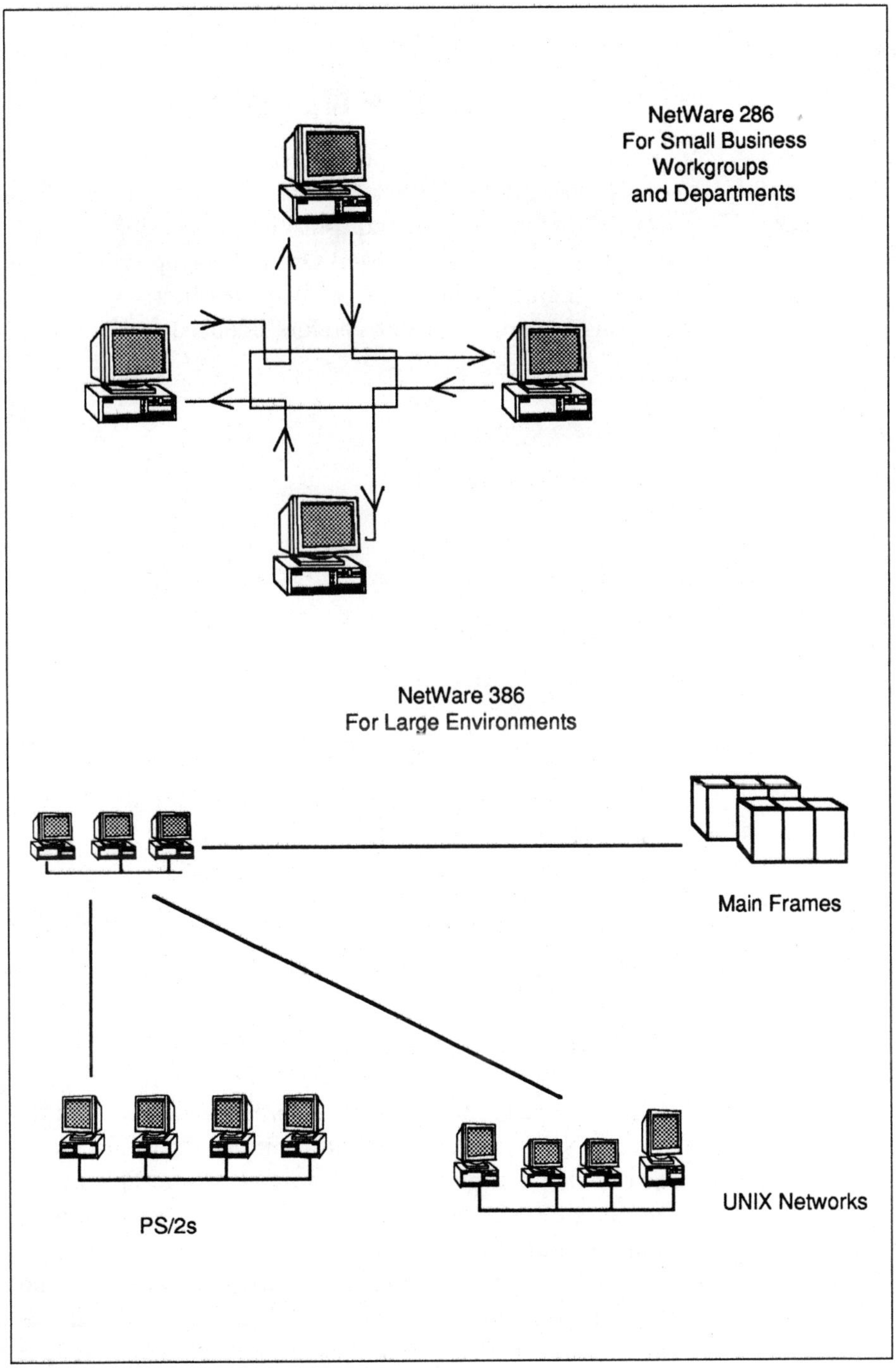

USING PORTABLE NETWARE

Portable NetWare is a C source-code version of the basic NetWare Services from NetWare 386. NetWare Services are the portions of the NetWare kernel that provide for real-time multi-tasking processing and file services. This version is being licensed to Novell Original Equipment Manufacturers (OEMs), who will then port Portable NetWare to their own hardware platforms and operating systems. Current vendors licensed for Portable NetWare include:

- ALTOS
- Data General
- Hewlett-Packard
- IBM
- ICL
- Interactive
- Intergraph
- Mips
- NCR
- Prime
- Pyramid
- Unisys
- Wang

By integrating hardware that runs Portable NetWare, you can make significant gains in productivity and integration of computing resources. The integration is achieved because Portable NetWare computing devices are using the same NetWare Services that traditional NetWare file servers are utilizing, meaning that common file access procedures and common Applications Programmers Interfaces (APIs) can be used by applications programs across a number of hardware platforms.

With Novell's Macintosh connectivity (and the attendant LocalTalk and Ethernet Macintosh hardware), the first level of this seamless data interchange has been achieved. For example, I use a 286 computer, and my graphic designers, without exception, use Macintosh; on a NetWare v2.15 network, it's easy to take the MS-DOS text files and the Macintosh graphics files and combine them into one cohesive document. (As mentioned earlier, I can now combine Mac graphics and DOS text without a network, but that hardware resolution was a long, painful time coming, because no one I talked to was aware that such a solution existed.)

Remember, however, that as far as Macintosh users are concerned, no reason is strong enough to make them WANT to deal with other operating systems. It's been my experience that almost all Mac users qualify as "evangelists" (Apple's term for its super salesmen), and they're very perplexed when you talk about the virtues of other types of computers or operating systems. Don't buy NetWare v2.15 or Portable NetWare with the expectation of converting Macintosh users to another operating system; it's not going to happen. Check with Macintosh experts for alternative, Mac-based connectivity solutions.

However, DOS users with an occasional need to access Macintosh files will find NetWare v2.15 easy to use (once installed). Portable NetWare allows this same level of data transparency to become a part of non-NetWare operating system platforms, such as the UNIX and OS/2 host operating system environments. Portable NetWare also serves as an easy bridge to common data interchange formats, such as TCP/IP.

Currently, in many cases, the only way to transfer data files between different platforms, such as UNIX and MS-DOS, is SneakerWare—again reduce the data file transfer to the lowest common denominator, then reload and recode the data so that it can be manipulated by a LAN system. Portable NetWare provides a better solution.

For example, if one of the computing platforms in your company is based on Portable NetWare, you know that the file formats and file access techniques are compatible with NetWare systems and that establishing a physical connection between your NetWare LAN and Portable NetWare allows common applications programs (as well as data files) to be accessed by both the host computer users and the LAN users.

Applications programs (such as WordPerfect) that can run in more than one operating system (such as UNIX and DOS) can manipulate files from each operating system; that is, you can take your DOS WordPerfect document to a UNIX machine where the DOS WordPerfect file can be read easily.

The reason that UNIX can't talk to NetWare, DOS can't talk to Macintosh, and Macintosh can't talk to OS/2 without help is because of the protocols that each uses. In most cases, NetWare uses its own protocol called IPX/SPX (Internet Packet Exchange/Sequenced Packet Exchange) to communicate on an Ethernet or Token-Ring cable (usually Ethernet, although several of the Portable NetWare OEMs use Token-Ring). UNIX uses TCP/IP (Transmission Control Protocol/Internet Protocol) to communicate on an Ethernet cable. It's quite possible to have one Ethernet backbone with DOS machines and UNIX machines, each machine cabled to its own network and each network passing packets up and down the same cable, without any communication taking place between the UNIX and the NetWare networks. This is because the protocols can't understand each other.

In most UNIX versions of Portable NetWare, the primary protocol is TCP/IP. When Portable NetWare's IPX protocol is added to the TCP/IP protocol, the Portable NetWare/UNIX server can see and understand the IPX packets sent by the NetWare servers and clients.

At the same time, if the applications themselves (such as WordPerfect) support both protocols, NetWare users can see minicomputer data files and can also run UNIX programs through terminal emulation programs traditionally run through serial communications links.

In a sign of a more open market, a larger number of UNIX machines are shipping with built-in Ethernet interfaces. This accomplishes two things for users: They no longer have to use serial communications links, and they have more compatibility/connectivity options. Serial communications links transmit at 9600 baud, which is considerably slower than Ethernet's 10 Mbps. Switching to Ethernet allows for faster throughput on the whole network. The second benefit derives from the fact that all Ethernet users are communicating down the same cable. An Ethernet connection can really expand the data processing options open to users (if the application and protocol differences can be resolved).

While Ethernet is currently the usual cabling choice for Portable NetWare, keep an eye on Token-Ring, which is achieving growing prominence in the industry; a number of computer vendors are starting to provide built-in Token-Ring connectivity. (Ethernet will probably maintain its large market share in its traditional UNIX environments.)

FUTURE OF PORTABLE NETWARE

The future of Portable NetWare really belongs to the software developers, specifically those developers interested in gateway programs; i.e., LAN mail programs, TCP/IP-based SMTP (Simple Mail Transport Protocol), and other UNIX-based mail systems. These gateway programs would then allow for the transport of electronic mail across different operating platforms and environments, and the benefits of that data compatibility are indeed huge in corporate environments.

Another potential for Portable NetWare is in database engines, which could take advantage of the power and speed of larger computers and still be able to move the data to the commonly accepted LAN platforms.

There isn't as much future in commonly running applications programs. Currently, only a small number of applications programs run in different operating system environments. Users from different environments gravitate to different applications, so that even if more applications programs ran in more than one operating system environment, many users wouldn't take advantage of them.

Portable NetWare is a portion of Novell's overall NetWare Open Systems strategy, which leads to an added degree of integration in the computer industry. Through Portable NetWare, Novell will be able to extend connections from its basic LAN roots into the minicomputer and mainframe environments. Whether Novell is successful in its efforts, though, is going to depend upon the marketplace.

IX

Related Technology

OVERVIEW

Networking technology is extremely fast moving. Just about the time you think that you understand what's going on, you realize that a new field has popped up and a whole bunch of people are speaking in tongues—again. FDDI, WANS, Wireless LANS, fax servers, and ISDN are all joining the mainstream of local area networking technology; this time last year, those products existed only for the insiders who were trying to market this new technology, mostly in the wide-area network arena. In San Jose, California (where I live), FDDI is a term that has suddenly started to appear on the billboards next to the freeway. No explanation, of course, because we're all techies here in the Silicon Valley, and we know our networking terminology.

But what if you don't live in the Silicon Valley or weren't able to acquire this terminology by osmosis? What if you only pay attention to computer technology that has been proven to be useful to your needs? Read on; some of this technology may be useful to your needs now, while some may be useful to your needs after your network has grown a bit. (Networks very rarely get smaller; they usually grow very quickly.)

Depending on the size of your LAN, you may not be interested in any of these new, and generally still quite expensive, technologies that allow your network to vastly expand its communications capabilities.

If you use Novell's Entry Level System (ELS) NetWare, the next expansion step is to a full-fledged version of NetWare, not to a high-speed or wide-area network. ELS, being old technology itself, will probably not support most technology that is still on the cutting edge. As mentioned earlier, it is very difficult for software (or hardware) to be upwardly compatible; that is, compatible with products that didn't exist when the software or hardware was created. And although NetWare's ELS is a big market, it is frequently overlooked by vendors with new and advanced products because these products have to specifically include downward compatibility with ELS, a product that is out of the technological mainstream and has a lot of restrictions.

However, if you use NetWare 286 or particularly NetWare 386, these new technologies (or parts of these technologies) may be just what you need. Each of the technologies mentioned above—FDDI, Wireless LANs, WANs, fax servers, and ISDN—are discussed in more detail in the sections that follow.

FDDI

FDDI, which stands for Fiber Data Distribution Interface, is a fancy term for running data over fiber-optic cable at 100 megabits per second (Mbps), considerably faster than the top speed (16 Mbps) of any of the three most popular network types on the market today—ARCNET, Ethernet, and Token-Ring. As a concept, FDDI has been around forever; today, however, some firms have discovered a real need for this high-speed, expensive network. The market for the FDDI networking type, which features a ring configuration with fault tolerance (a form of data duplication that minimizes lost information), is for those who do a lot of video animation, simulations, and medical imaging types of applications. Engineers, scientists, and the true power users among us are likely to find FDDI to be practical.

However, if you are running 286 and 386 machines and haven't been considerably inconvenienced by the speed limitations of your current network type, it's unlikely that you need to expand to FDDI. Experts think that 286 and 386 workstations are just not powerful enough to warrant such a fast system. (In other words, PC hardware technology hasn't caught up with the cabling hardware technology.)

Another drawback to FDDI is that the components are expensive. Interface boards to run FDDI cost around \$11,000 or \$12,000 each (an Ethernet interface board costs around \$500); a workstation/communication server designed to allow a number of workstations to communicate via FDDI without an interface board is being marketed by Fibronics International for between \$20,000 and \$30,000 (about \$2,500 for each workstation). Forrester Research, Inc., a market research firm, says that the average current cost per port for FDDI is \$11,650, including everything—fiber-optic interface boards, hubs, cables, and connectors.

The price could be halved if FDDI used shielded or unshielded twisted-pair wiring instead of fiber-optic cable. FDDI manufacturers have proposed that ANSI create a standard to allow FDDI to run on twisted-pair wiring, although problems exist with meeting the Federal Communications Commission requirements using twisted pair. Additional problems exist with trying to run high-speed communications over unshielded twisted-pair wiring, which doesn't block out electromagnetic and radio frequency interference. Shielded twisted-pair wiring would solve that problem, and SynOptics Communications, Inc., is working on a technology that would allow FDDI to run on IBM's Type 1 shielded twisted-pair cabling (also used for Token-Ring networks).

Still, putting a board that costs even $6,000 (instead of $12,000) into a workstation that costs $800 or $5,000 will bother some people, especially since neither the $800 or the $5,000 workstations currently can take advantage of the capabilities offered by FDDI.

However, if you need the technology and the cost doesn't bother you, Thomas-Conrad, among others of the 37 FDDI companies in the marketplace, is selling a 100-Mbps board that can use the company's existing ARCNET device drivers. Note that you cannot mix and match 100-Mbps boards with Thomas-Conrad's 2.5-Mbps boards, because the Thomas-Conrad Network System (TCNS) is not downwardly compatible with the installed base of ARCNET hardware and cables. The TCNS, with throughput of 40 times that of the standard 2.5-Mbps ARCNET board, is designed to be used as a subnetwork for workgroups that require the extra bandwidth. (Thomas-Conrad is marketing its TCNS toward those who handle image files for CAD, engineering, or graphics applications.)

The most common use of FDDI technology is as a backbone that connects two disparate networks in two different buildings or in situations where high security or insulation from electronic noise is very important. As the cost comes down and those who do a lot of video animation, simulations, and medical imaging types of applications increase in numbers, it is certain that FDDI use will become much more common.

For those who would like to ease into FDDI, SynOptics Communications has an intelligent hub that allows Ethernet, Token-Ring, and FDDI networks to coexist within a single intelligent wiring concentrator. The concentrator, illustrated in Figure 9.1, is designed to be a single network management station for large and complex networks. ("Complex" refers to the requirements generated when you combine Ethernet, Token-Ring, and FDDI networks, bridges, routers, and the various different kinds of network management supported by each network type.)

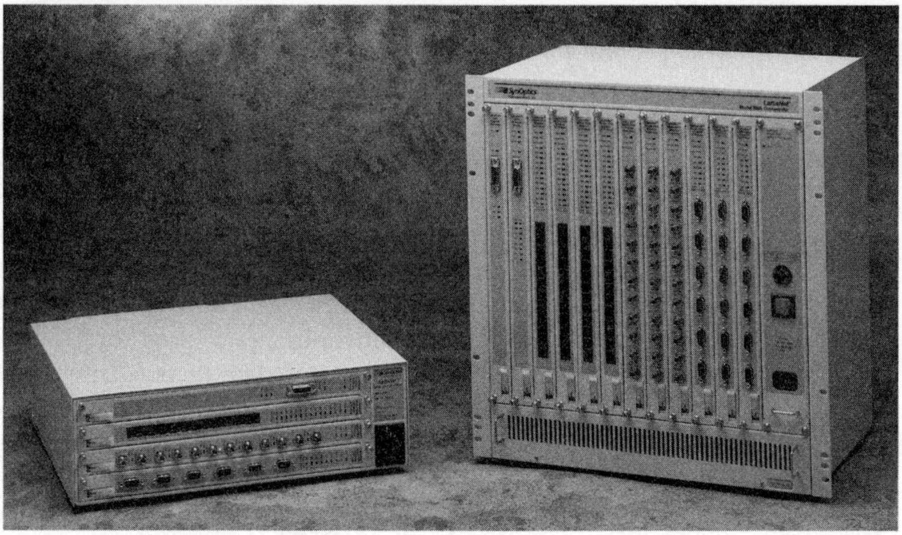

Figure 9.1. LattisNet System 3000 Intelligent Wiring Hub Courtesy of SynOptics Communications, Inc.

Theoretically, ELS networks run just fine on FDDI, especially since (in Thomas-Conrad's case) the high-speed interface could use the same software as Thomas-Conrad's ARCNET boards. However, if you have ELS and think you need FDDI, you probably need a full-fledged network operating system even more. ELS comes with a lot of limitations built in regarding number of users, hard disk drives, third-party device drivers, and, like all other versions of NetWare 286, total amount of memory on the system. Removing limitations by upgrading your network operating system may be all you need. It's certainly a more logical first step.

Without question, NetWare 286 and 386 networks can run on FDDI, and for some small (remembering how much each node will cost) networks with large graphics-type files, FDDI may be the answer.

WIRELESS LANS

Wireless LANs, although a fledgling industry, use several different methods to connect its networks: infrared light, infrared lasers, and spread-spectrum radio frequencies. The one that is gathering the most interest in the established LAN field is spread-spectrum radio, although Photonics, using infrared light, has a wireless LAN aimed at the Apple market, and LCI, using infrared lasers, has a wireless LAN to be used with Ethernet and Token-Ring networks. (LCI's product is in the FDDI price range at $14,000 and up.)

Most of the wireless LAN entries—O'Neill Communications Inc.'s Local Area Wireless Network (LAWN), Telesystems SLW Inc.'s Advanced Radio LAN (ARLAN), and NCR's WaveLAN—use spread-spectrum radio frequencies to connect their networks. Spread-spectrum radio frequencies are controlled by the Federal Communications Commission and range from .90 gigahertz (GHz), 2.4 GHz, and 5.8 GHz, and, since Motorola announced its product, to the 18 GHz spectrums. The LANs at the top of the spectrum (Motorola's WIN) are going to be faster than those at the bottom (O'Neill Communications Inc.'s LAWN and NCR's WaveLAN); they're going to cost more, too. Motorola's WIN is claimed to run at 15 Mbps, slightly less than Token-Ring's 16-Mbps speed, and Motorola brags that the WIN has been tested at speeds of 50 Mbps. NCR's WaveLAN runs at 2 Mbps, slightly less than ARCNET, while the LAWN product runs at 38.4 kilobits per second, about as fast as a terrific modem.

As an aside, let me say here that Motorola's product, at any speed, was not shipping when this book was written; the real product may not live up to its advance speed claims. VaporWare is presented as technology that Motorola or someone else may someday create, and someday usually comes very quickly when you're dealing with computer technology.

Leaving aside infrared technology, since it is being marketed by so few firms and seems to have so many drawbacks (usually concerning atmospheric conditions), and also leaving aside Motorola's speed claims since it is not a shipping product, the products using spread-spectrum radio—WaveLAN and LAWN, among others—have a couple of marked advantages and a couple of marked disadvantages, so much so that a quick summary should be enough to tell you if this technology is for you.

The main advantage is that you do not need cables. Cabling is the weakest link in a network, and people are always inadvertently doing things to cables that vendors warn you against—rolling over them with chairs, placing them close to heat and fluorescent light sources, pulling the wrong end of the terminator, and just plain tripping over them. Not having cables to trip over, splice, remove, or add can only be a blessing.

Also, keep in mind that older buildings built before the computer technology explosion may not able to physically accommodate additional wiring requirements generated by ARCNET, Ethernet, Token-Ring, or FDDI (although fiber-optic wiring takes up less room than coaxial or twisted-pair cable).

Finally, with a wireless LAN, personnel and computers can be moved around a floor, without the network administrator being forced to remove and install cabling with every move. (Before you embrace this technology for just this one reason, remember that networks using twisted-pair are also easy to maneuver, not quite as easy as a wireless, but easy enough so that maneuverability shouldn't be a showstopper.)

Disadvantages to wireless LANs, however, are much more extensive than the advantages:

- Price
- Speed
- Line-of-sight technology
- Electronic interference

One of the main drawbacks to a wireless LAN is price. Your typical Ethernet board costs about $500; these wireless LAN products range from $1400 to $2500, which seems like a lot to pay for a unproven technology. (I read somewhere that you should *never* buy version 1.0 of *anything*; there's a lot of sense to that statement, especially when it's your money and the technology is unproven.)

Going along with the price drawback is the fact that the current wireless LANs are slow. Leaving aside Motorola's claims of a 15- to 50-and-beyond-Mbps speed, wireless LANs using spread-spectrum radio frequencies range from 2 Mbps (slightly slower than ARCNET) downward to 38.4 Kbps (the same as your faster modems). However, NCR says that 2 Mbps isn't as slow as it sounds, because in throughput tests it comes in at 600-or-so Kbps, just slightly slower than Ethernet's 800-or-so Kbps throughput speed. (Remember that Ethernet runs at 10 Mbps, before you start running throughput speed tests on it. Remember also that throughput testing varies from vendor to vendor.)

Just the same, technology is heading the other direction, with FDDI turning in speed claims of 100 Mbps, Token-Ring quadrupling its speed to 16 Mbps, and ARCNET planning a board with 20-Mbps power (nearly a five-fold increase over its current 2.5 Mbps speed). Wireless LANs will have to find a niche where speed isn't of paramount importance.

The last two drawbacks concern two other aspects of the technology: line-of-sight and electrical interference.

Line-of-sight means, as a practical limitation, that the network in question should only be on one floor in one building, and that one floor should not have a lot of "structural blocks," such as walls made of thick metal or concrete. This, in turn, means that administrators of larger networks are likely to be uninterested in this technology until wireless LAN vendors can engineer workarounds to the problem.

NCR's WaveLAN, in fact, is avoiding the issue of larger LANs by targeting its wireless LAN for offices (with cubicles) rather than factories and walled offices, and it says that WaveLAN is best suited to small departmental LANs and to supplementing existing wiring schemes. However, its directional antenna is good for distances of up to 800 feet, and an optional line-of-sight antenna is meant for distances of up to five miles. The hardware required for a standard WaveLAN network is illustrated in Figure 9.2.

Electrical interference is a more enduring problem, one that wireless LAN engineers have already tried to correct. Motorola's WIN, at 18 GHz, is sharing the spectrum with military radar, microwave, and satellite control links. However, Motorola plans to obtain a license that will give it exclusive rights for a 35-mile radius around the licensed area, saying that this will cut down or eliminate most interference problems. Most other electrical interference problems can be eliminated by specialized antennas that allow the transceiver to lock onto the strongest signal.

Nearly all of these wireless LANs, no matter where they fit on the spectrum, support NetWare, which is only logical since NetWare is the standard in network operating systems. NCR's WaveLAN ships with drivers that support ELS Level I and Level II, NetWare 286, and NetWare 386. O'Neill Communications' LAWN product claims NetWare compatibility as of the end of 1990. As time goes on, other vendors will enter the market; if they don't advertise NetWare compatibility, ask them.

Still, the market for a wireless LAN is limited to those with specialized needs (a building that is difficult to cable with a workgroup that is closely spaced) and it still costs too much; while not fussing with cables is a marvelous benefit, you'll need to decide if the cost is worth it.

WANS

Wide-Area Networks (WANs) are not new networking technology; however, WANs seem to have entered the mainstream with a vengeance, and as technology has improved, ways of connecting your local area network to a wider-area network have proliferated. In fact, WANs have basically become the other half of LANs. If you have branch offices, or for that matter, a computer user who does a lot of work at home and needs to send the files to the office on a regular basis, you require a WAN.

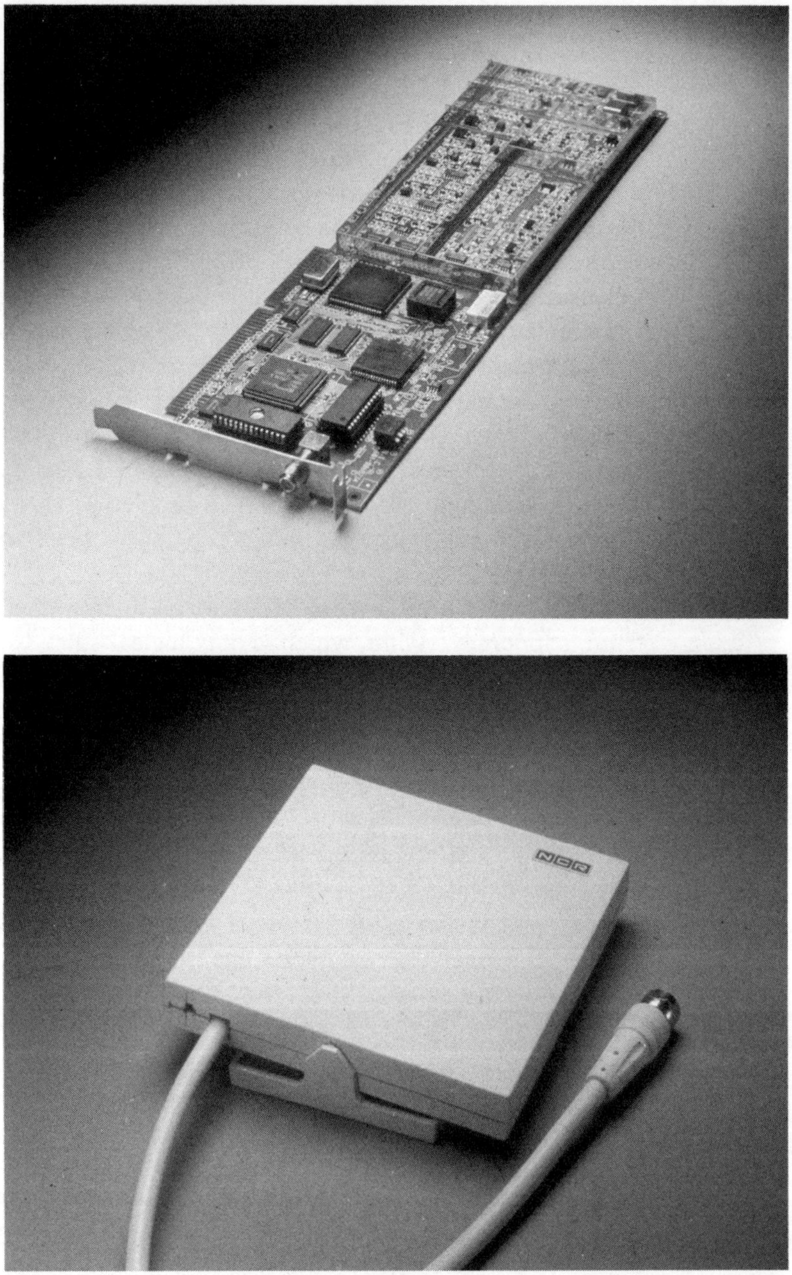

Figure 9.2. NCR WaveLAN Hardware (Interface Board and Directional Antenna) Courtesy of NCR Corporation

Novell has always thought the WAN market important and has provided a complete line of communications options to make it easier for people to communicate across long distances, including bridges and remote access software (NetWare Access, discussed in Chapter I).

Basically, a WAN requires a lot of planning and foresight so that you are not paying for more than you can use and you are not locking yourself into a system that is too soon too small.

WANs run on three different communication lines—voice, X.25 or Digital Data Service (DDS), and T-1—depending on the amount of traffic being sent. The cost of each of these lines is in direct proportion to the speed at which they transmit.

Voice, which transmits at up to 19.2 Kbps, is for small branch offices or the single user at home trying to communicate with headquarters. This kind of transmission is referred to as point-to-point voice-grade line communications.

X.25 or DDS transmits at 56 Kbps (US) or 64 Kbps (Europe) and is aimed at those networks that are facing much more traffic than those using a voice line. A regional office or two connected to headquarters would use medium-speed DDS lines, instead of point-to-point voice-grade lines. X.25 or DDS lines are referred to as point-to-point medium-speed communications. X.25 services can be bought from companies such as CompuServe and BT Tymnet. Both of these companies can provide connections to their nationwide and worldwide telecommunications services.

T-1 is the line for heavy-duty traffic, transmitting at 1.5 Mbps (US) or 2 Mbps (Europe), and is referred to as the high-speed connection. Keep in mind that if your Ethernet network runs at 10 Mbps and you send data to the WAN, the data are going to be transmitted at 1.5 Mbps across the T-1 cable. Also keep in mind that a T-1 line can cost many thousands of dollars a month more than a line transmitting at 56 Kbps and that there's something to be said for living with a slower data transmission rate.

WANs are not designed with the ELS network in mind, although some administrators who manage ELS networks along with their other, larger networks have tried to bridge into them. It is not easy to do because of the limitations that ELS contains.

NetWare 286 and 386 networks are designed so that WANs can be easily set up; however, *easily* is a relative term, and I would consult a professional before I started.

FAX SERVERS

Fax servers are fax modems that everyone on a network can use. A fax machine on every desk is not needed, and neither is a fax board in every PC.

All that is required is a computer to act as the fax server, a workstation to access it, and a few thousand dollars to buy the fax server board and software.

Right away the immediate convenience is apparent: If you compose faxes at your desk, you can send your fax as soon as you have finished composing it. You do not have to print your fax, get up, go to the printer for your copy, and then go to the fax machine to send it, or put it on the desk of the person in charge of controlling the fax machine's use and hope that it will be sent sometime soon. (I suppose that in some companies fax-use control could be an issue, but that's one reason networks have passwords and assigned rights.)

The Castelle Faxpress 2000, which is an unusual fax server in that it is a self-contained box with everything you need to plug it into your network, is illustrated in Figure 9.3. (Although it takes up a node on the network, it's much smaller than an HP printer.)

Fax servers have another advantage over standalone fax machines: The text is going to be far clearer and make a better impression on recipients; the scanner on traditional fax machines can't match that of computer-generated material.

However, for all the increase in convenience of sending faxes, fax servers aren't quite as good about receiving them. The main problem is that no fax

Figure 9.3. The Castelle Faxpress 2000
Courtesy of Castelle, Inc.

server in existence can accurately read the Route To name when it is written the way that humans usually write. (Some can read codes from Touchtone and PBX phones, but electronic codes are not human scrawls.) This means that a person who can read the instructions must screen all faxes and direct them to the appropriate workstation, which brings us back to the desk of the person in charge of faxes, who may or may not read the faxes at the same time.

Alternatively to a fax server, standalone fax boards are also becoming more popular, although they do not work well when you try to network them, because they cannot figure out where to send the incoming faxes. (In other words, you need network-specific software.) Some programs, such as Windows-based Facsys, from Optus Software, Inc., provide the software for standalone fax boards that can let up to 32 users send and receive faxes on a NetWare network.

For the majority of NetWare 286 and 386 users, a fax server is a technology whose time has come. However, for those using ELS, two problems immediately pop up: First, some (not all) fax servers require a message handling service, which means that ELS I networks can't use them at all and ELS II networks will have to purchase a message handling service option; and second, neither the four- nor the eight-person version of ELS is likely to have the space on the network to accommodate the added machinery, with or without the message handling service. For ELS users without a message handling service or without the room for one more node on the network, a standalone fax board in your workstation with NetWare-specific fax software may be the only alternative to sending faxes the old-fashioned way.

But if sending great-looking faxes is important, check with the resellers; explain your networking needs and restrictions and let them help you find solutions.

ISDN

ISDN, which stands for Integrated Services Digital Network, is the farthest from commercial acceptance in the networking world of all the technologies discussed in this chapter.

What ISDN does is allow users the capability of transmitting two 64-Kbps channels and one 16-Kbps channel down a single telephone line without requiring a modem. (Standard voice-grade transmission is 19.2 Kbps on a single telephone line.) As you can imagine, this is important technology for the various firms involved with telephone communications—Northern Telecom,

Hayes Microcomputer Products, Fujitsu Network Switching of America, and AT&T and all the Baby Bells—but it's not so important for the networking public, which has not really had the means or the opportunity to figure out what to do with this technology. Acceptance is further limited by the fact that this service is available in only small parts of a few very large cities.

Ideally, when ISDN networking does get here, you can plug any communications device—computer, fax machine, video device, or phone—into that network and allow it to work. The result will be that the current physical restrictions of the phone system will vanish and that any computer with an ISDN connection can talk to any other computer with an ISDN connection at 64 Kbps.

Kbps is thousands of bits per second instead of millions of bits per second, which is what most LANs run at. This means that an ISDN network has to create a niche where speed isn't important. The companies involved see ISDN's immediate future in point-to-point PC communications, used for WANs and in other areas where its slow speed (relative to full-fledged network types of ARCNET, Ethernet, and Token-Ring) is not a major drawback.

What is a major drawback, at least now, is the incompatibility between the various companies involved in making that technology a reality; specifically the telephone companies, which provide the physical ISDN lines and services, and the hardware communications vendors. Neither the telephone companies nor the hardware communications vendors can agree on a standard, so products from one company are not compatible with those of another, even if they are complementary rather than competing products. The biggest problem at the moment is signaling between the switches and the protocols.

But some LAN vendors, among them Banyan, are already beginning to work with this technology. At the Interop '90 show, Banyan demonstrated how clients on its Vines LAN can communicate with other PCs across an ISDN link. Novell hasn't made its ISDN plans public, but ELS would be as likely as NetWare 286 or 386 to be able to run on ISDN.

If you're interested in this technology, talk to your local phone company and your NetWare dealer. If the phone company doesn't have ISDN lines and also has ISDN tariffs from the public utility commission in place (ISDN tariffs are more important than ISDN lines, at least from the point of view of the regulatory agencies), then you can't use this technology.

APPENDIX A

Glossary

These definitions have been compiled from several sources: good computer dictionaries and other periodicals, Novell, various hardware and software engineers, and my own understanding.

Archival: Long-term storage for those who need a permanent record or for those who need a history. A good example would be a technical manual—any changes need to be made as soon as they're identified, but the manufacturer needs to know exactly what the document contains at each revision.

ARCNET: Attached Resource Computer NETwork. One of the main networking network types supported by NetWare. It runs at 2.5 Mbps (although a 20-Mbps speed is on the drawing board), features a token-passing scheme, and is usually wired in a star for easy troubleshooting.

Asynchronous: This is a very popular word in networking. It technically means happenings that occur in an irregular time sequence; for example, when you send electronic mail to someone but they don't read it for several hours or days, you are involved in asynchronous communications. Asynchronous is the capability to have an irregular time sequence like the one described.

Backbone: A building-wide network cable referring to Ethernet or ARCNET (when using a bus topology). The computers on the network connect to the main network cable from subsidiary cables.

Backup (see also Tape Backup): The preventative measure of making an extra copy of current files in case something happens to the original. Backups can be done manually (with floppies or small backup units) or automatically (with some of the fancier backup units on the market today).

Baseband networks: All of NetWare's most popular supported networking types—ARCNET, Ethernet, and Token-Ring—use a baseband transmission.

BIOS: Basic Input Output System. Located in every PC, the BIOS conducts the computer's self-testing routine and also controls its low-level operations. Very frequently, when we say "the computer won't support" such-and-such a feature, we mean that the BIOS doesn't support the feature, for one reason or another.

Board: Any printed circuit board placed in a computer to allow the computer to interface with another device, such as a monitor or a network. Boards are also called cards, NICs (network interface cards), and adapters. (Adapter is a term that is gaining strength in the disk controller board industry, especially for SCSI hard disk drives, as the need for a board that controls the hard disk drive disappears and the need for a board to help adapt the hard disk drive to various environments increases.)

Bridge: A bridge connects two similar networks together (i.e., networks that share the same communication system). The bridge can be internal (placed in a file server) or external (placed in a workstation), dedicated or non-dedicated. A dedicated, external bridge is the most efficient, because it only has one function.

Broadband networks: Network operating systems running on a broadband network, which use carrier frequencies and audio transmission, include Wang Computer's WangNET. NetWare supports broadband networking types as well, but they aren't as popular as the baseband types because they are more expensive and harder to install.

Bus: The pathway between devices (hard disk drives and the CPU, for example) that allows the devices to communicate with each other. The bus is usually divided into two parts, one locating the data and the other allowing the data to be transferred.

Bus mastering: Used in Micro Channel and EISA machines only and supported only by systems designed for Micro Channel and EISA applications.

Bus mastering allows network interface boards to bypass the CPU and take over the bus, speeding up the system throughput considerably.

Cache: This memory-speedup feature, once rare, is now found in most of the more powerful computers on the market. It is also found in hard disk drives and hard disk drive controller or adapter boards. Caching allows information that is likely to be used over and over to be retrieved quickly because the information is stored in RAM, which is quick. Caching can speed up system throughput.

Channel: In this book, a channel refers to the data transmission pathway (I/O address) in computers.

Channels also refer to the data transmission pathways I/O addresses controlled by a hard disk drive controller. In this case, ELS supports one channel, and other versions of NetWare 286 support four. NetWare 386 has abolished the term. Instead, NetWare 386 supports as many host adapter boards as you can get into the system that do not conflict with other boards already there.

Clock speed: How fast the computer runs. In most cases, faster is better, because the program will run faster. While some systems have two clocks, one to govern the CPU/memory and the other to control the bus, others have only one. Usually, the speed of the CPU will be half the clock speed, and the bus will be one-third the clock speed.

Clone: A computer that is functionally extremely similar to the industry standard, usually IBM (most clones are IBM AT-compatible, for example.) No clone can be 100% compatible (it wouldn't be a clone, then, but an IBM AT). The problem arises in functionality; if IBM's ATs can run Ethernet, for example, then the clone will advertise that it can too, and this may not be the case. Clones are cheaper, but before you buy one, make sure that it functions well in the areas that are important to you.

Closed architecture: An architecture whose technical specifications are not made public, preventing third-party vendors from creating enhancements. In this book, a good example of closed architecture is ELS, and the reason for it being closed architecture is obvious. If third-party vendors could create truly significant enhancements to this cut-rate beginner's version of NetWare, then no one would buy the more expensive versions.

Coaxial cable: An insulated (shielded) connecting cable used in ARCNET and Ethernet networking types. Coax has a larger transmission capacity than twisted-pair wiring and the shielding means it is good for electronically noisy environments, but it's so difficult to work with and so expensive that twisted-pair cable is becoming the cabling of choice. (If you have cable TV in your home, you have coax.)

Cold boot: The process of turning the computer on from the power switch, allowing it to check its memory and hardware configuration. The opposite, warm boot, is a method of rebooting the computer (by pressing the Ctrl, Alt, and Del keys simultaneously) so it can skip some of its self-testing procedures. A warm boot is a "first-resort" procedure to get the computer started after an application freezes the screen. If the keyboard is also locked, you'll have to do a cold boot, turning off the computer and starting over.

Computer: In this book, computer refers to that batch of electronics that allows you to receive electronic mail and work in a variety of applications. Technically, the desktop batch of electronics is a microcomputer. Minicomputers take up a whole room, and mainframe computers can take up a whole building.

CPU: Central Processing Unit. It's contained in the microprocessor chip on the motherboard of the computer and is the heart of the computer. The CPU controls all activity within the computer.

Data transfer rate: A hard disk drive term that refers to the amount of time it takes to transfer data to and from the hard disk drive. The rate is expressed in megabits per second (mbps).

Device: Any kind of hardware. In this book, a device refers to the computers, printers, modems, and the like that occupy a physical place on the network.

Disk controller board: An expansion board placed in a computer that acts as an interface between the computer and the hard disk drive. Since hard disk drives are more and more often carrying their own intelligence, disk controller boards are becoming disk "adapter" boards and taking on other functions to increase computer throughput.

Disk coprocessor board: A SCSI disk controller board originally created by Novell (but now licensed by ADIC and Samsung Information Systems America) that interfaces directly with NetWare instead of MS-DOS. This feature does a lot to speed up system throughput. Currently, three versions of these boards exist: one for the NetWare 386 market (EDCB, by ADIC), one for the Micro Channel market (DCB/2, by ADIC), and one for the ISA market (DCB, by ADIC and Samsung Information Systems America). A fourth version for EISA and bus mastering architecture is rumored to be in the works by Samsung.

Disk drive array: Four sets of two hard disk drives each attached to a special controller board. These multiple hard disk drives share the load of the file server. An array can handle multiple requests simultaneously, speeding up system throughput considerably.

Disk duplexing: A method (supported by SFT NetWare 286 and NetWare 386) of saving data to two different hard disks on different channels. This method requires a hard disk outside the original computer; for example, in another file server or in an attached disk subsystem.

Disk mirroring: A method (supported by SFT NetWare 286 and NetWare 386) of saving data to two different hard disks on the same channel. Mirroring isn't as fail safe a backup method as disk duplexing, and neither addresses some other backup issues such as archiving.

Downtime: The length of time that your personal computer or your network is not functioning. If your hard disk drive crashes, the time it takes you to fix or replace the hard disk and recreate any lost data is known as downtime.

Driver: The software required to run the hardware. If you add an Ethernet board to your file server, you have to add the driver to the list of drivers that NetWare maintains in order for the board to work.

EISA: Enhanced Industry Standard Architecture. The "latest and greatest" method of making your computer faster and more powerful. Created as an answer to IBM's Micro Channel architecture, it has a 32-bit bus that features bus mastering and is designed for multiprocessing; most of the 486 computers are EISA-architecture machines.

ELS: Entry Level System. This version of NetWare comes in two flavors: for four users and for eight users. Called "Beginner's NetWare" in the industry, it's not readily expandable, and you are limited to the storage that you can cram into your computer, although a few firms have developed workarounds.

ESDI: Enhanced Small Device Interface. A hard disk drive that utilizes the RLL method of encoding data on the disk. The term ESDI refers to the way that the disk interfaces with the computer. It has a data transfer rate of 10 Mbps, with a 15-Mbps rate planned.

Ethernet: One of the main networking types supported by NetWare. It transfers data at 10 Mbps, using a bus topology, on coax or unshielded twisted-pair cable.

Fault tolerant: See SFT.

Fax servers. Hardware (usually a board in a dedicated PC) and software that allows network users to fax data without having to create the copy, print it, and physically take it to the fax machine. Refer to Chapter IX for more information on fax servers.

FDDI. Fiber Data Distribution Interface. A networking technology that runs data over fiber-optic cable at 100 Mbps. Refer to Chapter IX for more information on FDDI.

Fiber-optic cable: Cable that is designed for long distances, electronically noisy environments and for networks where security is a concern. Fiber-optic cable also has a wider bandwidth than coax or twisted-pair wiring. Fiber-optic cabling is known as the best (and most expensive) cable on the market today.

Fiber-optic links: A link of fiber-optic cable can be the whole thing (backbone) or just a segment that connects two other (usually dissimilar) networks.

File server: A computer that runs the network operating system and provides data storage for the users. It's supposed to be much more powerful than the workstations it supports. In the marketplace, today's file server is tomorrow's workstation.

Gigabyte: One billion bytes or GB. Gigabyte is an increasingly more common label as mass storage reaches higher and higher size capabilities.

IDE: Integrated Device Electronics. One of the newest hard disk drive types, it has a maximum disk capacity of 425MB and a data transfer rate of 10

Mbps. It's become very popular in the industry because of its good performance (most IDE drives support disk caching) and low price.

IEEE: Institute of Electrical and Electronic Engineers. The Computer Society of the IEEE sets standards for the computer industry, including Ethernet and Token-Ring cabling.

IMSP: Independent Manufacturers Support Program. Created by Novell, the IMSP is essentially a certification lab. Those manufacturers with hardware products can have them tested (for a fee) with the various versions of NetWare.

I/O address: The location in computer memory for various devices. Each LAN and disk controller/host adapter board in the system has a unique I/O address.

IRQ: Interrupt Request Line. Local Area Network boards in a system must each be set to an IRQ that is unique to them. It's a circuit used by the LAN board and other I/O devices to send interrupt signals to the CPU, temporarily interrupting the CPU's program.

ISA: Industry Standard Architecture. At the same time that the EISA architecture standard was approved, ISA sprang into being. It's the plain old AT-standard architecture that we've had all along. The name was changed to conform to the EISA name.

ISDN: Integrated Services Digital Network. This is a network with the capability of transmitting two 64-Kbps channels and one 16-Kbps channel down a single telephone line without requiring a modem. Refer to Chapter IX for more information on this new technology.

KB: Kilobyte or 1,000 bytes.

LAN: Local Area Network. Personal computers in a particular geographical area that share storage and printer functions. The maximum wiring distance on a LAN is about 20,000 feet.

Logical ring: The way a networking type determines token access. A network may look like a physical star, but logically it's a ring.

MB: Megabyte or 1,000 kilobytes (one million bytes).

Megabit: One million bits, written as Mb. (A bit is one digit in a binary number. A byte is eight bits.)

Mbps: Megabit per second. The data transfer rate of a hard disk drive is expressed in Mbps.

Magnetic hard disk drives: This term is only used in discussions about optical drives, which use laser as the data transfer medium. Magnetic hard disk simply refers to any hard disk drive that's not an optical drive. Erasable optical drives are referred to as Magneto-optical drives, which means these drives use the heat of absorbed laser light together with a magnetic field to make changes.

Memory address: The location where the computer's CPU can send instructions to a device. Many LAN and disk controller/host adapter boards in the system have unique memory addresses.

MHz: MegaHertz or millions of Hertz (cycles) per second.

MFM: Modified Frequency Modulated. One of the earliest hard disk drives (for the purposes of this book), MFM is a method of encoding data on a hard disk drive. This technology has generally been supplanted by another hard disk drive encoding method called RLL.

Micro Channel: IBM's new, improved (compared to the AT-bus) architecture designed for multiprocessing. EISA architecture was formulated as an answer to the Micro Channel architecture. Neither AT- nor EISA-compatible boards can be used in a Micro Channel machine. The Micro Channel Bus runs at 14.5 MHz, while the AT-Bus usually runs at 8 MHz and the EISA bus runs as 16 to 25 MHz.

Motherboard: The printer circuit board on the floor of the chassis of your computer. It contains the bus and all chips that are used for controlling peripherals (i.e., keyboard, serial, and parallel port interfaces). It also contains expansion slots to hold additional printed circuit boards.

Multiprocessing: Two or more processors in one computer or two or more computers working together, sharing the workload. NetWare is promising a multiprocessing support feature, but hasn't said when it will ship.

Next ID identifier: This 8-bit register contains the address of the next station on the logical (not physical) ring. ARCNET uses the next identifier to identify the next station to receive the token.

NIC: Network Interface Card. One of the many names for an interface board, it usually refers to a LAN board.

Node: Any device on a network: file servers, workstations, printers, modems, and even the repeaters that connect the wiring together can be called nodes.

Node address: The identifier of each node on the network, in most cases known only to the computers.

Optical drive: A disk read or written by laser. The most popular optical drive is called a WORM (Write Once, Read Many), but erasable disks and CD-ROM drives are also available. Optical drives use SCSI interfaces, which means (theoretically, anyway) they can be attached to a computer easily.

OS/2: Operating System/2. The operating system for IBM's Micro Channel architecture machines (Personal System/2). OS/2 replaces MS-DOS on that series of machines.

Peripheral: Any device that attaches to a computer. A keyboard is a peripheral, as is a hard disk drive, a printer, and a mouse.

Platform: The standard, either hardware or software, to which programmers and developers design their products. IBM's PS/2 is the Micro Channel architecture platform; developers are now attempting to design functionally similar hardware.

Portable NetWare: A version, in C source code, of the basic NetWare Services from NetWare 386. NetWare Services are the portions of the NetWare kernel that provide for real-time, multi-tasking processing and file services.

Power surge protector: More accurately called a surge suppressor, this device protects a computer from surges/spikes in the power line. It prevents surges, and the better ones can even warn you in the event of brownouts. To prevent brownouts as well as surges, you need a voltage regulator. To prevent the computer from going down in the event of a power failure, you need an uninterruptible power supply unit.

Power user: Someone very familiar with computers. Network administrators usually find that power users are a challenge to deal with; power users usually have their own ideas about what kind of computers they should be given, what kind of peripherals should be attached to their computers, and frequently, how the network should be set up.

PROM: Programmable Read Only Memory. A chip that contains computer instructions.

Remote boot: Terminology exclusive to workstations, it allows the workstation to boot from the file server without using a local disk.

Remote Reset Boot PROM: The chip located on the LAN board that allows a remote boot to take place.

RLL: Run Length Limited. An encoding method for putting data on a hard disk drive. It is RLL technology that allows hard disk drives to achieve the maximum hard disk drive capacity on the market today.

SCSI I and SCSI II: Small Computer System Interface. The I and II indicate different versions. SCSI I has a data transfer rate of 5 Mbps, while SCSI II has a data transfer rate of 10 Mbps. The advantage of SCSI over ESDI drives is that SCSI is easy to install and is able to work with a wide variety of other SCSI devices. The drawback is that SCSI technology was adapted to hard disk drives from the electronics industry, instead of being exclusive to hard disk drives the way that ESDI and IDE are.

Seek time: The amount of time a hard disk takes to locate requested data. A full hard disk always has a slower seek time than a comparable empty disk; in addition, the seek time varies among the different types of hard disk drives. Faster is usually better.

SFT: System Fault Tolerant. Novell's umbrella term for disk duplexing, disk mirroring, and transaction tracking. Each of these functions provides a form of duplicating or saving data so that the data are available even if one drive fails.

SIMM: Single Inline Memory Modules. Memory chips located on a printed circuit board. SIMMs are much cheaper than conventional add-on memory chips, and they are a lot easier to install in the system.

StarLAN: AT&T's name for 1-Mbps Ethernet running on twisted pair. AT&T has transferred the name to the proposed 10Base-T Ethernet standard, but everyone else refers to 10Base-T as plain old twisted pair. 1-Mbps twisted pair is a technology whose time has gone.

System Fault Tolerant: See **SFT**.

Tape Backup: Usually a separate box attached to a workstation or file server that is used to make archives of current files on the disk. Backup units can use either magnetic or optical media; the medium used isn't as important as making the backup.

TCP/IP: Transmission Control Protocol/Internet Protocol. A method of controlling communication on a cable.

Terabyte: 1,000 gigabytes, abbreviated TB. 32TB is the term used to represent the maximum amount of data storage allowed by NetWare 386. Today's technology can't provide 1TB of data storage, let alone 32.

Token-Ring: One of the main wiring networking types supported by NetWare. It features a token-passing scheme wired in a ring, a 4-Mbps and a 16-Mbps data transmission rate, and shielded twisted-pair wiring, although, if you know what you're doing, you can also use unshielded twisted-pair wiring.

Topology: The way network wires are laid out—ring, star, or bus. Each has different strengths and weaknesses.

Throughput: The speed with which data are processed by the file server, the workstation, disk controller board, and/or the hard disk drive. If you're discussing network throughput, you also have to take the transmission speed of the network topology into account.

Twisted-pair wiring: A kind of wire where each pair of wires twists around each other. Phone wiring is twisted-pair wiring and is commonly used for LAN wiring.

UNIX: An operating system, like MS-DOS, that runs on many types of computer systems but is frequently found on mini- and mainframe computer systems.

UPS: Uninterruptible Power Supply. A peripheral that keeps the file server running in the event of a power failure. Most UPS units have battery power that allows the unit to alert the network administrator and network users to save their files and exit. Some custom-designed units can be attached to a generator and provide power indefinitely.

Wait state: The amount of time the computer waits before processing any more data. Many of the newest systems are now at zero wait states, meaning that there is no delay before data can be processed.

WAN: Wide-Area Network. A network that connects businesses across large areas.

WNIM: Wide-area Network Interface Module. This Novell product is a LAN board used in workstations to route asynchronous communications. NetWare Access Server uses WNIM boards.

Wireless LANs: Networking without cables. Wireless LANs use infrared light, lasers, and spread-spectrum radio frequencies to transmit data. Because of technological limitations, wireless LANs currently are slow and limited to short distances. Refer to Chapter IX for more information.

Workstation: A single-user personal computer (any size) that is networked to a file server. Workstations can either have a hard disk or can have only a floppy disk.

WORM: Write Once, Read Many. An optical disk that allows you to write data to it but does not allow that data to be erased. You can read the data on the disk as often as you like.

APPENDIX B

NetWare Requirements

This appendix is a listing of NetWare hardware requirements and the advantages and disadvantages of each networking type.

Each version of NetWare has different requirements; usually, the more powerful the machine, the happier you will be.

As a general rule, if your hardware type isn't listed here, check with the Novell dealer and/or the hardware manufacturer as to the product's compatibility with NetWare. Keep in mind the difference between 100% compatible and functionally compatible. No machine is 100% compatible with IBM or Compaq, for example, but a lot of machines will work just fine as substitutes for them. (IBM and Compaq don't believe it, but it's true.)

Also remember that not all compatibles are created equal. You should not have a problem with NetWare or other software compatibility as long as your compatible is a well-known brand whose manufacturer has quality control procedures firmly in place. You might have a problem if you buy through mail order or if you build the machine yourself.

Finally, remember that technology is changing constantly, both in hardware and in software. Hardware and software incompatibilities may mysteriously disappear (and occur) as new revisions are released into the marketplace. Hardware that is incompatible with some types of NetWare today may be universally supported by NetWare tomorrow as the hardware gains acceptance and the demand for support grows.

Before you buy anything, cross check hardware and software to be sure that they will work with each other. Don't buy them just because the vendor says they "ought" to work with each other, unless you get that statement in the form of a money-back guarantee.

If the manufacturers of hardware and software don't know all the products that are incompatible with their own products, you can't expect even the most up-to-date vendor to do better. The best you can hope for is a definite statement of compatibility, or lack thereof, about products that are being sold by the vendor.

HARDWARE REQUIREMENTS

The following list shows the official hardware requirements stated by Novell for each version of NetWare. The recommendations that follow are my own.

NETWARE 386

NETWARE 386 V3.0 AND V3.1

File server: Compaq 386/20
IBM model 70 or 80 that runs OS/2

Memory: 2MB

Recommended: IBM PC/AT-type (486)
IBM PS/2 Model 80

Workstation: IBM PC, PC XT, PC AT, or compatible
IBM PS/2 or compatible

Memory: 512KB

Recommended: IBM PC/AT-type (286 or 386)
IBM PS/2 Model 60

NETWARE ACCESS SERVER (V1.0)

Hardware:

File Server: 386 computer with multiport WNIM boards
3MB RAM for every four users, up to a maximum of 12MB RAM for 15 users

Workstations: 386 computer with multiport WNIM boards modem
640KB
1 hard disk enabled

Software:

Modify your CONFIG.SYS file to exclude C600-C7FF and E000-E7FF conflicting memory addresses (if you have a VGA monitor board in your system).

NETWARE 286

ADVANCED, SFT, NETWARE FOR MACINTOSH

File server: IBM PC/AT or compatible
IBM PS/2 Model 30 (286), 50Z, 70, or 80*

Memory: 1MB

Recommended: IBM PC/AT-type (386)
IBM PS/2 Model 70 or 80

Workstation: IBM PC/XT/AT or compatible
IBM PS/2
Macintosh Plus**
Macintosh II (any model)**
Macintosh SE (any model)**

Memory: 384KB

Recommended: IBM PC/AT-type (286)
IBM PS/2 Model 50Z

*The 286 installation manual also says that the PS/2 Model 50 and Model 60 are supported; however, they have been discontinued.

**NetWare v2.15 for Macintosh allows you to connect Macs to your network; however, because NetWare naturally takes a MS-DOS approach, it forces the Macs to play by DOS rules (slow down) rather than speeding the network up. Mac people aren't happy with NetWare.

NETWARE ANYWARE

Hardware:

Dedicated workstation
256KB RAM
Modem

ELS I AND II

File server: IBM PC/AT or compatible
IBM Personal System/2 Model 30 (286), 50Z, 70, or 80*

Memory: 2MB (if non-dedicated)
1MB (if dedicated)

Recommended: IBM PC/AT-type (386SX)
IBM PS/2 Model 70

*The ELS installation manual also says that the PS/2 Model 50 and Model 60 are supported; however, they have been discontinued.

Workstation: IBM PC/XT/AT or compatible
IBM PS/2

Memory: 384KB

Recommended: IBM PC/AT-type (286)
IBM PS/2

Disk Drives:

1 or 2 internal drives:	IBM PS/2 MFM IBM PS/2 MFM 286 IBM PS/2 ESDI ISA Compatible
Disk Controller:	Western Digital or compatible

ELS I and II, in non-dedicated mode, have a three-pronged problem with slow keyboard input (how long it takes for the computer to recognize that something's been typed). (The fault lies jointly with the keyboard, NetWare, and the keyboard chip.) Test any file server that will be running in non-dedicated mode before purchasing it.

ELS I AND II SUPPORT

The next list, of what ELS I and ELS II do and do not support was gleaned from various sources; this market is changing rapidly, and things that are on the *Does not support* list move up to the *Supports* list with amazing rapidity.

ELS LEVEL I, v2.12*

Supports

- Four users
- MFM hard disk drives
- RLL hard disk drives
- ESDI hard disk drives
- IDE hard disk drives**
- MS-DOS 3.x, MS-DOS 4.x
- E-Mail+
- Message Handling Service Software (connectivity with electronic mail services)+

Does not support

- Eight users
- SCSI hard disk drives
- disk duplexing
- disk mirroring++
- third-party drivers
- disk drive subsystems
- NetWare for Macintosh Value Added Process (VAP)

*ELS Level I, v2.0, is considered obsolete; it was supposed to stop shipping in March 1990. (I found a copy in the stores in June 1990.) It basically supported the same things as v2.12, except for MS-DOS 4.x and some of the hard disk drive types. Its hard disk drive capacity limit was around 100MB.

**Some IDE drives have a NetWare driver problem that precludes them from working with ELS NetWare. Try them out with ELS before you buy.

+ELS Level I, v2.12, supports the software engine that runs MHS; however, it is an option that you have to purchase separately.

++Although Novell spokesmen say that disk mirroring isn't supported through software *or* hardware, I would ask third-party vendors before giving up.

ELS LEVEL II, v2.15

Supports

- Eight users
- MS-DOS 4.x
- MFM hard disk drives
- RLL hard disk drives
- ESDI hard disk drives
- IDE hard disk drives*
- IBM PS/2 SCSI hard disk drives

- NetWare for Macintosh Value Added Process (VAP)
- Message Handling Service Software

Does not support

- Disk drive subsystems**
- Third-party drivers**
- Disk duplexing
- Disk mirroring+
- SCSI hard disk drives that are not IBM PS/2 SCSI compatible

*Some IDE drives have a NetWare driver problem that precludes them from working with ELS NetWare. Try them out with ELS before you buy.

**Several firms have developed workarounds for ELS II (not ELS I) that allow it to support disk drive subsystems. Plus Development, for example, with Novell's official blessing, substitutes its device drivers for the device drivers shipped with ELS II.

+Although Novell spokesmen say that disk mirroring isn't supported through software *or* hardware, I would ask third-party vendors before giving up.

NETWORK TYPES

Novell's NetWare supports a number of network types (I read somewhere that NetWare is basically promiscuous; it supports everything). However, the most popular network types are ARCNET, Ethernet, and Token-Ring. These wiring systems are briefly summarized below.

ARCNET

Advantages

- Easy to install
- Easy to troubleshoot

- Flexibile (can mix and match wiring)
- Inexpensive
- For small to medium (255 node) networks

Disadvantage

- Slow (2.5 Mbps; 20 Mbps planned)

Wiring choices

- Coaxial cable (thin cable for small networks)
- Unshielded twisted-pair cable (preferred for all situations)
- Fiber optic (special situations: distance, security, noise)

ETHERNET

Advantages

- DEC connectivity
- Historically, small to medium networks; using unshielded twisted-pair wiring may change its reputation
- Reliable performance
- Supported by Portable NetWare

Disadvantage

- Difficult to troubleshoot (with coax cable)

Wiring choices

- Coaxial cable (thin cable, for stable networks of less than 25 users)
- Unshielded twisted-pair cable (for more than 25 users or for networks that are expected to grow)

- Fiber optic (special situations: distance, security, noise)

TOKEN-RING

Advantages

- IBM connectivity
- Built-in network intelligence
- Reliable performance
- Large networks
- Some OEMs support Token-Ring with Portable NetWare

Disadvantage

- Expensive

Wiring choices

- Shielded twisted-pair cable (for all situations)
- Unshielded twisted-pair cable (a specifications draft is being prepared now)
- Fiber optic (special situations: distance, security, noise)

APPENDIX C

Hardware Incompatibilities

Nothing works perfectly all the time. Software exists out there that can stump any hardware. However, by the same token, if your machine is stumped by something, you can probably find a product that does work with it and accomplishes your purpose just as well as the product that does not work.

NEW COMPUTERS AND OLD BOARDS

If your computer is of the super-powerful EISA architecture, it is going to be very fast. A lot of today's peripherals cannot really keep up with EISA computers. Watch out for LAN boards. Watch out for any boards without bus mastering; some of them may work in the machine, but they will slow everything down and defeat the purpose of buying the ultra-fast machine.

One of the current workarounds to fast machines and slow boards is to disable the computer's built-in memory cache. Since this also defeats one of the features of the computer, it should only be used strictly as a temporary solution (for the length of time it takes you to go out and buy a faster board, for example).

NEW BOARDS AND OLD COMPUTERS

The opposite problem also exists: older computers and newer boards may not work well together because the boards are so fast and the computers are so slow.

If you are buying new boards for an old machine, ask the vendor about slower boards, on the philosophy of not buying more than you can use. Eight-bit boards are usually slower than 16-bit boards. They can get the job done, just not as quickly as today's technological marvels. (If you're updating piece by piece, I would buy the fastest products that work so that when you get around to replacing the computer, you really do have a faster, better machine.)

Thirty-two bit boards are only recently on the market; it is unlikely that an old computer will have a 32-bit slot on the motherboard. If it does, the slot is undoubtedly proprietary, which means it only works with boards that the manufacturer of the computer knows about and is willing to sell you. Putting a 16-bit board into the slot can destroy both the 16-bit board and the motherboard. Installing a 32-bit board that wasn't designed by the manufacturers of the system can also do terrible things to the boards in the computer.

NEW COMPUTERS AND OLD SOFTWARE

If you have a super-powerful computer, you will have problems getting maximum performance out of some older versions of some software, which were not designed with some features (like bus mastering) in mind and will not be able to take advantage of increased bus speeds.

Remember that software isn't upwardly compatible with other software; this may affect the new hardware as well. For example, ELS I, v2.0a (now considered obsolete), didn't support MS-DOS 4.x, which came out a few years later. This means that version of ELS wouldn't support any computer that used MS-DOS 4.x as the computer's operating system, including, for example, a lot of the 486 computers. Check new products for compatibility with the old products before you buy anything.

NEW HARD DISK DRIVES AND OLD COMPUTERS

If your computer is four or five years old, it was built in the days when only a couple of hard disk drive types existed. The computer will undoubtedly support all drives labeled AT- or ISA-compatible, but check to be sure that the drive is compatible enough. Before you stick any newer-type hard disk drive in your old computer, make sure that the computer will support that hard disk drive type.

Even if the computer supports the right hard disk drive type, it may not support the larger-capacity hard disk drives. Standard ISA drives are up to 600MB and are heading for 1GB, a quantum jump from the early days of 20MB, 40MB, and 80MB hard disk drives. These older drives are also called ISA drives. (At least that is what they're called today. They used to be called plain old MFM and RLL drives.)

Check the documentation about what kinds of hard disk drives are supported by your system. Also, the built-in setup procedure that ships with most computers includes a hard disk drive table that can be used to identify drives that are supported by the computer's BIOS.

NEW COMPUTERS AND OLD HARD DISK DRIVES

Most of the older good-quality hard disk drives will run in today's newer computers. They are not going to be fast; they are not going to be high-capacity; they will slow down the system throughput; but they will work. Again, check the documentation or the hard disk drive table that shipped with your computer's setup procedure for a list of supported hard disk drives.

IBM

IBM's products work best with other IBM products. And IBM puts out so many different products that, once you commit to it, you can use IBM exclusively for all your computer needs and not worry too much about compatibility. If things are not compatible, you can complain and should get a positive response from IBM. The tradeoff is that IBM's products are expensive.

The computer industry is large, and there are other products out there that do the same things as IBM's products, are cheaper, and do not have any more inherent quality control problems than IBM has. There is a tradeoff here; you will have to do more compatibility testing to be sure that the products that you want to buy will work with each other.

APPENDIX D

Shared Printer Devices: Alternative to Networking

If you are just starting out in the networking world, but are not sure you need everything that a network can offer, consider the alternatives to networking before you buy. For example, if your primary concern is printing (the main reason that a lot of people go to networking), you may be able to buy a device that lets everyone print from the same printer. This option should only be considered if you do not really care about electronic mail and if every person in your small office uses a different applications program. (If several people use the same program, it makes sense to offer it from a network file server.)

These shared printer devices range in price from very inexpensive to costing considerably more than NetWare. They are also sold in versions from one node (hardly helpful) to 16 or more. Some of the most complex and expensive shared printer devices even come with electronic mail, which is more than you can say for Novell's Entry Level System. (ELS, Level I, doesn't even come with the software for message handling services, although it can be purchased separately. ELS, Level II, does ship with message handling services software.)

If you have a small office, one that's likely to remain stable in size for some time, consider a shared printer device. If, on the other hand, you have a small office today but tomorrow will have a larger one, stay away from what can only be a temporary solution. Larger offices need, in addition to shared printers, electronic mail, shared data storage, and security that keeps unauthorized users from fiddling with files that do not belong to them (in personnel or accounting, for example). (Remember that a standalone computer is one that anyone can use. A knowledgeable PC user can access any file in any directory in any computer that does not have password protection or is not physically locked away.)

The deciding factor may very well be money. A real networking system costs less than some of the shared printer devices serving a maximum number of users. However, this does not take into account the network management cost. A shared printer device, once configured, can usually be left alone. A network can *never* be left alone; someone is going to have to be in charge of providing passwords and keeping the system up and running after installation. If your network is small, this will not be a full-time job; the job grows with the network.

Installation is another story. Because shared printer devices are, by definition, less complex than a networking system, they are going to be less difficult to install, especially if you start with twisted-pair wiring. Installing a network requires advance planning—choosing a network topology, choosing cabling, designing the physical layout of the network—as well as software installation. These decisions are minimized with shared printer devices.

If you have decided upon a shared printer device, look for one that prints as transparently as possible; that is, the user doesn't have to direct the document to the default printer. Also look for software with the device that allows users to select different printers or automatically routes jobs from a busy to an idle printer.

APPENDIX E

Techs, Techies, and Other Resources

No book is going to give you enough information on networking, especially if you are trying to combine your old computers with new computers, new peripherals, and new software (as in NetWare). Books are always involved with tomorrow's technology. They have to be, because as soon as they are published, they become a record of yesterday's technology.

Technology is always finding better ways to do things. Computers are much more powerful now than they were expected to be 10 years ago. Software does things that couldn't even be imagined then. Peripherals, particularly printers, are much different now than they used to be, and there are essential peripherals out there, such as internal fax boards, that didn't exist a few years ago.

Computers that are a couple of generations behind, say four or five years old, were never designed to do the things that today's computers do. So, sometimes they fit in, and sometimes they don't. The older the computer, the less likely it will fit in with today's technology.

Before you junk your old products, however, ask around. There may be things that you can do to salvage them for at least a while. An example is the four mbps Token-Ring board. While hardly obsolete yet, its much-quicker replacement is on the horizon and moving fast.

If you buy new Token-Ring boards that run at 16 mbps, you'll find that many of them are switchable between 16 and four megabits, which means that you can buy the new boards and put them on your old Token-Ring network. This gives you time to replace the older boards. You don't get to enjoy the new technology while you're replacing the older boards, but at least you have a functioning network during the transition period, which can last as long as you want. (You don't want to wait too long or you'll find the newest technology isn't 16 mbps but 32.)

TECHS

Another solution, at least if you are the administrator of a larger network, is to subscribe to TECHS, a database of information about old and new technology. I say larger, because according to an article by Lisa Dillon (*LAN TIMES*, April 1990), subscribing to this service will cost you more than $1500 per year.

Both hardware and software vendors (including Novell) participate in this service, sending "solution screens" for problems that have cropped up among their users. Madge Networks, among those sending solution screens, said that one of the great things about TECHS is that the database contains information on older products, both hardware and software. That is, information is not deleted from the database just because a product has been declared obsolete by a vendor. The Madge Networks spokesman thought that TECHS would be perfect for those who were trying to combine their old technology with the new. TECHS can be reached by calling (714) 777-7700.

TECHIES

If you think your technology problems are not going to be of such duration that you need to subscribe to TECHS, you might want to consider hiring a consultant. While expensive, a consultant should have a background in networking, which means that he or she may know about your particular "old" technology and may know how to combine it peaceably into the "new" technology. If specific knowledge is not forthcoming, consultants may be able to provide workarounds that will render your old technology useful.

And even if these techies cannot provide a solution that will keep your old hardware working, they are still going to know more than you do about the ins and outs of networking connectivity. If you have not expanded your network lately, you are behind on your technology knowledge.

A consultant who keeps up with the software and hardware networking technology can answer all the networking questions for you, especially if he or she specializes in your problem area. A consultant is not cheap in up-front costs, but on the other hand, up-front costs are not as important or as expensive as life-of-network costs. They would like you to sign on for an extended relationship, but will be willing to sell you short-term advice as well. Consultants can be found through users' groups and in the yellow pages of your phone book.

OTHER RESOURCES

Don't overlook users' groups as a resource. You may find someone in the group who had just your problem and who is happy to tell you the solution. Among all the literature that you received when you purchased your networking package will undoubtedly be a list of users' groups.

If not, or if you threw that literature away long ago, you'll have to do some research. *LAN TIMES* prints a list of worldwide users' groups for Novell, Banyan's Vines, and 3Com in the back of every issue. Or you can try calling the technical support department for the product in question and asking them for a list of users' groups.

Beyond users' groups are various publications and your local technical bookstore. The just-mentioned *LAN TIMES* is a monthly periodical that goes into depth about networking news. (It is aimed at the volume buyer but still provides good information for those who are just interested in the field.) It also provides reviews of LAN technology products, runs tutorials on networking technology, and gives technological updates of different aspects of networking. Until mid-1989 it was owned by Novell and mainly printed news for and about Novell and NetWare. Now owned by McGraw-Hill, *LAN TIMES* has branched out more than it could have when owned by Novell, although Novell is still a primary focus. One reason for continuing to talk about Novell a lot, besides the fact that many of the staffers were transferred along with the magazine, is that Novell is the industry leader.

PC Week and *PC Magazine* are consumers' periodicals that give you general computer news as well as running reviews of the latest and greatest products (all kinds) on the market today. Doing the same thing, only specializing in networking, are *LAN, LAN Technology,* and *Network Computing.*

InfoWorld, whose reviews are mentioned in this book, is a controlled circulation newspaper whose purpose is the same as *PC Week*'s and *PC Magazine*'s but is aimed specifically at those in the computer industry rather than those who might be interested in computers. Controlled circulation means you can get your copies of the paper free if you are responsible for purchasing $250,000 or so of computer products a year. If you don't meet the criteria, you aren't supposed to get a copy at all, but if you really push, *InfoWorld*'s circulation department will sell you a subscription for $150 a year.

NOVELL

Novell has put all the test bulletins from the IMSP into a book and is selling them, both in hard copy and over NetWire. The test bulletins are a summary of the testing that each product submitted to Novell for certification has gone through.

In the bulletin is the product's configuration, including any hardware that is shipping with it (hard disk drives, LAN boards, etc.) and any limitations (a test that the product didn't pass). The limitation is not enough to prevent the product from being certified by Novell, but does show product limits (a computer that doesn't support a LAN board while running as a workstation). If a product didn't receive certification, that is also noted on the test bulletin.

The test bulletins are invaluable for anyone purchasing new equipment for a network; it won't help much if most of your equipment is four or five years old. Novell's testing program didn't become a runaway success (with everyone in the industry submitting products for certification) until mid-1989 or so.

For more information on the test bulletin book, check NetWire or call Novell at 801-429-7670.

NETWIRE

NetWire is a bulletin board published by Novell. Listed on it, among other things, are bugs fixes and software patches, specific to problems acknowledged by the various versions of NetWare. The bugs and patches are usually incorporated into their respective versions of NetWare once a year; in the meantime, they can be taken off NetWire and used now.

Most Novell dealers subscribe to NetWire.

If you're interested in NetWire, you'll need to have access to the CompuServe Information Service; you'll also need a modem and a communications program. Then call 1-800-848-8199, and ask for operator 58.

WIRING RESOURCES

If you need information about wiring specifications, you can contact the following groups:

IEEE (for Token-Ring and Ethernet standards)

445 Hoes Lane
Piscataway, NJ 08855
(201) 981-0060

Ethernet is the 802.3 standard; Token-Ring is the 802.5 standard.

ARCNET Trade Association
3365 N. Arlington Heights Road, Suite J
Arlington Heights, IL 60004
(708) 255-3003

APPENDIX F

Compatibility Issues

This appendix lists machines that had compatibility problems during Novell's testing with LAN boards or the version of NetWare that they were running.

The information shown here is subject to change. Always confirm with the manufacturer or authorized dealer to be sure that this information is still correct. In particular, any limitations that refer to NetWare 386 most likely have changed, because both Novell and computer manufacturers are striving for compatibility. In addition, Novell has released another version of NetWare 386, probably correcting some of the problems that have appeared in the v3.0 version.

These problems discussed affect only the particular model listed. Other machines by the same manufacturer very likely do not have this problem. When in doubt, ask.

IBM

PCN II

The PC Network Adapter II Board (PCN II) is fairly old technology, and the network type it supports has fallen out of the market mainstream. A number of computers, most of them fast, were unable to handle the PCN II board properly; none of the vendors that I checked with thought that this failure made any difference to them financially. Some didn't even know what the board is for. Although you can check, I doubt that the vendors are going to correct this compatibility problem.

Problem: **Can't run the board in any mode**

Solution:

None

Machines affected:

Club American Technologies (325C)
CSR (386-25C)
Hewlett-Packard (HP Vectra 486)
Olivetti Office Limited (M290S)
Samsung (PCTerminal/386SX)

Problem: **Computer is too fast for the board**

Solutions:

Disable the memory cache
Change the system speed

Machines affected:

Mitac (MPC 4000G 386/33)
Research Machines (VX 486)

Problem: **Computer can only run board in file server mode**

Solution:

Choose a different, compatible board for your workstations

Machines affected:

Apricot Computers PLC (Qi 660i)
Everex (Step386 33)
Storage Dimensions (FileMaster)

Problem: **Computer can run board in workstation mode only with updated drivers**

Solution:

Check with IBM to be sure systems have correct workstation shell drivers

Machines affected:

Model 70 A21
Model 80 A21
Model 80 A31

TOKEN-RING

Token-Ring is the network type of the future, as far as IBM is concerned. Since most of the machines on the list are the biggest and fastest in today's market, I think most of the problems caused with this board were caused by technological glitches that may have indeed been resolved. Check before you buy.

Problem: **Computer cannot run the board in any mode**

Solution:

Buy a different brand Token-Ring board

Machines affected:

Hewlett-Packard (HP Vectra 486)
NEC Technologies (PowerMate 386/25)*
Olivetti Office Limited (M290S)
Philips Electronics (P3345) (NetWare v2.15)
Research Machines (VX 486)
Tulip Computers International (AT Compact 3)

*The PowerMate 386/25 doesn't work with NetWare 386 and the Token-Ring board; it works with NetWare 286 and the Token-Ring board after you disable video shadowing.

Problem: **Computer is too fast for the board**

Solution:

Disable the memory cache

Machine affected:

NCR (486 ALR)

Problem: **Computer can only run board in file server mode**

Solution:

Buy a different brand Token-Ring board

Machine affected:
Enigma Technologies' Dimension 286

3COM

3Com's boards had some problems with the computers when the machines were running in non-dedicated mode with NetWare's ELS. I would not buy any computer to run with ELS before I tested it in the configuration I was going to use with the boards I planned to install. ELS is very touchy.

Problem: **Computer can't run ELS in non-dedicated mode with board listed**

Solutions:
Run ELS in dedicated mode only (a wise idea in any case)
Choose a different board

Board/Machines affected:
3C505
Acer America
NEC Technologies
3C503
HP Vectra 486
3C523 MC
Tandy/Radio Shack (5000 MC)
486 by NCR

NOVELL

NE2000

The following systems listed could run the board with conditions such as: "works when the date of the driver is after such-and-such-a-date," to "works when you change the board's default configuration," and "AppleTalk problems":

Intel (302/25 and 303)

NEC (Powermate and Powermate SX)

Northgate (386/33)

Zenith Data Systems (Z386/SX)

Problem: **Computer can't support the board in any mode**

Solution:

Buy a different brand Ethernet board

Machines affected:

Apricot Computers PLC (XEN-S 250)
Epson U.K. (AX3/20 and AX3/25)
Leading Technology (12/286MX)

DCB

Novell's DCB, a SCSI host adapter board, is tested with every system that comes through Novell's testing program to be certified as a file server. It is not surprising that some computers are not able to support it. It is also unlikely that the computer manufacturers in question care. There are many disk controller and host adapter boards in the marketplace today; you can find, without much difficulty, a disk controller board that works in your system and supports the channels you need supported in your NetWare 286 installation.

Problem: **Channel Support**

Solution:

Choose a different disk controller or SCSI host adapter board

Machines affected:

Acer America (1100SX) (Channel 1 and Channel 4)
Acer America (915P) (Channel 4)
Epson U.K. (AX3/25) (Channel 2)

Problem: **Board Not Supported**

Solution:

Choose a different disk controller or SCSI host adapter board

Machines affected:

Philips Electronics (P3345) (NetWare 386)
Epson U.K. (AX3/35)

ELS

ELS has one major compatibility problem with the computers on the market today, and that is that how machines respond when they are run as non-dedicated file servers. Most of them don't respond well, which can be the fault of NetWare just as easily as the fault of the computer manufacturer. Novell admits that the keyboard input on ELS machines is frequently slow in terms of how long it takes for the computer to recognize that something's been typed and says that it is partly a problem with the software. ELS is being killed by Novell. In the future, NetWare 286 will be consolidated so that every version has the same features, only the number of users will differ. Any solutions will have to come from the computer manufacturers.

Problem: **Slow keyboard input in non-dedicated mode**

Solutions:

Different keyboard
Different keyboard chip
Don't run in non-dedicated mode

Machines affected:

Northgate (386/33) (not certified for use with ELS in non-dedicated mode)
Tulip Computers International (SX Compact 2) (not certified for use with ELS in non-dedicated mode)
ALR (Flex Cache 386/33)
CSS (MAXSYS 386T-33)
Commodore Business Machines (PC 50II)
Epson U.K. Limited (AX3/20)
Everex (Step386 33/Stepserver)
Hewlett Packard (Vectra RS/25C and Vectra QS/16S)
Intel (302/20)
Memorex Telex (7045)
Tulip Computers International (AT 386 SX)
Victor Technologies Ltd (T386/25)
Victor UK Ltd. (V386T)
Wang (280/20)

NETWARE 386, V3.0

NetWare 386 v3.0 and some of IBM's biggest files servers have a difficulty that is more Novell's problem than IBM's. A driver (IBMSCSI.DSK) written by Novell, causes you to have to reload the drivers every time the file server is rebooted if the file server is an IBM Model 65 or 80. As a note, file servers aren't usually rebooted every day, unlike workstations, so we aren't talking about a problem of insurmountable magnitude, but it is a serious inconvenience even if it happens only once a month.

The problem has been corrected with NetWare 386, v3.1, and Novell is urging IBM owners of Models 65 and 80 to upgrade to v3.1 as soon as possible.

Problem: **Every time file server reboots drivers have to be reloaded**

Solution:

Upgrade to v3.1

Machines affected:

Model 65
Model 80 A21
Model 80 A31
Model 80 121

Index

D

E

F

H

I

L

M

N

T

U

V

W